Jerusalem Won: Signed In Blood

The Epic Quest for Lasting Peace

By

Roy H. Ferguson

with

Malcolm McGough

Co Author and Editor

Copyright © 2025 by

Roy H. Ferguson

ALL RIGHTS RESERVED. NO part of this book may be reproduced or transmitted in any form by any means, electronic or mechanical, including photocopying and recording, or by any information storage and retrieval system, except as may be expressly permitted in writing from the author.

Hardcover ISBN : 978-1-967828-76-0

Paperback ISBN: 978-1-967828-78-4

Published by:

Pine Book Writing

www.PineBookWriting.com

R-10225 Yonge St Suite #250, Richmond Hill, ON L4C 3B2, Canada.

Printed in the United States of America

Born and raised in Jamaica, author Roy H. Ferguson will donate a portion of the proceeds from this book to aid ongoing relief and rebuilding efforts in his home country following the devastation caused by Hurricane Melissa.

Dedication

In memory of Charlie Kirk (1994–2025), whose courageous witness affirms that though the cost of truth may be high, the reward is eternal.

May the angels who worship before the throne (Revelation 5:11–12) remind us that Jerusalem is WON, and that Christ will soon declare: "Behold, I make all things new" (Revelation 21:5).

Memorial Preface

On September 10, 2025, America was shaken by the shocking death of Charlie Kirk, Founder of Turning Point USA. At just thirty-one years old, his life was cut short on the campus of Utah Valley University.

To the world, Charlie was recognized as a bold and unyielding witness for truth, a voice that refused compromise in an age of deception. His words and actions carried the weight of conviction, confronting the rising tide of secularism with a testimony rooted in faith and courage. But to those who knew his convictions more deeply, Charlie was also a man who came to honor the Sabbath as God's appointed rest, rooted in Creation and enshrined in His eternal law (Genesis 2:2–3; Exodus 20:8–11). Encouraged by friends and mentors, he studied biblical literature earnestly and came to believe that the Sabbath was truly God's direction of rest in His honor. Through his study of God's Word, he became convinced that a time would come when there would be conflict between tradition and command, especially in regard to Sunday worship—'man's tradition and laws versus God's command.' His choice to embrace the biblical Sabbath was a testimony that the Spirit still leads seekers back to God's covenant sign, and in love, Charlie never deviated from this.

Charlie's life and death remind us that truth is costly. To honor God above human decree often places one at odds with the world. Yet as Christ promised: "In the world ye shall have tribulation: but be of good cheer; I have overcome the world" (John 16:33). Like Jerusalem herself—God's prophetic clock—his witness points to the coming conflict over worship (Revelation 13:15–17; 14:6–12). Though Charlie's death is not that final crisis, it foreshadows a world increasingly hostile to those who keep God's commandments and the faith of Jesus.

We mourn his passing yet lift our eyes beyond the grave. For there remains a Sabbath rest for the people of God (Hebrews 4:9). Even now, angels worship before the throne, declaring the victory of the Lamb and reminding us that Jerusalem is not only history, but destiny. One day soon, strife will cease, and Christ will proclaim: "Behold, I make all things new" (Revelation 21:5).

Until then, may Jerusalem WON stand as lamp and plumb line: light for the pilgrim path and measure for the faithful soul. Dedicated to the memory of Charlie Kirk—whose courageous witness affirms that though the cost of truth may be high, the reward is eternal.

May the Lord surround his family and friends with comfort, strengthen them with hope, and remind them that Charlie's witness and martyrdom lives on in eternity. Amen.

Table of Contents

FOREWORD

Jerusalem WON: Signed In Blood 💧 The Epic Quest for Lasting Peace

By Dr Bell.

In *Jerusalem WON: Signed in Blood 💧 — The Epic Quest for Lasting Peace*, authors **Roy H. Ferguson** and **Malcolm McGough** invite readers to embark on a gripping journey of faith, redemption, and the relentless pursuit of peace in a world fraught with turmoil. Roy, born in the vibrant community of Mount Salem, Jamaica, initially chased dreams of fame and success in Hollywood. However, a life-altering moment of impending blindness forced him to confront his true calling, redirecting his path toward a life dedicated to serving the marginalized. 20 years later he meets Malcolm, who helps Roy realize his dream by helping to author and edit, this book and his screenplay of the same name. But remember, this is Roy's story, a story manifested by tragic circumstances, and orchestrated by God himself, as he introduces Roy and Malcolm to complete this most important journey.

After major surgery at LA County USC Hospital, Roy took a break from the glitz of the entertainment industry to serve the homeless on Skid Row in downtown Los Angeles. It was here that he encountered Raymond Yeshua at St. Vincent's House Mission—a fellow seeker of spiritual truth and a Nazarite—who inspired Roy to embrace a vow of consecration unto God to discover his true purpose. Following his time at St. Vincent's, Roy joined the Christian Life Discipleship Program at the Union Rescue Mission, where he engaged in Bible study at this Christ-centered institution. During this transformative year, Roy unearthed the "Sacred Text for the Song of the Lamb," a revelation that would change the trajectory of his life.

As he faced the darkness of impending blindness, Roy called out to God and experienced a profound spiritual awakening. While his physical eyes were closing, his spiritual eyes opened, and he realized that he had been "dancing with the devil" in an attempt to please God. God heard his cry and led him back to the path of righteousness, redeeming him through the blood of the Lamb, Jesus Christ.

Roy's groundbreaking work caught the attention of influential leaders within the Seventh-day Adventist Church, leading him to Oakwood University in Huntsville, Alabama. There, he met with renowned figures like Dr. Delbert Baker president of Oakwood University and Dr. Eurydice Osterman who was commissioned to compose the music for the "Song of the Lamb," which was later performed at Pioneer Memorial

Church at Andrews University in Berrien Springs, Michigan. This powerful composition, alongside “Song of Moses” and the “Sonia of the Lamb” in Hebrew which was commissioned to be set to music by Dr. James Lee III encapsulates a divine message of hope and prophecy, resonating with the biblical promise of Israel’s ultimate redemption.

After returning from a 53-day fact-finding mission in Israel in 2023, where he further explored the Middle East crisis, Roy spent additional time at the Union Rescue Mission following a separation from his wife, Tara. In 2025, he pursued a career in cinema producing at the LA Film School, with the intent of adapting his journey into a dramatic film that would feature the soundtracks of the "Song of Moses" and the "Song of the Lamb" in Hebrew. This project aims to inspire a global revival and reformation, ushering in the return of Jesus Christ, the Prince of Peace.

At the heart of "Jerusalem WON" lies a compelling exploration of the prophetic fulfillment of Ezekiel 38 and 39. Ferguson boldly asserts that the return of Jesus Christ is not just a personal quest but a universal call to resolve conflict and restore hope for the nations. His vision extends beyond the present, envisioning a future where global revival and reformation will usher in peace after the apocalypse, culminating in the New Jerusalem.

As the narrative unfolds, readers are invited to witness the magnificent plan of God for humanity, including the ultimate confrontation between good and evil on the Mount of Olives, where Satan will summon his army to attack the Holy City. Divine fire will descend from heaven, consuming the wicked and cleansing the earth, transforming it into a new haven free of sorrow, pain, and death.

This book is more than a personal memoir; it is a clarion call to the Jewish people, reminding them that Jesus is the Messiah and the last bastion of hope in these challenging times. With fervent passion, Ferguson delivers a powerful message of revival and reformation, urging readers to embrace the spirit of the final three angels' messages.

This Foreword now yields to the story, so eloquently told and briefly captured in the Preface, Prelude and Prologue. This is a deliberate pause of the heart. In what follows, the reader is invited to prayerful stillness, so that when the narrative opens, it does not rush past the soul but takes root within it.

PREFACE

This book was not written out of ambition but out of obedience. *Jerusalem WON: Signed in Blood* 💧 *– The Epic Quest for Lasting Peace* is the story of my pilgrimage with God, a journey that has taken me from the hills of Jamaica to the streets of Los Angeles, through seasons of blindness and despair, and into the light of revelation and renewed hope.

For me, this work is not simply a memoir, nor is it only prophecy. It is a testimony of God's power to redeem, restore, and realign a life when all seems lost. My own path has been marked by failures and struggles, but also by profound encounters with the living Christ. Those experiences have impressed upon me the urgency of sharing the message that has carried me: that in the blood of the Lamb, peace and deliverance are not only possible but promised.

What sets this story apart is not who I am, but what God has done. Along the way, He has revealed visions of revival and reformation, rooted in the Three Angels' Messages of Revelation 14 and in the promise of the New Jerusalem. These are not distant prophecies, but present realities pressing upon us now. My testimony joins with the song of Moses and the song of the

Lamb, reminding us that praise itself becomes a weapon in the final conflict between light and darkness.

Although these pages tell my story, they would not exist in this form without my co-author, Malcolm McGough. Malcolm has helped to give structure, voice, and clarity to what God has entrusted to me. This book is the fruit of our collaboration, but its heartbeat remains the testimony of what Christ has done in my life. For his faithful labor and encouragement, I am deeply grateful.

My prayer is that this book will not merely inform but transform. May it stir in you the same urgency I have felt — to turn fully toward Christ, to hold fast to His promises, and to look with longing for the New Jerusalem. Read these pages as an invitation and summons, for the time is short and the call is clear.

Just as *Pilgrim's Progress* showed that every believer's path is marked by struggle, faith, and ultimate deliverance, so too this work reflects not only my pilgrimage, but also Malcolm's, and — we believe — yours as well. It is with that shared spirit of journey that we now invite you into the Prelude, where the greater story of Jerusalem and eternity unfolds.

With gratitude and faith,

Roy H. Ferguson

with **Malcolm McGough**

October 2025

Los Angeles, California

Introduction

This Introduction exists to provide the reader with orientation and purpose. It clarifies why Jerusalem stands at the center of this work and how prophecy, history, and present reality converge within its pages. The task here is not to answer every question, but to frame them rightly: Why Jerusalem? Why now? What does her story demand of those who believe, those who doubt, and those who simply watch? You will encounter Scripture placed in the context of lived experience, not to sensationalize the times, but to sanctify the reader's attention. The aim is preparation, not prediction; fidelity, not fear. Read, then, with a steady heart. Let the following chapters be both lamp and plumb line—light for the path and measure for the soul—so that the narrative which follows is received as more than history, and the Epilogue as more than an ending.

Why Jerusalem? Why now? These questions lie at the very heart of this work. Jerusalem is not merely a city among cities. She is a covenantal signpost, a meeting place of heaven and earth, a stage where empires have risen and fallen, and where prophets have declared the words of the Living God. To speak of Jerusalem is to speak of the pulse of redemption history itself.

In this moment of history, her significance presses upon the conscience of the world with renewed urgency. Political powers wrestle over her boundaries. Faith traditions claim her as sacred ground. Prophetic voices warn and promise. The stones of her streets are not silent relics; they are witnesses. And the world, knowingly or unknowingly, leans toward her as though she were a clock striking the hour.

Why now? Because the signs of the age converge in ways that make Jerusalem not only a matter of history but of destiny. Global conflict, spiritual hunger, and cultural fracture all find strange resonance in her gates. To ignore her story is to ignore the axis on which the human drama now turns.

But what does her story demand of us? It does not permit indifference. For the believer, Jerusalem summons faith — a reminder that God's promises do not fail. For the doubter, she provokes the question: why does this city endure when all logic says she should have been erased? For the watcher on the sidelines, she insists upon decision — to watch is to be implicated, for Jerusalem's destiny entwines with the destiny of nations.

This Introduction therefore sets the terms of our journey. It is not enough to admire Jerusalem from afar. One must wrestle with her claims, her prophecies, and her place in both divine intention and human history. This is why this work begins here: with the acknowledgment that Jerusalem is not only central to the story we tell, but also to the story in which we live.

Roy's journey, as told in the Prologue, mirrors this call. His pilgrimage is not only his own but a reflection of us all: a passage through denial, doubt, faith, and deliverance. The story is both personal and prophetic, showing us, that Jerusalem is not a distant reality but a present invitation. In Roy's footsteps we discern our own, and in his progress we see the pattern of the pilgrim's path.

Prelude
The Tapestry of Destiny

In the shadow of Jerusalem, where ancient stones whisper secrets of glory and despair, a cosmic struggle rages—a battle not merely waged in the hearts of men, but in the very fabric of existence. Before the foundation of the world, Roy found himself entwined in a tale of ambition and rebellion—a tale that began with Lucifer, the covered cherub, radiant in his splendor yet consumed by an insatiable desire to ascend to the throne of God. "For you have said in your heart, 'I will ascend to heaven; above the stars of God, I will set my throne on high; I will sit on the mount of assembly in the far reaches of the north; I will ascend above the heights of the clouds; I will make myself like the Most High.'" (Isaiah 14:13-14). His pride ignited a war in heaven, a cataclysmic clash that would cast him from celestial heights to the abyss below, dragging a third of the angels with him into the darkness.

Now, as the dragon, he roams the earth; a master deceiver cloaked in charm, whispering seductive lies that echo through the ages. With cunning, he ensnared our forebears, Adam and Eve, in the garden where innocence bloomed. "For all that is in the world—the desires of the flesh and the desires of the eyes and pride of life—is not from the Father but is from the world." (1 John 2:16). Through the lust of the eyes, the pride of life, and the cravings of the flesh, he spun a web of deceit that has entangled humanity for six millennia. It is this very deception that fuels his relentless desire to thwart the sovereignty of God, to delay the coming of the New Jerusalem—a city of peace, the final dwelling place of the redeemed.

But why, you may ask, is peace so elusive in this sacred land? The answer lies in a covenant sealed in blood—a divine promise etched into the heart of Israel. "I will establish my covenant between me and you and your offspring after you throughout their generations for an everlasting covenant." (Genesis 17:7). Here, in the cradle of salvation, the blood of Jesus—the second Adam—would soon be shed, reclaiming a world that had been forfeited by the first. This blood-bought land, chosen by the God of Abraham, Isaac, and Jacob, is destined to become the epicenter of eternity, where the King of kings will reign upon the throne of David, establishing the New Jerusalem upon the Mount of Olives.

As the world spirals toward chaos, the Antichrist—a puppet of the dragon—rises from the shadows, wielding deception as his greatest weapon. With the help of a false prophet, he will enforce a law that contradicts the very essence of God's commandments, leading the masses into the snare of worship on a day that honors the sun rather than the Creator. "And he causes all, both small and great, rich and poor, free and slave, to receive a mark on their right hand or on their foreheads." (Revelation 13:16). In this pivotal hour, the faithful remnant—the saints—will rise, armed with the truth of the Three Angels' Messages, declaring a clarion call to all who will listen amidst the cacophony of lies.

As the millennium dawns, the saints will ascend to heaven, witnessing the judgment of the wicked, their questions answered in the light of divine justice. "Do you not know that the saints will judge the world?" (1 Corinthians 6:2). They will reign with Christ, unraveling the threads of history and understanding the depths of grace and mercy that shaped their lives. Meanwhile, the dragon, furious and desperate, will unleash his final assault, proclaiming himself as God within the temple of Jerusalem—a blasphemous act destined to ignite the final conflict.

In the face of this turmoil, Jerusalem stands as a beacon of hope and a battleground for souls. "And at that time shall arise Michael, the great prince who has charge of your people. And there shall be a time of trouble, such as never has been since there was a nation till that time." (Daniel 12:1). It is here, where heaven and earth converge, that the ultimate triumph of good over evil will be played out. As the saints flee to the mountains, as foretold in prophecy, the archangel Michael will rise up for His people, delivering all whose names are inscribed in the Book of Life.

Jerusalem WON—a declaration that transcends time and space—is not merely a title; it is the promise of a world order rooted in the New Jerusalem, a stark contrast to the deceptive New World Order. "And I saw the holy city, New Jerusalem, coming down out of heaven from God, prepared as a bride adorned for her husband." (Revelation 21:2). As the curtain rises on the final act of this grand narrative, the question remains: In this theater of divine destiny, will you recognize the truth, or will you be swept away in the tide of deception? The choice is yours, and the time is now.

With this foundation laid, we now step into the unfolding of Jerusalem's story—a narrative both ancient and immediate.

We are reminded that each journey toward Jerusalem is, in truth, our own pilgrimage. Roy's story, told in the Prologue, mirrors the spiritual progress of every soul— from denial to faith, from doubt to deliverance. The Prelude therefore whispers: this is not his story alone, but ours as well.

In this way, Roy's pilgrimage becomes more than a single traveler's tale. It is a reflection of our own spiritual journey—the Pilgrim's progress through doubt and faith, through weakness and deliverance. His footsteps mirror ours, reminding us that the call of Jerusalem is not abstract but deeply personal. It is a summons we each must answer.

Prologue

In a world where darkness so often overshadows hope and challenges seem endless, there remain those who dare to believe change is possible. They are the dreamers, the seekers, the ones who refuse to surrender to despair. Roy Ferguson once counted himself among them.

In the quiet hills of Jamaica, beneath skies brushed with the hues of dawn, a little boy stood on a grassy rise as his mother's voice echoed in his ears:

"You will do something great for God."

At only three years old, Roy could not comprehend the weight of his mother's prophecy. Yet those words settled deep within him, a seed planted by faith, waiting for its season to bloom.

But as the years passed, the laughter of childhood gave way to shadows. His parents' marriage fractured, and with every argument and tearful goodbye, the foundation of his world trembled. Though his mother labored endlessly to hold the family together, the cracks deepened, leaving Roy searching for stability — and for God.

By his teenage years, bitterness had replaced innocence. The promise spoken over him felt distant, almost mocking. "If God truly called me," Roy thought, "why has He abandoned us?" Disappointment became rebellion, and rebellion led him to doors better left unopened.

At first, it seemed harmless: a flicker of candlelight, whispered names, and the thrill of forbidden things. But what began in curiosity grew into a darkness that consumed him. One dark night of soul in restless defiance, he bit into his finger, the metallic taste of blood filling his mouth. Trembling, he signed in blood on the mirror words that would haunt his soul:

"I will serve you, Satan."

A pact was sealed. Innocence surrendered.

Roy fled Jamaica for America, drawn by Hollywood's promise of reinvention. But beneath the glittering lights, he found a deeper emptiness. Fame whispered; power beckoned. Yet each achievement faded like smoke, leaving him hollow.

The Mirror and the Invitation

One night, back in his apartment, Roy's gaze drifted toward the mirror across the room.

His reflection stared back at him — a cruel reminder of the wild man he had become. Haunted. Weary. A stranger to the bright-eyed dreamer he once was.

"You're too far gone, Roy," he muttered. "This is it."

He reached for a photo frame on his cluttered desk — a snapshot of him and his friends, their youthful faces radiant with hope. A fleeting smile crossed his lips, but it quickly twisted into a grimace. He tossed the photo aside, and the glass shattered against the floor.

His hand brushed against an invitation — the one he knew he should never have accepted. Clutching it, he left the apartment, aimless, heart pounding with the weight of a decision he sensed would change everything.

As he drifted down Hollywood Boulevard beneath the midday sun, neon lights blurred into meaninglessness. Tourists, street performers, and hollow smiles blurred together, each step carrying him closer to something inevitable.

He stopped before a street magician, his tricks drawing a captivated crowd. For a moment, Roy watched the illusion unfolding — smoke, mirrors, and sleight of hand. And deep down, he felt it: This is the game I'm about to enter — one of promises that vanish into nothing.

The Whisper of Power

That night, in a dimly lit bar, he nursed a drink while eavesdropping on two actors nearby.

"What's a little soul sacrifice for a shot at the big time?" one joked.

Roy leaned in, his heart quickening.

"You think it's funny?" the other replied. "You have no idea what it takes to survive here."

Their words clung to him like a siren's call. He thought of the invitation burning in his pocket — a chance to meet the enigmatic agent known for delivering success... at a price.

Opportunity without risk is nothing, he told himself. But what if the risk swallows everything?

The Mansion of Shadows

The party was opulent, alive with music, beauty, and ambition — but shadows lurked in every corner. Beautiful souls smiled behind masks of desperation. Roy moved through the crowd, each step heavier than the last, until whispers led him toward a quiet back room.

The agent was waiting. Enigmatic. Charming. Dangerous.

"You want fame, don't you, Roy?" the man asked, his words like silk. "All it takes is a little... sacrifice."

Roy's throat tightened. "What's the cost?"

The agent leaned in closely, his whisper soft but sharp — secrets promising everything Roy had ever wanted. Whatever was said was not heard by the ears but understood by the soul.

Later, back in his apartment, Roy collapsed onto his bed, the invitation clutched in trembling hands. Shadows stretched across the ceiling as doubt whispered louder than hope.

I could be lost forever, he thought. But what if... what if I'm already too far gone?

The Room of the Pact

It wasn't a single choice that led Roy here — it was a thousand tiny compromises, each one leading him deeper into darkness. In time, he returned to a room he had avoided for months — a sanctuary of forbidden knowledge.

Books on witchcraft lined the shelves, an amulet stained in ram's blood lay nearby, and a five-pointed star covered the floor. A single candle flickered, stretching shadows like skeletal fingers across the walls.

On the table sat a large leather-bound book, heavy with secrets and promises. Beside it, a vial of crimson liquid pulsed faintly in the candlelight. Roy's hand trembled as he reached for it, the scent of iron filling the room.

"This is my only chance," he whispered.

With the vial uncapped, he dipped the quill and hovered over the page. Shadows danced wildly as a voice — low, smooth, and unyielding — spoke from nowhere and everywhere:

“You understand what you are giving up, don’t you, Roy? Your soul is the price of your ambition.”

He froze. His hand shook. But the promise of power was louder than the warning. With a final breath, he pressed the quill to parchment. Blood touched paper. Fate was sealed.

“For what will it profit a man if he gains the whole world, and forfeits his soul?” — Matthew 16:26

The Breaking Point

Not long after, a diagnosis threatened to take his sight. Fear drove him to his knees. In the silence of his apartment, he whispered through tears:

“God... spare my vision” and I will serve you as long as I live! But if I should go Blind I will go back to Jamaica and my mother will lead me.

In that moment, the true miracle unfolded: though his physical sight waned, his spiritual eyes opened. The God he had abandoned had never abandoned him.

From the edge of destruction, Roy’s story turned toward redemption. He walked away from the illusions of fame and into the sunbaked streets of Skid Row, where the forgotten waited for hope. There he met Raymond Yeshu; a Nazarite whose wisdom helped him consecrate his life back to God.

Roy's journey became a testament: that no shadow is too deep, no pact too binding, no distance too great for God's light to break through.

"The light shines in the darkness, and the darkness has not overcome it." — John 1:5

Jerusalem Won: Signed in Blood is the chronicle of that journey — a war between calling and compromise, darkness and redemption. It is a reminder that before the promise is fulfilled, the wilderness must be faced, and that to step into the light, one must first confront the weight of the shadows.

Chapter 1
Memories from Jamaica

One Thursday, the noonday sun shone fiercely on the old, modest apartment in Mount Salem, Jamaica. The apartment was cramped, a one-bedroom unit with chipped walls and creaking floors, but to Gloria, it was home; it was a space she fiercely protected for her children. That day, however, the air inside was heavy with tension. Her ten-year-old son sat cross-legged on the floor with his siblings as he attempted his math homework. His pencil tapped nervously against the paper indicating his restless heart and thoughts that were racing.

Gloria was seated at the small dining table across the room while she was sorting through a towering pile of bills. She was trying hard to do the math with her fingers, but her mind was miles away. When little Roy finally broke the silence, his voice was small and hesitant, but it cut through her thoughts like a knife.

"Mom?"

Gloria suddenly looked up with a startled face. The weariness in her eyes softened when she met her son's curious gaze.

"Yes, sweetheart?"

Roy hesitated to speak further with his pencil now still in his hand. He glanced at the floor before turning his head toward his mother again as if deciding whether to speak his mind.

"Why did Dad say I'm not his son?"

The question landed like a stone in a still pond, sending ripples of shock and sadness through Gloria. Her math calculations suddenly stopped as her fingers froze midway. But she quickly recovered and placed the bills aside and leaned forward.

"Roy," she said gently, "come here."

The little boy obeyed and approached her, dragging his small stool closer to her. Gloria reached out, cupping his face in her hands. She searched his eyes, looking for the right words to soothe the storm she knew was brewing inside him.

"Sometimes," she began, her voice calm but steady, "adults say things out of anger or fear. Things that aren't true. What matters is that I know who you are, and you are my son. I love you."

Roy frowned and looked down at the floor, trying to grapple her words in his young mind. "But why would he say that? Is it because I'm not good enough?"

"No!" Gloria's voice rose slightly, but not out of anger—out of desperation to make him understand. "Roy, you are more than enough. Never let anyone make you think otherwise."

"You are special, Roy. God has plans for you," she further stated.

Roy nodded, but the doubt still lingered in his mind. Gloria pulled him closer and hugged him tightly as if her embrace could shield him from the harshness of the world. But deep down, she knew it wasn't enough.

Later that evening, the family sat around the small dining table for dinner. Gloria had managed to stretch the last of their provisions into a simple meal of rice and peas. Roy's younger siblings—eight-year-old Desrine, six-year-old Andrea, and four-year-old Dwight—chattered excitedly about their day and were blissfully unaware of the tension that had earlier consumed the household. Roy, on the other hand, was unusually quiet, pushing his food around on his plate.

"Roy, you're not eating," Gloria said, her voice laced with concern.

"I'm not hungry," he replied dully while still looking at his plate.

Desrine chimed in with her mouth somewhat full of rice. "Roy got in trouble at school today again, Mom."

Gloria's eyes widened. "Is that true, Roy?"

Roy dropped his shoulders. "It wasn't my fault," he mumbled. "David said something mean about you."

"What did he say?" Gloria asked her tone firm but not accusatory.

"He said you're a liar and that..." Roy hesitated as his voice faltered. "That I'm not really part of this family."

The table fell silent. Even Desrine and the siblings stopped eating, their young, innocent eyes darting between Roy and Gloria. Gloria's jaw tightened, but she quickly softened her expression, not wanting to alarm her children.

"And what did you do then?" she asked calmly.

"I hit him," Roy admitted, his voice barely above a whisper. "I know I shouldn't have, but he wouldn't stop, Mom."

Gloria sighed, reaching across the table to take his hand. "Roy, I'm proud of you for standing up for me, but violence is never the answer. Next time, you come to me or your teacher, okay?"

Roy nodded reluctantly. "Okay."

Gloria smiled faintly and squeezed his hand softly. "Good. Now eat your dinner. You'll need your strength for tomorrow."

"And tomorrow, we will have a feast, just you all wait!" she said with high spirits, but deep down only she knew how hard it was for her to say it to her children.

The next morning, Gloria walked Roy to school with her hand firmly gripping his. The streets of Mount Salem were alive with the sounds of vendors hawking their goods and children laughing on their way to class. Gloria glanced down at Roy; his small face set in a determined expression.

"Remember what I said," she told him. "If anyone gives you trouble, you handle it the right way. Promise me."

"I promise, Mom," Roy said, though his tone lacked conviction.

As they approached the school gates, Gloria knelt to his level, adjusting his collar and wiped the sweat from his brow. "You're going to have a great day, my little warrior. Just keep your head high and remember who you are."

Roy managed a small smile. "Okay, Mom."

Roy walked away, and Gloria watched as he disappeared into the schoolyard, her heart heavy with worry. She knew the world could be cruel, especially to a boy like Roy, but she also knew he had a strength within him that would one day shine.

That afternoon, Roy's teacher, Mrs. Clarke, called Gloria into the school. As Gloria entered the classroom, she was greeted by the sight of Roy sitting in a chair, his head bowed. Beside him stood David, the boy he had fought with, with a light bruise on his left cheek.

"Mrs. Ferguson," Mrs. Clarke began in her professional but stern tone. "We need to discuss what happened today."

"I'm sorry about this," Gloria said, glancing at Roy. "He's... been going through a lot."

"I understand," Mrs. Clarke replied, softening slightly. "But violence is not acceptable in this school. Roy needs to learn to express himself without resorting to his fists."

Gloria nodded. "I'll talk to him."

Mrs. Clarke sighed, and her gaze shifted to Roy. "He's a bright boy Mrs. Ferguson; he has so much potential. I just want to see him succeed."

As they left the school, Gloria placed a hand on Roy's shoulder. "We're going to fix this," she said firmly. "Together."

That evening, Gloria and Roy sat on the worn couch in their living room. The younger children were asleep, and the quiet allowed them to talk openly.

"Roy," Gloria began, her voice soft, "why didn't you come to me when David was bothering you?"

"Because I didn't want to seem weak," Roy admitted. "And because... I'm tired of people saying things about us."

Gloria's heart pained for her son. She took his hands in hers, looking him straight in the eye.

"Roy, being strong doesn't mean fighting back with your fists. It means knowing when to walk away and when to speak up. It means standing tall even when people try to bring you down. Do you understand?"

"*And always remember that being honest is the best thing you can do for yourself and everyone*," she stated further.

Roy nodded slowly. "I love you, Mom, you're the best."

As Gloria heard his words, she smiled from ear to ear. "I love you more. No matter what anyone says, you are my son. Nothing can change that."

Roy hugged her tightly and felt a fleeting moment of comfort in her embrace. Yet, Gloria could not stop thinking about making ends meet, the gnawing hunger that had become their unwelcome companion.

The days passed quietly and routinely. On one such morning, when Roy was off from school, he was playing in the backyard all alone, trying to draw different patterns with a stick in the sand. Suddenly, he noticed a big tree across the boundary with juicy seasonal mangoes hanging. As he stared at the fresh fruit, his stomach groaned with hunger as it reminded him that even a simple breakfast like plain toast with a thin layer of strawberry jam had been out of reach for breakfast that morning. He walked up to the neighbor's backyard and stared at the mangoes with bright eyes.

"If I could get just a small piece . . ." His daydreaming was interrupted as he heard the loud voice of an old man, Mr. Thompson.

"Hey! What are you doing, kid?"

Roy was startled and stumbled back a step. His mouth opened, but no words came at first. "I... I was just looking.

"Well, you can have one, but you better ask your mom first," Mr. Thompson said gruffly.

Roy nodded but his cheeks were burning with embarrassment. He plucked a mango and held it tightly as if it were a treasure. *Indeed, for him, it was.* He ran towards his house in excitement and approached his mother.

"Mom, mom, see what I got. Mr. Thompson gave this to me, but he said I must ask you first before I eat it," Roy said with a short breath.

Gloria saw the juicy fruit, and she herself could not stop staring at it. Days without a proper meal led her stomach to make a sound, but her love for her son was nothing compared to it. She could see the spark in his eyes as Roy waited for her response patiently, and as she stared at his innocent face, her heart ached when she thought of denying him even the smallest joy. Her thoughts were torn between the looming bills and the hunger gnawing inside. Even fruit was beyond their reach.

"That's very nice, sweetheart," she said softly, forcing a smile. "Of course you can have it Roy, just make sure you thank Mr. Thompson."

That night, Roy lay in bed as he stared at the ceiling. The shadows from a flickering lamp danced across the walls. He could hear the muffled sound of his parents arguing. Words like "divorce" and "abandonment" cut through the night, each one piercing Roy's heart. He clenched his fists, swallowing the lump in his throat as he tried to sleep.

The following weeks were no kinder. At school, Roy did his best to blend in, but the whispers always found him.

Once again, one day after school, Roy was hit by a reality check.

"That's him," David murmured to another. "The illegitimate one."

"His dad doesn't even want him," one of David's cronies sneered.

"I think you need another smack in the head, David," Roy said harshly.

David and his friends looked at him with anger as he started walking away.

Roy kept his head down all the way back home, but their words dug deep, which stirred a storm inside him.

When he got home, he found his mother sitting on the couch, clutching a framed photo of their family. Her fingers traced the edges of the picture as if willing the image to come alive.

"Mom," Roy said, his voice breaking the quiet. "What special thing am I going to do for God?"

Gloria looked up with her eyes glistening with unshed tears. She reached out, pulling Roy into a hug.

"You'll understand when the time comes," she whispered. "Just know that God is always with you, no matter what."

Years passed, and the seeds Gloria had planted in Roy's heart began to grow. As a teenager, he found solace and purpose in the church. He stood at the altar one evening, his voice strong and steady as he led a group of troubled youths in prayer.

"God is our Father," he said passionately. "He loves us no matter what!"

The room pulsed with sacred anticipation. A quiet hope hung in the air, fragile but real—like a candle in a storm, defiant and trembling. Faces were lifted; hearts were softening. But just as the atmosphere swelled with spiritual promise, a violent sound shattered it.

The heavy doors of the church exploded open with a crash, slamming against the walls like thunderclaps. Cold air rushed in with the gang that followed. Their boots echoed off the hardwood floor, and their laughter—sharp, mocking—ripped through the sanctuary.

The leader sauntered forward with a swagger of dominance, eyes sweeping the pews like a predator sizing up prey.

"Well, well," he said, voice dripping with sarcasm. "What's this? A prayer meeting?" His smirk curled as he looked around at the silent congregation.

A collective hush blanketed the room. No one moved. Fear rose like mist—unspoken but thick in the air.

Roy stood firm at the altar, his palms sweating, but his heart steady now—not by human strength, but by something greater.

"You're not alone," he said, his voice calm but piercing. "You don't have to keep living like this. You can change. There's still time."

A chorus of laughter erupted from the gang. It bounced off the walls, crude and wild.

But then—like a needle scratching across a record—the laughter stopped.

The gang leader's eyes had locked onto Roy. He took a step forward, staring, not in menace anymore but in confusion—maybe even curiosity. There was something in Roy's face. Not defiance. Not fear. Something purer. Something unfamiliar. 'Conviction.'

All of a sudden, Roy remembered his mother's words, "Whenever you're lost, remember God is your Father," Gloria said during a storm while comforting her little boy.

"You mean that?" the leader asked, his tone suddenly stripped of sarcasm.

"I do," Roy replied, softer now, but every syllable weighed with truth. "I was once like you. Lost and searching. But I found a family in God," Roy said as he started walking down the altar. "You were made for more than this. I can see it in you; and so can He!"

He gestured gently toward the cross behind him. Roy took a step closer, his pulse pounding in his ears. "Without Jesus you'll always feel empty," he said in his soft voice but resolutely. "But there's hope for you, just like there was for me."

The others looked to their leader, their posturing momentarily deflated. The room, which just seconds earlier had felt like a tinderbox, now held its breath in a different kind of tension—not of violence, but of possibility.

The apprehension in the room was thick, but a flicker of something, curiosity, maybe even hope crossed the gang leader's face. He didn't say anything, just stared at Roy before turning and walking out. One by one, the other gang members followed – 'A Seed had been planted'.

Years later, Roy, with his adult physique and a more mature attire, sat with his mother in their small apartment. The same framed photo from years ago sat between them. They smiled, their bond strengthened by the trials they had faced together.

"Through pain and rejection, I learned that family isn't just blood ..., a truth I experienced many years later in my own family."

Outside the church, Roy stood surrounded by a group of young people, their faces bright with hope. He looked up at the sky and a smile spread across his face.

"...but love. And love can conquer all."

In his apartment, Roy sat on the couch with his back slightly hunched while he was reviving his memory. A small table in the middle of the living room was cluttered with schoolbooks and a single, wilted flower drooped in a dry, cracked vase. His eyes stared at the framed photo of his family resting on the table in front of him. It's the same photo from years ago, now slightly yellowed with age. The image shows his younger self beside his mother, Gloria, a version of her that seemed more hopeful, her smile untainted by the years of hardship. Roy touched the frame gently, his fingers brushing the glass as if trying to connect with that memory, that life he can never quite return to.

If I knew then what I know now about rebelling against God, I would have done things differently.

Chapter 2
The Forbidden Game

It was almost dusk and the roads were empty. Roy stood at the rusted wrought iron gate of the neighbor's house, his fingers hesitating over the latch. The temptation to step inside burned in him, the allure of adventure far too strong to resist. His eyes gleamed with mischief as he glanced toward a ripe mango hanging from a tree nearby. The fifteen-year-old then remembered what happened the last time he asked for a mango from Mr. Thompson and what his mother told him. As he smiled at the thought of Mr. Thompson, his mind was suddenly jolted back to the reason for being at his neighbor's house.

He had been watching them for weeks—Liam, Nora, Carrie, and Diego. They were always so mysterious, always whispering, always with that damn Ouija board. He had heard rumors. Some said it was just a game, a way to pass the time. Others whispered that it could contact spirits, that it could predict the future, even manipulate events. It was something that his mother, Gloria, would never allow him to play with. And yet, here he was, drawn like a moth to a flame.

The gate creaked open as Roy pushed it, stepping onto the property. He looked around quickly to make sure no one saw him before creeping toward the living room window. Inside, the soft glow of candlelight flickered through the curtains. It was the same as the other times, the same strange ritual.

Roy knew he shouldn't be here. Something deep within him warned him to turn away, yet another voice — softer, darker — urged him closer. His breath quickened as he crept toward the door, careful not to stir the old floorboards beneath his feet. The low murmur of voices leaked through the narrow crack at the bottom, weaving through the stillness like a living thing. He pressed his ear to the wood. Nora's voice came faint but clear. "I think it's ready. We should try again."

Inside, four teenagers sat cross-legged in a circle on the worn carpet laid across the living room floor. The faint, wavering candlelight illuminated their faces, casting restless shadows that danced along the walls. In the center of the circle lay the Ouija board, its glossy surface catching the trembling glow of the flames. The board was arranged with deliberate care, the letters and numbers drawn in bold, dark ink.

Though Roy could not see it from where he stood, he could feel its presence seeping through the door — a strange and silent lure that seemed to reach for him, stirring something deep and unguarded within. He did not know it then, but in that moment, the first thread of temptation had tightened around his soul — a whisper from the darkness that would one day demand a price written in blood.

Liam, the oldest and perhaps the most serious of the group, spoke first. With his low and steady voice, he said, “Alright, we’ve done this before. We need to focus. Everyone clear their minds.”

Carrie, who was sitting beside him, bit her lip nervously. “I don’t know, Liam. What if it’s real this time? What if... we actually make contact?”

“You’re freaking yourself out,” Liam said with a chuckle. “It’s just a game. Remember, that’s all it is.”

“I don’t know...” Carrie trailed off as she looked at others. Nora, who was sitting opposite her, smiled reassuringly.

“Don’t worry, Carrie. It’s harmless. Just a way to have some fun.”

Nora’s voice was sweet and coaxing. Roy recognized her as one of the more approachable ones in the group, but even her calm demeanor couldn't hide the excitement in her eyes about what was to come.

The planchette, the little triangular piece that would move across the board, was placed in the center. The group’s fingers hovered over it. The atmosphere in the room felt heavy with the tension of expectation arising.

"Is anyone there?" Nora asked softly, her voice barely above a whisper. She sounded both hopeful and apprehensive, as though she was testing the waters of some forbidden pool.

A deep silence followed her questions and they looked at each other, breathing heavily. But then, to everyone's shock, the planchette moved. Both Nora and Carrie let out a short but fearful scream as the triangle began to move across the surface, as if guided by invisible fingers until it settled on the letter "Y."

Everyone gasped collectively, and for a moment, time seemed to stand still. The board was real. It was working. It wasn't just a game anymore to pass the time, like people said.

The planchette continued to glide across the board, spelling out words, one letter at a time: "Y-E-S."

Carrie's breath caught in her throat. "Oh my God, it's real."

"Alright, alright," Liam said, trying to regain some composure. He leaned forward, his eyes narrowing with curiosity. "Who are you?"

The planchette jerked and then moved again, this time spelling out: "I-A-M."

"I am?" Nora repeated with a confused look. "Who is this?"

The planchette moved once more, slowly, deliberately: "T-H-A-T."

"That?" Diego, who had been silent until now, said. "What does that mean?"

All four of them gave a look of uncertainty to each other, and with their eyes back on the board, they waited for the planchette to move.

Before they could get a complete answer, a loud creak echoed through the room as the front door swung open, startling them all.

"Hey," a voice called out, startling everyone. It was Roy standing in the doorway, his wide eyes betraying a mixture of curiosity and caution. He looked over at the board and then at the group with great concern.

"Roy!" Liam said, clearly startled but not upset. "What are you doing here?"

Roy, caught off guard, stammered. "I... I saw the lights. What's going on? Is this a game?"

Carrie forced a smile, but there was a sharpness to her tone that didn't quite match the friendliness in her eyes. "Come in. We're just... trying something. You should join us."

"I don't know..." Roy's gaze flickered between the Ouija board and the group, his hands nervously gripping the doorframe. "Isn't this... what is this? Some sort of spirit thing?" His voice lowered, suddenly aware of how serious it all seemed, how much darker it had become after the incident earlier.

Nora let out a nervous laugh. She brushed it off too quickly, her voice too light. "It's just for fun, Roy. Don't be such a scaredy-cat. You don't have to believe in it." She looked away right after saying it, as if trying to convince herself more than him.

Carrie nodded, though her expression was tight, her voice holding an edge of discomfort. "Yeah, we're not really expecting anything. It's just to see if it works. It's not a big deal." But there was a flicker of doubt in her eyes that made Roy question her words even more.

Something about their energy felt off—like they were all trying too hard to make it sound casual when everything inside him screamed that it wasn't. Roy hesitated but he could feel that something about this game called to him, like a siren's song. He took a seat next to Carrie and his eyes were glued to the board.

The air in the room felt thick with tension. He could almost taste the excitement, the fear, and the thrill in the air.

As soon as he sat down, Liam gave him a nod. "Alright, Roy. If you're in, place your fingers on the planchette. We're trying to figure out who's here."

Roy hesitated but finally placed his fingers lightly on the planchette, joining the circle. The room fell silent as they all waited, breaths held.

The planchette moved again.

"Is this game dangerous?" Roy asked, his voice low and a little shaky. His fingers were still on the planchette, and he could feel it moving beneath his touch as though something unseen was guiding it.

"No," Liam said firmly, though his eyes betrayed some doubt. "Look, Roy, I get it. I saw what happened too, but... it's just a game. You can't let it freak you out like that."

But Roy's heart was pounding in his chest. He wasn't sure if it was fear or excitement, but something about the whole situation felt wrong.

Days later, Roy couldn't shake the feeling that something was off. The memory of the Ouija board, the way it had moved so effortlessly, haunted him. What had they contacted? What had he been a part of?

There, in his room, Roy sat on the edge of his bed, his eyes locked on the Ouija board resting across his lap. The memory of that night at the neighbor's house still clung to him — the flickering candlelight, the chill that ran through the air, the strange movement of the planchette beneath their trembling fingers. He had meant only to watch, but when the door creaked and all eyes turned toward him, they had called him in. What followed had left an imprint on his soul — the sensation that something unseen had brushed against him, aware of his presence, almost welcoming him.

He hadn't been able to shake it. The whispers lingered in his mind, weaving through his thoughts in the quiet hours of the night. Curiosity turned into a restless ache, a pull he could neither explain nor resist. It was as if the board itself had followed him home, whispering for him to return.

When the package finally arrived, he tore it open with trembling hands. The glossy surface of the new board gleamed as though alive, the bold letters seeming to pulse beneath his gaze. He traced them slowly with his fingertips, his heartbeat quickening.

The air around him felt charged — waiting. A thrill of fear and fascination coursed through him, and though he told himself it was only a game, deep inside, he knew something far darker had already begun.

Roy had always been the kind of boy who sought answers to questions no one else dared to ask. Maybe it was curiosity. Maybe it was the quiet frustration of a world that felt too small, too predictable. His family was struggling, scraping by with what little they had, and the thought that this strange board might hold a link to something greater — something that could reveal truth, power, or even the promise of wealth — was intoxicating. It was more than curiosity now; it was hope wrapped in darkness, a promise that whispered to his longing soul.

As he stared at the board, Roy thought about his mother. He glanced at a family photo kept on his dresser, his mother's warm smile contrasting with the darkness growing within him. She had always believed that God had a plan for him, that he was destined for greatness. But in his heart, Roy felt lost, uncertain of that path.

His fingers hovered over the bold letters. The secret of having his own Ouija board gave him a rush like he was holding a key to something bigger than his small world. But the guilt gnawed at him. What would his mother say if she found out? Would she understand? Would she believe him when he said it was just a game?

He turned the board over, its glossy surface reflecting the dim light in his room. He wasn't sure what he was hoping for. Answers? A sign? Or was it simply the thrill of the unknown, the temptation to step into a world where everything wasn't so dull, so painfully predictable?

Later that evening, Gloria was preparing dinner—the usual plain rice with mashed potatoes and steamed vegetables. After carefully hiding the Ouija board under his bed, Roy walked into the kitchen his heart thumping in his chest as he tried to act normal.

Gloria glanced over her shoulder, noticing his unusual silence. She raised an eyebrow with concern.

"Roy," she said softly, her voice full of motherly warmth. "You okay? You've been quiet lately."

Roy hesitated for a moment, trying to hide the turmoil inside him. "Yeah, just... thinking about school," he replied, his voice lacking conviction.

Gloria turned to face him fully now and her eyes scanned him for any hint of distress. She put the spatula down and walked over, placing a hand on his shoulder.

"You know you're destined for something special, right?" she said. "God has a plan for you, Roy."

Roy sensed that her words carried a heavy meaning. His mind drifted to the stark contrast between her unwavering faith and his own sense of doubt too apparent to ignore. He wanted to believe her. He wanted to feel the certainty she did, to know that everything in his life—his struggles, his pain, the feeling of being trapped—had a purpose.

But deep down, Roy wasn't so sure.

He thought God would bless him, help him make his family's life better and pull them out of poverty. He thought he was meant for something greater, that maybe his talents or his drive would open doors that were closed to others.

Instead, they were still dirt poor. Still scraping by. And now, Roy found himself reaching out to something darker, something that promised power and knowledge in exchange for his faith, in exchange for his curiosity.

Gloria gave him a soft smile, squeezing his shoulder. "You'll see, Roy. God has big plans for you. Just trust in Him."

Roy forced a smile back, but it felt hollow. "Yeah, I know, Mom."

He turned away quickly, unwilling to let her see the storm brewing inside him. As he headed to his room, his thoughts turned back to the Ouija board, the weight of his expectations of the board and what it might provide, along with the heaviness of the evil he knew it contained, a constant reminder that he was entering into an uncertain world. But he was already planning his next move.

His rebellious spirit decided to get back to the board. It wasn't just curiosity this time. It was the need to understand, a need to be in control of his destiny, to get answers he and his friends couldn't get the last time they breached the boundaries of what he knew to be true; they had breached the spirit world.

The next week, Roy, along with Liam, Carrie, Nora and Diego, went to a horse race taking place in the city. The racetrack was alive with energy. Horses galloped past, and the crowd cheered. The scent of fresh hay and sweat hung in the air, thick with the excitement of the races.

Roy, now carrying the Ouija board with him, pushed through the bustling crowd until he found a quiet spot near the fence. The other four followed and joined him shortly after.

"Roy," Diego said, looking over at him. "Are you sure about this? I mean, we're in the middle of a racetrack—this is a little crazy."

Carrie chimed in, trying to lighten the mood. "It's for fun, Diego. What's the worst that can happen?"

Roy wasn't sure, but he didn't want to admit it. He didn't want to seem like the scared one. So, he nodded. "Let's do it."

He set the Ouija board down on the grass, and the group gathered around it, their faces a mix of excitement and nervousness. The noise of the racetrack faded into the background as Roy placed his fingers on the planchette.

"Let's see what, or whoever is in there, can do for us," he murmured.

"We don't have much," Liam said, pulling a few crumpled bills from his pocket. He looked at the others, hesitant. "But if we're gonna do this, we need to pool what we've got."

Carrie bit her lip and searched through her bag, producing a small stash of coins and a single dollar bill. "It's not much, but it's something," she said, placing it on the table.

Nora added her contribution—a five-dollar bill she had been saving for weeks. "This is all I've got," she said softly.

Diego reached into his jacket, revealing a ten-dollar bill. "This is from my dad's emergency stash," he admitted, glancing nervously at the group. "But I'm in. Let's see if this thing really works."

Roy hesitated. He had the idea of how much his family struggled, and every penny he had could mean the difference between food on the table and an empty stomach. But the allure of the Ouija board was convincing enough. He added his own five-dollar bill to the growing pile.

"Okay," Roy said, his voice steady but his hands trembling. "That's twenty-two dollars. We'll bet it on whatever the thing on the board says."

They asked a simple question. "Which horse is going to win this race?"

The planchette moved ever so slowly, spelling out "N-U-M-B-E-R T-H-R-E-E."

"That's it," Carrie whispered, her voice trembling. "It said number three."

They all nodded in agreement and approached the betting counter. Roy handed over the money, his heart pounding.

"Twenty-two dollars on number three," he said, his voice wavering.

The clerk, a middle-aged man with a skeptical look, raised an eyebrow but placed the bet without a word.

After about thirty minutes, the horses lined up at the gate. Ember's Glory, a sleek chestnut stallion, stood among them. It was a favorite, but still, it seemed too easy.

The race began with a thunderous roar, hooves pounding against the dirt track. Ember's Glory surged forward, its powerful strides eating up the distance.

Roy's pulse quickened as he watched, a strange sense of fate settling over him. It was happening. The board had predicted it. Ember's Glory was in the lead, and it looked unstoppable. For a fleeting moment, Roy wondered about the life he had always dreamed of. A good life for his family that he was about to begin, with the little money he could win from this race.

But then, disaster struck.

In a split second, the horse stumbled. Its legs buckled beneath it, and the jockey was thrown violently from the saddle. Ember's Glory crashed to the ground with a sickening thud, the crowd gasping in shock.

Roy stood frozen, his heart in his throat. The board had been wrong. "This can't be happening."

Roy watched as the medics rushed to the fallen jockey and the race veterinarian attended to the stricken horse, now, knowingly, surrounded by a 'green screen' trying desperately to stabilize and save it. The excitement of the race had been replaced by tension, fear, and confusion.

"Roy, what the hell?" Diego exclaimed. "This isn't what we expected."

Roy didn't know what to say. He had been part of it, part of the prediction. And now it had gone terribly wrong.

Nora grabbed his arm, her face pale. "We need to stop. This isn't a game anymore."

Roy couldn't disagree. He could feel the weight of the consequences pressing down on him. It wasn't just a game. It had never been just a game.

He rushed back to his home and busted through the door of his room with a short breath and heavy sweat. With his trembling hands, he threw the Ouija board across the room. It was nighttime now and the room was silent, save for the ticking of the clock.

"I thought I could control it, but now it felt like it was controlling me..."

The board sat there, mocking him, daring him to try again. But this time, he knew better.

From the kitchen, Gloria sensed Roy's distress as she watched him rush to his room. She entered his room and said, "What's wrong, Roy?"

Roy stared at the floor, conflicted. He wanted to tell her everything—the growing darkness inside him, the way the Ouija board seemed to be pulling him in. But something held him back.

Gloria crossed her arms. "Roy," she said, her voice steady yet tinged with concern, "what's going on? You've been different. I can feel it."

"I… I was just trying to help us," he muttered, still avoiding her gaze.

Gloria's eyes narrowed a little, and she stepped closer. "Help us how, Roy? Don't think I haven't noticed the way you've been sneaking around, the late nights, the lies. What are you involved in?"

Roy finally looked up and his face was pale. "It's nothing, Mom. Just… just a way to make things better. For you. For all of us."

Her eyes fell on the corner of his room, where the edge of the Ouija board peeked out from under a pile of clothes. Her breath hitched as she realized.

"Is that...?" she started, her voice trembling before hardening. "Roy, is that a Ouija board?"

He didn't answer, but the guilt in his eyes gave her the answer.

Gloria's face darkened with a mixture of anger and fear. "Do you have any idea what you've done? Do you know what that thing is? It's not a game, Roy. It's dangerous. You're meddling with things you don't understand!"

He recoiled as he realized how bad things were now. He had never seen his mother like that.

"Mom, I was just trying to—"

"To what?" she interrupted, her voice trembling now with emotion. "To help us? God is the only one who can help us, Roy. Not some board, not some spirits. You don't need that to find your way."

The weight of her words settled over him, the truth in them cutting deeper than any warning.

Roy hesitated to speak further and whispered, "But I was too far gone...I'm sorry," he whispered, his voice barely audible.

Gloria took a deep breath to calm herself down. She reached out, placing a hand on his shoulder. "Roy, you're my son, and I love you. But you need to get rid of that board. Tonight. Promise me."

Roy hesitated for a moment, then nodded, his throat tight.

"Good," she said firmly. "Because if I ever see that thing in this house again, I'll burn it myself."

As she turned to leave, Roy dropped himself on the bed with his hands on his head. He knew she was right, but the pull of the board still lingered, like a whisper in the back of his mind, tempting him.

The same night, he rushed back to the neighbor's house. He couldn't shake the feeling that he had to stop what was happening, even if it meant going against the group he had joined.

With the Ouija board in his hands, Roy made his way back through the dark, to his neighbor's house, where his rebellion first began. As the house loomed ahead, the dim light from the windows barely cutting through the night, his heart began to beat harder.

As he walked up the steps, he hesitated for a moment. He knew things had gotten out of hand. What was once a curious game now felt like something dangerous, something evil and a crossing into the occult, and Roy wondered if he just might not be able to get back from what he had become involved in.

Inside, the atmosphere was intense. The group of friends—Liam, Carrie, Nora, and Diego—were gathered in the same spot they had been before, around the Ouija board. But this time, the air was different. It felt heavier and colder. They were all quiet, their faces pale, eyes wide as they glanced at each other nervously.

Roy stepped into the room, his voice urgent and full of fear.

"We need to stop," he said, his words barely above a whisper. "This is dangerous."

The group turned to look at him, their expressions a mix of confusion and fear.

"What do you mean?" asked Liam, his voice shaky.

"I saw what it can do," Roy shouted, his heart pounding in his chest. "It's not just a game anymore. Ask them Liam. You were not there at the race."

Before anyone could respond, the lights in the room flickered violently, and the candles that had been lighting the space went out, plunging them into darkness. The only light came from the faint glow of the Ouija board.

Suddenly, the planchette on the board moved on its own, sliding across the surface. Everyone gasped as the board began to spell out a chilling message: "G-E-T O-U-T."

Fear swept over the group as they watched the planchette move uncontrollably.

"What's happening?" Carrie cried out, her voice laced with panic.

Roy felt a wave of dread spread through him. The darkness seemed to close in on him, and it felt like the very air was thick with something evil. His mind raced. He had to get out—get them all out—before things got worse.

Without thinking, Roy grabbed the Ouija board and turned to the others.

“Come on,” he urged, his voice desperate. “We need to leave now.”

The group scrambled to their feet frantically as fear overcame their hesitation. Roy's urgency was contagious, and without waiting for anyone to argue or question his judgment, he rushed towards the front door.

"Come on!" he shouted, sounding commanding.

The others followed immediately but their eyes remained fixed on the dimly lit room, as if expecting something to emerge from the shadows. The planchette on the Ouija board was at the table, eerily still, yet its silence felt alarming.

Roy burst through the door first, stepping outside the house. The others followed close behind with their footsteps echoing loud in the silence.

Outside, the world was creepily quiet. No crickets chirped, no dogs barked in the distance. The usual buzz of the neighborhood was absent, replaced by a stillness that felt oppressive.

Roy glanced over his shoulder, his breath coming in short, sharp gasps. The others huddled together with their pale faces. Nora clutched Diego's arm and her knuckles turned white with the tight grip. Carrie stood there with tears rolling down her face. Liam was the one standing closest to Roy with his jaw clenched tightly.

"What just happened?" Liam finally asked, his voice shaky.

Roy didn't answer as his mind raced with fragments of what had just occurred—the flickering lights, the candles extinguishing, the planchette moving on its own to spell 'GET OUT'.

"We shouldn't have done it," Roy muttered after a while.

"What do you mean?" Nora whispered. Her voice was barely audible.

Roy turned to them and said, "I saw what it can do. I saw the darkness."

The group exchanged uneasy glances. No one dared to ask him to elaborate.

They were all standing there in complete disbelief. The silence wasn't calming; it was suffocating, as though the world itself was holding its breath, waiting.

Roy thought, "*This wasn't just a bad decision or a mistake born of curiosity. It was something deeper, something far more dangerous.*" He was now sure that he had opened a door that should have remained shut; uncertain how to close it.

"We can't go back," Roy said suddenly.

Carrie looked up, her face streaked with tears. "What do you mean? We can't just leave it like that!"

"We don't have a choice," Roy replied firmly. "Whatever's in there... it's not something we can fight.

As they stood on the front lawn, Roy cast one final glance at the house. Its windows loomed like vacant eyes, the echoes of laughter and life swallowed by an oppressive silence that seemed to breathe from within.

This was no longer just a house—it was a battleground, and the darkness would not claim victory.

Clutching the board in trembling hands, Roy stepped forward, his voice low but defiant. "I renounce you," he growled into the void.

The board convulsed violently, as though a force unseen fought to cling to him, but Roy's grip tightened. He refused to falter. A gust of wind whipped around him, sharp and cold, before suddenly ceasing.

And then, as if a shroud had been lifted, the air grew still. The suffocating weight that had hung over him for days dissolved, replaced by something faint yet undeniable: *peace.*

The nightmare had ended.

The next morning, Gloria found Roy at the breakfast table, his eyes clearer than they had been in weeks. She studied him, her smile soft but certain. "See? God has a plan for you, Roy," she said gently. "You don't need anything else for your God given purpose to be fulfilled, especially not a Ouija board."

Roy met her gaze, a spark of something new—something resolute—burning within him. “I know, Mom. I know,” he replied, his voice firm with conviction.

And as the days unfolded, Roy began the arduous work of rebuilding. The darkness that had once clawed at his soul was gone, banished by faith and a purpose he hadn’t known he was searching for.

Chapter 3
The Aftermath

The Jamaican sunset covered the sky with the hues of orange and pink, casting its warm glow over the lush countryside. Roy pedaled furiously down the back roads with his bike vibrating and unsteady on the uneven gravel. The wind passed through his hair, matching the wild determination in his eyes. His speed was increasing with every passing minute as if running away from something. He was not just running away from a place but from his life. His upbringing, his faith, the poverty that hit his family like a never-ending storm, all were weighing him down and he didn't know how to escape.

However, Roy's thoughts raced faster than his bike.

I won't let you win, he thought, gripping the handlebars tightly.

A stark realization hit him reminding him that he was no longer the boy who recited Bible verses in church or hummed the melodies his mother lovingly composed. He was something else now, someone driven by an invisible force that whispered promises of wealth, fame, and escape. Everything he ever wanted.

Later that evening, the racetrack buzzed with life under the glow of neon lights. The place was packed with people and the air was electric with their excitement. People cheered as horses thundered down the track, their hooves pounding against the dirt in a rhythm that matched Roy's heartbeat.

Roy stood at the edge of the track with a winning ticket clutched in his hand. His eyes gleamed with exhilaration as the horse he bet on finally crossed the finish line. The thrill of victory washed over him but it was getting intoxicating and addictive for him.

He stuffed the winning cash into his pocket, the bills crumpled but precious.

This is it, he thought. *This is the life I've been waiting for.*

But as the night was ending and the adrenaline faded, another feeling crept in—one he couldn't quite shake.

Back home, long after his family had gone to bed, Roy sat alone in the living room under the low, amber light of a single lamp. Candles flickered on the floor, their uneven glow casting strange, wavering shapes across the walls. Before him lay his Ouija board — the very one he had once sworn to his mother he would destroy yet had defiantly hidden away instead. In the days leading up to this night, he had brought it out again, curious to test its power. When the board had revealed the winner of a local horse race, and the outcome proved true, something inside him had shifted. The thrill of it was intoxicating — part wonder, part fear — as though an unseen force had confirmed his daring.

Now, as he sat before it once more, the glossy surface gleamed in the candlelight, almost alive beneath his gaze. The temptation to do it again was intoxicating and again he told himself it was harmless, that he wasn't doing anything wrong, but his heart knew otherwise. The board seemed to hum softly in the stillness, patient and knowing, like an old secret waiting to be acknowledged a secret that would cause his downfall at the track.

He placed his fingers on the planchette. He moved his fingers deliberately but anxiously with the fear of his mother getting up in the middle of the night and seeing him doing this again.

"Tell me," he whispered, his voice barely audible. "Which horse will win tomorrow?"

The board remained still. The candles flickered, but the planchette didn't move.

Frustration bubbled within him. He tried again and again, night after night, but the board offered no answers. The dark force he had once felt so connected to seemed distant, almost mocking him with its silence, and he could only wonder *why*.

Several weeks passed, and Roy's luck at the racetrack turned sour. His winnings dwindled, and soon, he was losing money he couldn't afford to lose given his family's financial condition.

One night, when Roy had reached his limits, he threw the Ouija board into the corner of his room. It landed with a dull thud, a symbol of his mounting frustrations.

Roy's room was a chaotic mix of who he had been and who he was becoming, but he did not seem to stop. Posters of rock stars and Hollywood icons covered the walls, replacing the Bible verses and family photographs that once held pride of place.

He sat on the edge of his bed with a notebook balanced on his knees. The pages were filled with scribbled song lyrics—angry, defiant, and dripping with ambition.

I'll make it, he thought. *I'll get us out of this poverty, no matter what it takes.*

But his mind drifted to his mother who was in her 40s. He reminded himself of how she worked tirelessly to keep the family afloat.

The next morning, the smell of something simple and usual drifted through the house. Gloria stood at the stove, humming a hymn as she prepared breakfast for everyone.

Roy entered the kitchen sluggishly and leaned against the doorway, watching her with a mix of admiration and guilt.

"Morning, Roy," Gloria said as she looked at him with a warm smile.

"Morning, Mom," he replied, his voice low.

Gloria turned back to the stove, her humming filling the silence as she flipped the eggs.

Roy hesitated before speaking. "Mom, do you ever feel like... like you're stuck?"

Gloria paused as she heard him with her hands resting on the counter. She then turned to face him.

"Life isn't always easy, Roy," she said gently. "But God has a plan for us. Even in the struggles, there's purpose."

Roy looked away. He wanted to believe her words, but thinking about his failures and the life he had chosen for himself did not let him think straight.

As Roy retreated to his room, memories of his childhood flooded his mind. He remembered standing nervously in front of the church congregation, reciting Bible verses his mother had taught him. Gloria had always been his biggest supporter and her pride was evident in the way she smiled at him from the pews every time Roy stood there reciting.

She used to set Bible verses to music, turning scripture into songs that captivated Roy's young mind. But those days felt like a lifetime ago.

Now, his room gave a completely different vibe. The notebook on his desk was open to a fresh page, and Roy began to write furiously. The lyrics came easily, each line a reflection of his rebellion and desire.

Suddenly, his eyes flicked to an advertisement in Tiger Beat magazine pinned to the wall. It called for young musicians to submit their work for a chance to collaborate with industry professionals.

Days turned into weeks as he delved deep into this new passion. This path would not let him rest as the only thing he could think of was to get a life far removed from the one he knew. He stayed up late every night, trying to perfect the lyrics.

But the darkness he had attracted—the Ouija board, the obsession with wealth and success—lingered in the corners of his mind.

One night, unable to sleep, Roy found himself staring at the board in the corner of his room. It seemed to beckon him, its presence a reminder of the path he had chosen.

He approached it cautiously, his heart pounding.

"This isn't over," he thought.

He placed the board back in its box and shoved it in his closet. He didn't want to get rid of it, *not yet*. But for now, he needed to focus on the life he was trying to build—a life filled with music, ambition, and the hope of a better future.

Roy's journey was far from over. The darkness still loomed, and the choices he made in the coming days would shape his destiny. But for now, he clung to the dream of escape, even as the past threatened to pull him back.

Chapter 4

The Memory Montage And Signing In Blood

One day Roy sat in his room, his legs shaking furiously with the stress of somehow making his life better. He had been hustling to get his work acknowledged and praised, but all his efforts and sleep sacrifices proved to be useless. He aimed for a chance at something bigger, but every door he knocked on stayed shut. As he leaned against the wooden headboard of his bed, his gaze landed on the crumpled rejection letter from Five Stars Music Master. He had sent them his song, "Hooked on Your Love," hoping it would be his big break, but the response had been anything but promising.

The paper was creased from how many times he had squeezed it in frustration, a painful reminder that his dreams were not as easy to grasp as he had once thought. He had poured his heart into that song, imagining a future where he would rise above his family's struggles, where his mother, Gloria, wouldn't have to work herself to exhaustion just to put food on the table.

He wanted the best for his siblings—a life so fulfilling that they would forget they ever lived like this.

However, fate had other plans.

"But my song, 'Hooked on Your Love,' never lived up to my dream."

These words kept repeating in his mind as he let the paper slip from his fingers and onto the floor.

At the side table lay another important invitation of his life. The letter from the Wicca Convent in Chicago felt heavier than it should have, as if it carried something more dangerous than the Ouija board. His fingers traced over the edges of the paper, and his heart pounded with the possibilities. He had sent the application weeks ago, drawn in by the idea of something greater than himself, something so powerful. The words in the ad had promised knowledge, enlightenment, and a path to secrets beyond the ordinary world. It had felt like a calling. But as he looked at it now, he felt a wave of restlessness.

The invitation was a doorway to a deeper darkness. Gavin and Yvonne, a warlock and a witch who ran the convent, had responded to his inquiries with a package that unsettled him the moment he opened it. Inside was a book, The Magic and Power of Witchcraft, its cover worn and looking ancient. The pages smelled of old parchment, laced with an aroma of herbs and something metallic, blood maybe. Along with the book was a Pentagram, its metal stained in the deep crimson of a ram's blood, a talisman meant to be worn after the book was opened, for protection. But protection from what?

At first, Roy had hesitated. The moment his fingers brushed the Pentagram; a cold shiver ran down his spine. But curiosity—no, hunger—overpowered caution. He devoured the book's contents, absorbing every detail about summoning, sigils, and spells crafted to bend reality. It wasn't just knowledge; it was power. His small experiments soon turned into something much bigger—his own sanctuary. Hidden away from his mother's watchful eyes, he collected herbs, oils, and rare plants, turning his room into a shrine of dark rituals.

The Ouija board had been the beginning, but this was the next step, the significant step. It was no longer a game. He was walking straight into the abyss.

He stood up from his bed and went straight to his cupboard, where he had buried the Ouija board deep under a pile of his clothes to keep it hidden from his mother. That night, he went out on the Jamaican backroads with the board held tight. He stopped at the neighbor's house and knocked on the door. An old Obeah Man opened the door, whose presence had always been unsettling. A warlock named Mr. Kerr had watched Roy closely; his dark eyes filled with something unreadable.

"You must burn the Ouija, boy," Mr. Kerr said, his voice thick with warning. "Secrets like that can consume you."

Roy had hesitated. The board had given him something—hope, maybe even answers. It had guided him, hadn't it?

"What if I need it?" Roy had asked, his voice small.

The Obeah man shook his head, his lined face grim.

"You don't play with fire and expect not to get burned."

This reminded him of the stern warning of his mother regarding the forbidden game. He rushed back to his house and locked his room. His heart was pounding when he decided to do what he should have done earlier.

Despite his doubt, Roy had done it. He had watched as the flames devoured the wooden board, the letters and numbers curling and blackening in the heat. The smell of smoke had filled his nostrils. The fire had crackled, and for a moment, he thought he heard something—a whisper, almost too soft to catch; what was it that was said in a whisper? An Omen? A Ghoulish message? A word from the 'other' side? Roy racked his brains to remember but he could not recall.

Even after it was gone, the feeling lingered. A weight in the air. "*My life had become one of secrets, dancing with the Devil...*"

Days passed, and Roy found himself slipping further into the pull of the unknown. The rejection, the disappointment, the need for something more; it all kept distressing him. He found himself torn between two worlds. One where his mother still believed he had a future, that he was destined for something great, and another where he was enticed by forces he barely understood.

He walked through the school corridors every day, feeling like a stranger. His friends laughed, gossiped, and talked about their plans for the future, completely unaware of the war raging inside him. He never had the courage to talk to anyone about this dark part and the harsh reality of his life. Moreover, he could not stop thinking about his mother, who had no idea how far he had strayed from the faith she was so proud of.

One day before going to bed, Gloria was doing the dishes and Roy was helping her clean the kitchen. Gloria, trying to talk things out with her son, asked him about his future with a light of hope in her eyes.

"You're destined for greatness, my boy. God has a plan for you."

"I know, Mom," he said dully. Lost in his thoughts, he replied to her with a voice she could barely hear, *"But I was in too deep to turn back now."*

Soon after, he went to bed with a heavy heart, questioning his existence.

Once again, while he was sleeping, he dreamt of landing a Boeing 737 of Caribbean Airlines. With the desire to be a pilot fresh in his mind, the next afternoon he found himself standing near the Jamaican, Sangster International airport observation platform, envisioning the landing he had dreamt about earlier that night.

At Sangster International Airport the next day, (a place Roy frequented often as he dreamed of his future) he watched as' Captain Carl Rhoden landed the Air Canada 747 with precision. Roy watched in awe with excitement gleaming in his eyes. The sight of the massive plane touching down so smoothly made something inside him stir. For the first time in a long time, he felt a spark of something real—something he could become. Maybe he could be a pilot. Maybe he could escape all of this.

But the darkness never let him go so easily.

A shiver ran down his spine, disrupting his moment of clarity. He tore his gaze away from the runway as he turned toward the main terminal and the nearest restroom. The feeling of being watched clung to him like a second skin, tightening with each step he took.

He pushed open the restroom door, the fluorescent lights buzzing overhead that cast a sickly glow over the tiled walls. The air inside smelled of industrial cleaner, mingled with the lingering traces of sweat and cheap cologne. Roy stepped inside, letting the door close behind him with a soft creak.

He moved toward the sink and turned the cold water on full blast. His hands were shaking as he splashed the icy liquid onto his face, the shock grounding him for a brief moment. He looked up, staring at his reflection in the mirror—his eyes were hollow, sunken with exhaustion. He barely recognized himself anymore.

Then, something shifted.

A strange shadow flickered behind him, just at the edge of his vision. He turned around quickly with his breath catching in his throat.

A man stood at the entrance of the restroom, his presence unsettlingly still. He wasn't old, but his face carried an ageless quality, like someone who had lived far too many lives. He had dark eyes that locked onto Roy with an intensity that made his stomach twist.

"You've got to make a choice, boy," the man said, his voice low, almost like a growl. "The power you seek comes with a price."

Roy could hear his own pulse in his ears. He wanted to move, to say something, but his body refused to obey. He had never seen this man before, and yet—something about him felt eerily familiar.

"I don't know what you're talking about," Roy said.

The man took a slow step forward and the air was growing thick and heavy, suffocating.

"Oh, but you do." A smirk curled at the corners of his lips. "You've already opened the door. Now, you have to decide whether you'll step through."

Roy swallowed hard as he heard those words. The lights above flickered, casting shifting shadows across the walls. His fingers dug into the cold porcelain of the sink, trying to be steady.

Then, just as suddenly as he appeared, the man stepped back, blending into the shadows, his figure fading into nothingness.

Roy's chest heaved, his breath ragged. He spun around, searching the empty restroom.

No one was there.

His fingers were trembling as he reached for his reflection in the mirror, touching the cool glass as if to make sure he was still real.

His mind quickly went back to the time he put the Ouija board on fire. He was pacing back and forth in his room, divided between his dreams and the darkness that beckons him. *Was this the life I wanted? Or was I just chasing shadows?* He thought as he watched the ashes still smoldering.

He felt the need to urinate after the horrific scene in the restroom. As he finished and started walking towards the door, a calm voice slithered into his ears, saying, “You have not washed your hands.”

He froze for a moment and then turned back, walking towards the sink. As he was washing his hands, again a voice echoed, but this time, it carried a sinister weight, thick with an unsettling presence.

"Bite your index finger... and write on the mirror with your blood."

The words crawled down his spine like ice, making him lose a bit of his breath.

Roy shook his head violently, whispering to himself, "No... no, this isn't real."

But his body didn't listen. His hand lifted on its own, his fingers trembling as they hovered over his mouth. He watched it all happen without his will.

"No, stop. Don't do this," he cried.

But a strange compulsion, a force stronger than his will, guided him. His teeth sank into his skin, piercing through the flesh of his index finger. Warm blood pooled at the wound, a single crimson droplet forming at the tip.

His breath quickened and heart pounded.

His trembling hand rose to the mirror.

And then, as if some unseen force had taken hold of him, he began to write on the mirror.

I WILL SERVE YOU, SATAN.

Each letter was a slash of red against the glass, the words glaring back at him, damning him.

The moment the last letter was complete, a wave of euphoria surged through his veins, intoxicating and electric. His vision blurred and body swayed.

And then—everything changed in the quiet of the restroom.

The lights above shattered, plunging the restroom into near darkness. Shadows swirled, twisting unnaturally along the walls.

Then, in the mirror—he saw something that made his blood run cold.

His reflection smirked back at him.

Not him his other self. A twisted, grinning version of him stared back, eyes gleaming with something dark, something sinister.

Roy stumbled backward, slamming against the sink, his breath ragged.

“What have I done?” he choked out.

The walls seemed to close in around him, whispers slithering from every direction.

"You belong to us now, Roy."

His head throbbed. His body ached. He squeezed his eyes shut, willing it all away.

And then—just as suddenly as it started—it stopped.

The lights flickered back on. The room returned to normal.

Except for the words.

The bloodied message on the mirror remained, staring back at him and mocking him.

Instantly, the restroom door swung open.

Roy turned around, and his heart was hammering against his ribs. A security guard stood in the doorway with his eyes narrowing as he took in the scene. He sensed something bad from outside as he was passing by and rushed inside.

"Hey," the guard said, stepping forward. "You okay in here?"

Roy's mouth opened, but no words came out. His body felt weak and drained. He frantically wiped the mirror with his sleeve, smearing the blood but failing to erase the words completely.

The guard frowned, taking another cautious step closer. "You ok?" he said again.

"I... I'm fine," Roy forced out, his voice hoarse. "Just needed a moment."

The guard looked at him with suspicion creeping into his expression.

"I... I just need to go," Roy said, feeling agitated.

He pushed past the man and rushed out the door, his mind spinning, body shaking. And before the guard could say anything further, Roy had bolted, vanished; just as the 'presence of evil' in the restroom had done a moment before.

The second he stepped out of the restroom and into the corridor to the main terminal, the bright, artificial lights blinded him for a moment, a subtle omen of what was to confront him in the future; and the people bustled past him, unaware of the nightmare that he had just witnessed inside the restroom.

Roy moved through the crowd in a daze, his breath shallow. He could still feel it—the darkness, clinging to him like a second skin.

And then, as he reached the exit, a familiar presence made his skin crawl.

He turned and his stomach dropped.

The shadowy figure from the restroom stood at the edge of the crowd, watching him.

He panicked and started running.

"Get away from me!" he shouted at it, hoping it would actually leave him alone.

But the figure didn't move. It simply grinned, eyes glinting like a predator savoring its prey.

He burst through the airport doors and the cold air slapped against his face. The moment he reached his bike in the parking lot, he collapsed beside it, gasping for breath. His hands clutched his head, trying to silence the echoing whispers in his mind.

"I couldn't escape it. The darkness was inside me now."

His phone buzzed in his pocket. With shaky hands, he pulled it out and saw a text from his mother.

"Where are you? Please come home."

"Home," he said to himself as he saw her text.

Could he even go back?

Roy glanced over his shoulder at the airport, half-expecting to see the shadowy figure again. But it was gone. For now, at least, until he realized darkness had now followed him home, it was within him.

This incident was the moment when everything escalated. When the whispers no longer stayed in his head but became a voice—a presence. When the bathroom stall became a threshold, he stood face-to-face with something beyond human understanding. Satan had manifested. There, in the flickering fluorescent lights, in the suffocating silence between his breaths. He hadn't just imagined it. He hadn't conjured it from fear. It was real.

Now, as he looked again at the letter from the Wicca Convent, his fingers clenched around the edges of the paper, and he realized the path he had chosen was not something he could turn back from so easily. Something had seen him. Something had marked him.

And it was waiting.

Chapter 5
Reflection and Regret

The rain continued its relentless assault on the windowpane, each droplet tapping against the glass like a quiet warning. Roy was sitting on his bed with his shoulders hunched, staring into the dimly lit room. The weight of his actions pressed heavily on him, making his limbs feel like lead. All the corners of his room were haunting him making him feel a presence but nothing was visible.

His gaze drifted across space, taking in the cluttered desk littered with old notebooks, the posters of rock bands peeling slightly at the corners, and the leftovers of the Ouija board box still tucked in the far corner, partially covered by a jacket. The memories of the board hit him, and now all he could do was wish he had never opened it.

He could still hear his mother's strict voice. "Roy, don't ever use that board again."

Gloria had always been religious. Her faith was an anchor in their turbulent life. She worked long hours, taking on extra shifts, trying to keep the family afloat. Despite their financial struggles, she never wavered in her belief that things would get better. But Roy had stopped believing in that a long time ago.

At first, the board had seemed like an escape, a way to feel control over something and change his fate. Now, it felt like shackles around his soul.

As he turned back to his nightstand, his eyes landed on the small, framed photo of his mother. She was smiling, her dark eyes filled with warmth and hope. His chest quickly tightened. She had given him everything she could, even when they barely had enough to get by. And how had he repaid her? By playing with forces he didn't understand?

A sudden wave of nausea washed over him and he felt sick.

He buried his face in his hands. His breath came out in short, uneven gasps as the memories of the airport confrontation with evil crashed over him—the whispers, the icy touch of unseen hands, the sensation of something lurking just beyond his vision. He tried a lot to convince himself that it was all in his head and nothing was real. But deep down, he knew better.

He had opened the door. And now, something was inside him.

The wind howled outside and the windows were rattling. He shivered, though the room wasn't cold. A strange sensation prickled along his skin, as if unseen eyes were watching him. He clenched his fists, trying to steady himself.

"I can't let this consume me," he muttered under his breath. But even as he said it, doubt crept in.

Despite the fear and guilt, he couldn't deny the power he had felt. The voice in his dream had promised him everything. It had spoken of wealth, success, and freedom from struggle.

And for that brief moment, he wanted it all.

He sucked in a sharp breath and reached for the pile of books on his desk. Roy thought, "*Maybe there was still a way out of this.*" Roy quickly flipped through the pages of an old encyclopedia, his eyes scanning for anything that might offer him answers. The faint candlelight cast long, flickering shadows across his face, highlighting the dark circles beneath his eyes from all those sleepless nights.

Everything inside him screamed that this was absurd, that he was just imagining things. But the voice, the whispers, the cold touch in the dead of night—none of it felt like a trick of the mind. All of it felt real.

He then turned to a book on the occult; its pages were yellowed with age.

"Signs of demonic possession."

His fingers trembled as he read the first page. The words were haunting.

Mood swings.

His chest tightened. He had been snapping at his mother more than usual. His emotions felt unpredictable as if they were not his own.

Hearing whispers or disembodied voices.

Roy's hands were shaking as he read that one. He had heard them—soft, coaxing, sometimes mocking. At first, they had been nothing more than faint murmurs, indistinct sounds that he brushed off as his imagination. But now, all the voices were clear.

He had seen them. The figures he saw in the airport restroom, and the reflection of his own in the mirror.

Feeling an invisible presence.

The hair on the back of his neck stood up. It was always there. Watching. Waiting.

Loss of faith.

He clenched his jaw at this one.

Gloria had instilled faith in him, making him believe in God no matter what happens. But now? He had doubted. He had questioned. And worst of all—he had turned away from his religion.

Some of the books he had borrowed from the library had been written by religious scholars, warning against dark forces. Others were personal stories from people who claimed to have experienced what he was going through.

"It starts with small things," one post read. "You think you're imagining it. A whisper here, a shadow there. But slowly it grows. You start feeling like you're losing control. Like something is inside you, influencing your thoughts and provoking you to do something sinful. The more you entertain it, the stronger it gets."

Roy's stomach twisted into knots as he read further.

Another book caught his eye. It was titled "Signs You Made a Pact Without Knowing." His blood ran cold as he skimmed through it.

"Sometimes, you don't even realize what you've done," it began. "A simple invitation. A moment of desperation. A whispered promise to an unknown force, asking for something in return. That's all it takes."

He breathed heavily as he read the list of symptoms.

Unusual success or luck after a request for help (*The test I didn't study for. The fight I won.*)

A persistent presence following you (*The feeling of being watched, even when alone.*)

Dreams of figures offering you things (*The shadow in my dream. The promise of power and wealth.*)

Uncontrollable urges or impulses (*The growing temptation to keep using the board, despite knowing I shouldn't.*)

A price to pay (*But what is the price?*)

Roy slammed the book shut, his breathing erratic. His hands were sweaty, his skin ice cold.

This wasn't just some stupid game anymore. Something was wrong. And it was real.

At some point, exhaustion overtook him, and he collapsed onto his bed. Sleep pulled him under like an unforgiving tide.

He was flying.

The air was crisp and the stars above him were dazzlingly bright. Below, the world stretched out in all directions, but it seemed so small, so distant. The weight of his guilt, his fear, his regrets—everything melted away.

For the first time in what felt like forever, he felt free.

The wind rushed through his hair as he soared higher and higher until the sky itself seemed within reach.

But then, the clouds thickened. The stars dimmed. The once beautiful night was swallowed by an invading darkness.

A voice whispered through the air, deep and velvety smooth.

"You could have it all, Roy. Just let go of your faith... and embrace the power."

He twisted in the air, trying to locate the source, but the darkness surrounded him on all sides.

Then finally he saw it.

A shadowy figure emerged from the void, its presence suffocating and its grin sinister.

His heart skipped a beat for a moment.

"Who are you?" he asked, though deep down, he already knew.

"A friend. A guide. A giver of all things."

The voice wrapped around him like a serpent, coiling, squeezing.

"You've already taken the first step. Why turn back now, Roy?"

The promise lingered in the air. The temptation was tangible.

Fame. Wealth. Power.

No more struggling. No more being broke. No more worrying about his mother working herself to exhaustion.

All he had to do was let go.

Roy clenched his fists. "No! I don’t want that!"

The darkness rushed forward.

He jolted awake from his sleep. His breath heavy and his forehead sweaty.

The room was silent, but the feeling of the dream clung to him like a second skin.

The rain still tapped against the window.

He swung his legs over the side of the bed and his whole body was shaking. He needed some air.

As he walked out of the room, he padded down the hall toward the kitchen. The dim glow of a lamp spilled from the doorway.

His mother was awake.

She sat at the table, her Bible open in front of her, though she wasn't reading it. She looked up as he entered her expression tired but concerned.

"Roy," she said softly. "You've been distant lately. What's going on?"

For a long moment, he hesitated. He wanted to tell her everything. He wanted to lay it all out, to confess the weight that had been dragging him down.

But he just couldn't do it.

She would never believe him.

"I don't know, Mom," he murmured. "I feel lost."

Gloria studied him, her eyes filled with something deep and unreadable. Finally, she reached out, placing a gentle hand over his.

"Sometimes, we stray from the path," she said. "But God is always there, waiting for us to return."

The words hit him like a punch to the gut.

He swallowed hard and nodded, though he wasn't sure if he really believed it.

Back in his room, he stood before the worn and torn Ouija Board box still shoved in the corner. His hands curled into fists.

He had gotten rid of the board but the memories lingered as he looked at the Ouija board box, the memories of power flooding back as the box morphed in his mind into the real and physical board. It was then that he realized, he had to get rid of everything that reminded him of the dark past.

Grabbing the box, he stared down at the worn torn edges. His fingers traced the letters, the symbols, remembering how they felt on the real board.

Memories surfaced—the whispers, the shadows, the thrill.

A determination came over him as he gathered up the Ouija Board box and anything that reminded him of the power the Board had over him. He knew what to do; and now, as he forced himself to throw the remaining memories into the fierce fire, he was eerily expecting some dire retribution from the spirit world that terrified his soul.

Despite this unsettling feeling of the retributions that might be coming his way, for the first time in days, he felt like he had taken a step in the right direction.

But suddenly, as if the board was fighting for its life and the life of Roy himself, he heard a whisper.

Soft.

Mocking.

"You're already mine."

Chapter 6

Shadows of the Past and Challenges of the Future

As he grew older, Roy's fascination with the supernatural deepened. Not because he wanted to summon spirits or make pacts with demons, but because he sought the hidden knowledge that whispered of power, recognition, and fortune. He yearned to know why he felt things others couldn't—why he could enter a room and feel an invisible heaviness pressing upon him. Why he felt so lost and empty, and most of all, why was he drifting away from God.

By the time he was in his fifties, Roy was wandering in a kind of wilderness. The screenplay that once burned in his heart lay unfinished. The Jerusalem WON project—first seeded nearly twenty years earlier through a small grant from a Mission donor—remained stalled. Even the book he longed to write seemed little more than a distant hope. His calling felt suspended in midair, waiting for a spark.

Roy remembered vividly how God had arranged that meeting at Union Rescue Mission in Los Angeles, where he crossed paths with Malcolm. Though the encounter was real and grounded, he often recalled it with a searching quality, like stepping into a hidden bookstore—one of those places where seekers stumbled upon more than books, where lives intersected under divine appointment. This memory returned to him often, reminding him that such an encounter would bear fruit in ways yet unseen.

Malcolm carried the weight of a man tested by both earthly and spiritual battle. A Lieutenant Colonel, CEO, and seasoned Department of Defense executive, he also bore the marks of someone who had stood against the same shadows that haunted Roy. Yet there was something deeper than credentials—there was faith that had been refined in the fire.

Malcolm had experienced tragedy in his family and Roy had just divorced Tara. They were both down on their luck and spending time at the URM gave them a solid footing for the next part of their journey.

The friendship that developed was no accident; it was God's design. Through Malcolm's encouragement, Roy found the courage to move again. The screenplay gained momentum, the book began to take shape, and doors opened to write and speak with political and spiritual leaders across the world about the urgency of the Jerusalem WON vision.

Together, they even took the opportunity to provide an informal briefing to the newly appointed CEO of Union Rescue

Mission—something Malcolm was uniquely equipped to lead, drawing on his lifetime of command and leadership. For Roy, meeting Malcolm was not just friendship; it was the catalyst that carried his calling forward in earnest, a living reminder that God's timing is never late.

The two men grew into brothers-in-arms, not only in faith but in life's battles. They studied together, prayed together, and challenged one another to stand when the shadows pressed close. Roy's wilderness years began to break open, not because of human willpower alone, but because God had joined his path with Malcolm's at the appointed time.

One evening, they sat together in Roy's office at the mission. Roy had been given a volunteer coordinator's position which came with an office, a place where Roy could be alone, to contemplate and mark out the path he would need to navigate next to fulfill God's purpose for him. The room was dim, lit only by a single lamp that cast long, trembling shadows across stacks of papers and the manuscript that weighed like iron before them. Silence stretched heavy, the kind of silence that carries memory and unspoken fears. Roy tapped the worn leather cover of his book, his voice low and uneven.

"You know, Malcolm," he said, "this chapter... it feels like a thread binding together everything we've lived, everything we've seen."

Malcolm leaned forward, his eyes keen, his pen poised over the page. "History repeats itself. Every generation thinks it can harness what lies beyond. But power always extracts its price."

Roy gave a dry laugh. "Six months ago, the Freemasons approached me. It was intoxicating... the secrets, the promise of belonging. I went twice." His jaw clenched. "It felt like signing a pact all over again."

Malcolm set his pen down slowly. The atmosphere seemed to shift, as though unseen eyes had leaned in to listen. "Roy... what about your soul?"

The question cut deep. Roy hesitated, then whispered, "I wonder if I've already lost it."

As the lamp flickered, both men felt the unseen press against the room. Their conversation turned to old memories—Mr. Robinson's tormented house in Jamaica, priests too weak to stand against darkness, the countless exorcisms and hauntings they had witnessed. Fear had been their companion, but faith was their shield.

And then Malcolm shared his heart. His friend's daughter, Mia, a young woman once vibrant with dreams, now wasted by a mysterious affliction that doctors could not explain. The nights filled with screams in voices not her own. Priests who refused to cross her threshold; her Parents exhausted and afraid.

Roy felt the chill creep down his spine. He placed a steadying hand on Malcolm's shoulder. "Then we help her."

But even as those words were spoken, the air split with a scream—piercing, near, and unearthly. Both men froze, knowing darkness had been listening. And yet, as they rose side by side, determination ignited in them once more.

"Then let's face it together," Roy said.

Two old warriors stood again—not in their strength, but in the Lord's—ready to confront the shadows that had hunted them for a lifetime.

The room fell quiet again, save for the hum of the ceiling fan. The scream outside had faded, but its echo still clung to the air. Roy, ever one to balance darkness with curiosity, reached for his phone. He pulled up an image that had been making the rounds online and showed it to Malcolm: a photo of President Biden with a caption beneath it.

"My role is to be the fall guy where I mess up and do all the wrong things, and Donald Trump comes along to be the savior of the world to usher in the New World Order."

Malcolm chuckled, shaking his head. "So, Biden's the scapegoat, huh? And Trump's the hero for the New World Order? I don't think so, mate. Sounds like a script for a bad movie."

Roy leaned in, eyes sharp with intensity. "But think about it. This is the perfect example of the Hegelian dialectic—thesis, antithesis, synthesis. It's the spin doctors at work!"

Malcolm raised an eyebrow, intrigued but skeptical. "You really believe it's that calculated? That they're playing us like puppets?"

"Absolutely," Roy said firmly. "Politicians create chaos, then position themselves as the solution. It's a cycle, a game they've mastered."

Malcolm crossed his arms, his tone still doubtful. "But consider this: if Trump is the savior, he's hardly Jesus Christ. More like a controversial figure riding a wave of populism."

Roy smiled knowingly. "True. But isn't that how every savior archetype emerges? From the ashes of chaos, they rise."

Malcolm let out a dry laugh. "Or they exploit the chaos to gain power. You're giving them too much credit."

Roy waved his hand dismissively, pacing the room now. "No, no—it's orchestrated. A New World Order. They're manipulating perception, controlling narrative."

Malcolm laughed softly with disbelief. "And what about the average citizen? Are we all just pawns in their game?"

Roy stopped pacing and locked eyes with him. "Exactly. People are waking up, but the powers keep them distracted with the next shiny object. Look around—Elon Musk, the tech giants—they're all in on it."

A silence stretched between them, heavy but not hopeless. Malcolm broke it at last. "But can we really blame them? Isn't it just politics as usual?"

Roy shook his head. "It's more than politics. It's a manipulation of reality itself. People cling to illusions as if they were truth."

Malcolm smirked. "So, what's the solution? A revolution? Or just a good old-fashioned debate?"

Roy gave a wry smile. "Maybe an awakening. An understanding that we're not just players in their game—we need to call out the game itself."

Malcolm's skepticism softened as he leaned forward. "You really think we can change the narrative?"

Roy's answer came without hesitation. "If enough of us see through the illusion, we can rewrite the script."

Malcolm nodded slowly, his voice steadier now. "Then let's start with what's in front of us. The screenplay. The book. The letters to spiritual and political leaders. And since all this began at Union Rescue Mission, let's prepare a more formal and comprehensive briefing for the CEO we met earlier. Maybe we can give something back—for all they've done and still do in people's lives. If we can't change the world straight away, let's do it one person at a time."

The two men sat back, the earlier tension giving way to a quieter resolve. Outside, the city's noise hummed on, but inside that dimly lit room, two old warriors had found their marching orders.

Chapter 7

Fulfilling Satan's Purpose - A Lust For Power

Roy sat in his office at the Mission, still turning over the words he and Malcolm had shared. Their conversations echoed like thunder in his spirit, awakening both dread and clarity. The battles of his past were not over—they had simply shifted shape.

The discussions with Malcolm had drawn a sharp line: the fight ahead was not just about writing or politics, but about truth and deception, light and darkness. Yet as Roy leaned back in his chair, staring into the shadows pooling at the edges of the room, his mind slipped into memory. The present always seemed to summon the past, and in those echoes lay the roots of his struggle.

Roy sensed, even in those moments, that Malcolm's role in his life was only beginning. Their conversations felt like the first chapter of a story God was still writing, one that would return with greater significance in days ahead. The weight of that realization pressed against him, stirring old echoes he could not escape.

He remembered his youth—the moments of hunger not only for knowledge but for power, recognition, and glory. The path that led him to dabble in the occult was not born merely of curiosity, but of a restless craving for more.

Why did he feel things others did not? Why could he walk into a room and sense a presence pressing upon him? Why did emptiness haunt him, and why, above all, did his heart drift so far from God?

Those questions began in boyhood, but their shadows stretched into manhood. And so, as Roy sat in the stillness of his office, the past rose again to meet him—an old story he could not escape, a warning to those who would walk the same path.

Young Roy walked through the crowded halls of his school with a lightness in his step that had been absent for a very long time. The air between the walls was buzzing with conversation, laughter bouncing off the lockers and filling the corridors with an infectious energy. He spotted familiar faces as he stood in front of his locker, and for the first time in weeks, he didn't shy away. Instead, he allowed himself to smile.

"Yo, Roy! What's up, man?" A classmate, Kevin, slapped him on the back as he passed.

"Nothing much," Roy responded, chuckling as he continued walking. The weight he had carried—the isolation, the fear—

seemed to have lifted, even if a little. For once, he felt like he fitted somewhere like he wasn't drowning in the darkness that had swallowed him whole.

Yet, as much as life seemed to be getting better for him, he couldn't shake the feeling that something still lurked in the shadows, waiting for a chance to pull him back into its dark realm.

As the day went by, the afternoon sun covered the park in a golden glow with a chill in the air. Roy sat alone on a bench with his notebook open on his lap and fingers gripping a pen as he scribbled down lyrics. Music had always been his escape, a place where his emotions could spill freely without consequence. The words came effortlessly, filled with longing, with hope, with the conflict that still burned inside him.

He inhaled deeply, the fresh air filling his lungs. For the first time in a while, he felt truly alive. However, that peace was fleeting.

As he wrote the lyrics, he glanced at a nearby group of teenagers flashing money and partying as they showed off to one another. Bottles clinked, and the scent of smoke hung in the air. The boys looked free, wild, untouchable. The seductive allure of it tugged at Roy, whispering at the back of his mind.

He swallowed hard.

He realized that the temptation hadn't disappeared. It was just waiting for him to slip.

The night fell soon. Roy lay in his bed, staring at the ceiling, and his mind was restless. The temptation, the craving for something more—something dark—still gnawed at him. As he turned to his right side, his eyes settled on his guitar propped against the wall. His fingers twitched, itching to play, drown in the music, and silence the storm inside.

But even that wasn't enough for him to overcome this emptiness.

Sitting up abruptly, he swung his legs over the edge of the bed. His chest tightened as he forced himself to his feet, his resolve leading him out of the room toward the kitchen.

Gloria stood at the counter, chopping vegetables for dinner. The sound of the knife hitting the cutting board was oddly satisfying. The smell of garlic and onions filled the air, grounding him momentarily. But he couldn't ignore the storm raging inside him.

"Mom," he said hesitantly.

She turned; her warm brown eyes filled with immediate concern. "What is it, Roy?"

He hesitated, his throat tight. "I need help. I feel like I'm being pulled in two directions."

Gloria set the knife down, wiping her hands on a dish towel before stepping closer. Her gaze softened, full of understanding. "You don't have to go through this alone," she said gently. "We can pray together. God can help you find your way back."

He wanted to believe her. He wanted to believe that he wasn't too far gone.

That night, Roy knelt beside his bed with Gloria by his side, her voice steady as she led the prayer. He squeezed his eyes shut, his heart pounding as he whispered the words:

"Dear Lord, and Father of mankind, forgive us for our foolish evil ways, reclothe in our rightful mind, in pure life, thy service fine, in deeper reverence, praise. In Jesus name Amen!"

But deep down, doubt still lingered.

That doubt followed him into sleep.

As he fell asleep, the dream returned. However, this time, it was not the same.

Roy wasn't flying. He wasn't soaring over the dark abyss. Instead, he stood firmly on solid ground, facing the shadowy figure that had haunted him for so long. The air crackled with tension, the darkness pressing in, trying to get to him.

But he didn't back down.

"I refuse to let you control me!" he shouted, his voice echoing through the void.

The figure hesitated, its form flickering, shrinking back as if recoiling from the strength in Roy's voice.

Then, suddenly, light erupted around him that pierced through the darkness. The figure let out a terrible screech, its form dissolving as the light consumed it.

For the first time, Roy felt power—not from the darkness, but from something greater.

Morning came, and Roy awoke with a clarity he hadn't felt in a long time. Sunlight streamed through his window, illuminating his room in golden hues. He sat up and exhaled deeply. The weight on his chest had lessened.

But the war was far from over.

That night, the darkness crept back in.

Roy's room was messy with remnants of his past—rock posters, an old Bible buried under piles of old notebooks, and the remnants of a Ouija board shoved into the corner. He stood before the mirror, his own reflection unknown to him.

His hands trembled as he held a parchment scroll. Its ink was fresh.

"A human sacrifice... preferably an innocent child, " Roy whispered, his voice hollow.

The memory of the Shadowy Figure's command echoed in his mind. A blood vow needed to be fulfilled every three days.

The cost of his success had finally come due.

The temptation, the power, the promises came rushing back as he walked around the school. Students laughed, gossiped, and lived their lives, oblivious to the war raging inside him.

"Did you hear about that witchcraft club?" a boy said.

"Yeah, they say it's all fake," another replied.

Roy clenched his jaw. If only they knew.

The fear tore through his chest. He had tried to balance on the edge, thinking he could dabble in the darkness without fully losing himself. But he was wrong.

That night, as he sat alone on his bed, the choice loomed before him.

He clutched a pentagram necklace dipped in ram's blood, a chilling reminder of his dark journey.

"I learned these rituals during my days studying witchcraft. It's a cardinal sin in Wicca to know these secrets without protection."

Could he really do this? Sacrifice an innocent child to save himself?

"I thought I could get a pass from the Devil. But it's either do or die."

"I thought I could straddle the fence, but poverty would become my lord and master if I didn't comply."

As the night darkened even more, he ran out of his house, through the darkened streets, toward the only place that might offer salvation.

The air inside the church was thick with anger, the scent both foreign and strangely comforting. Roy fell to his knees before the altar, his body trembling.

"Jesus," he whispered, his voice raw. "I need Your blood of forgiveness."

Tears burned his eyes as he looked up at the crucifix, his heart torn between the Devil's intoxicating promises and the hope that he could still be saved.

The choice was his.

When he returned home, he saw a child playing outside his window, laughter ringing in the silence.

The thought of sacrifice gnawed at him as he grabbed the window frame, battling his conscience.

Roy stepped outside and his heart was pounding. The child, innocent and unaware, played under the streetlight.

Was I really willing to go through with it?

Suddenly, the shadowy figure appeared beside him and whispered, "You know what you must do. Fulfill the oath or suffer the consequences."

Roy stumbled back in fear. "No! I won't do it!"

Once again, Roy raced back to the church with desperation in his eyes. He threw himself at the altar, praying fervently.

"Lord, forgive me! Help me break this curse," he cried.

Then, when he went back home, he picked up the pen with his shaking hands.

And then—

He tore the parchment in half.

"I choose life," he whispered.

The room felt so heavy, with the darkness pressing in, angered by his defiance.

The Shadowy Figure emerged before him, its form twisting, seething.

"You think you can just walk away?" it hissed.

Roy stood his ground. "I won't let you control me anymore."

The church bells rang in the distance. Light flooded his room. The dark figure let out a piercing scream as its form began to fracture, splintering like shattered glass. The sound echoed through the air, fading into nothing but a whisper of rage. Just before it vanished completely, its voice thundered one last time: "You will regret this!"

In an instant, Roy found himself standing inside the church. The voices of the congregation rose around him — a swelling chorus of hope and faith that filled the space with light.

"We renounce the darkness!" everyone chanted.

Roy exhaled, his entire body trembling.

"The battle was won, but the war for my soul would continue."

Chapter 8

Oath Card – Blood Oath

The bass from the speakers pounded against Roy's chest like a second heartbeat, which seemed to pull him closer to the chaos that was going to unfold.

Young Roy found himself standing aimlessly inside an abandoned warehouse that was alive with movement—bodies swaying, twisting, and convulsing under the strobing lights that painted the cracked concrete walls in eerie flashes of red, blue, and white.

All the noises blended together, forming a chilling symphony of reckless abandon. The space smelled of sweat, alcohol, and something rotten deep beneath the surface.

Roy stood at the edge of the wild crowd, unsure whether to step forward or turn back. The curious young boy was excited to be there and be seen. There was no denying the thrill—the intoxicating lure of the unknown—but there was also something else, something cold and whispering at the edges of his mind, warning him that this place was not meant for him.

He clenched his fists tightly, convincing himself to calm down.

"You can't afford to be weak. If you hesitate, you'll be devoured whole."

He knew this to be true. He had spent too long on the outside, watching others claim what they wanted, making their way to wealth and fame. And there he was, a nameless face in a sea of people who had already sold themselves to something bigger than them.

He stood there in confusion, his Adam's apple bobbing as he surveyed the scene. He was surrounded by partygoers who were lost in their own worlds, dancing and laughing, heedless of the shadows growing from every corner of the warehouse. Their faces flickered between euphoria and something more sinister, their grins too wide, their laughter a little too sharp.

He forced himself to remain still.

Why am I pretending? The truth is, I walked in here knowing exactly what I was getting into.

He did not need to pretend anymore, as he had made his choice long before he set foot in this warehouse. No one had forced him. No one had dragged him here. His own greed and ambition pushed him forward to walk into the lion's den.

They say God gave us free will. And I used mine to bow before the Devil. For what? A taste of power? A shortcut to glory?

His throat felt dry, but his eyes were wet as he thought back to the nights spent alone in his room full of posters, staring at the screens that promised him a life of excess, power, and adoration. He had seen his idols win by luck without any consequences, bending the world to their will. He had craved that power so badly which led him to the darkness. He had prayed for it—only he hadn't prayed to God.

Am I too far gone? Or is there still a way out?

A wave of nausea rolled through him as the reality of that thought settled deep in his gut. He looked around and suddenly felt as though the warehouse walls were closing in, and everything was slowly fading—music, laughter, lights. He started to feel suffocated.

Then, his eyes were locked on him.

A man stood alone behind the crowd at the far end of the room. He was dressed in a dark, tailored suit that looked far too expensive for this rundown place. He wasn't dancing. He wasn't drinking. He wasn't even speaking. He was just watching. Watching him.

Roy's breath caught in his throat as goosebumps prickled his skin. He didn't know who this man was, but something in his smirk, the way his eyes glowed like embers beneath the dim light, made him sweat with fear.

The deeper you go, the harder it is to tell the difference between darkness and light. Even fallen angels were once in heaven.

As he stared at the man, someone grabbed his hand, yanking him out of his trance.

"Come on, Roy!" A girl, her face half-hidden behind a curtain of wild curls, said as she took him to the back of the warehouse. He barely recognized her, but that didn't seem to matter. The crowd swallowed them whole, pushing them toward a hidden room beyond the chaos.

The moment he stepped inside the room, the atmosphere shifted. The air felt heavier. A small group of people were chanting and laughing, passing around a glass bottle filled with amber liquid. Their laughter was softer here, almost conspiratorial as if they were in on a secret Roy had yet to understand.

One of the guys raised the bottle toward him, an unspoken invitation.

Roy hesitated. He had a feeling the invitation was drawing him into danger.

The Devil doesn't deal in favors. If you dance to his tune, you pay his price.

His fingers twitched and his mind was screaming at him to walk away. But then he heard it again; the same murmuring whispers beneath the music, the slow, seductive voice of something ancient and hungry that he heard years ago when everything started. It coiled around him like invisible chains, luring him into darkness.

Might as well drink deep. The price is already set.

He walked up to the guy and took the bottle from him. He drank its contents like a thirsty boy.

The warmth spread through his veins, loosening the tension in his shoulders and dulling the whispering voice of caution within him. The room spun, and the faces around him transformed into something grotesque yet mesmerizing. The music seeped into his bones, and before he knew it, he was dancing.

The world around him blurred.

Laughter. Smoke. Hands pulling him closer.

Then—darkness.

He stumbled backward, and his vision warped as shadows stretched unnaturally around him, growing longer to grab him. He could hear his heartbeat, faster, faster—until suddenly, the air around him calmed.

He turned around in confusion and saw the man in the suit standing before him.

"You're doing well, Roy." His voice was smooth. "Keep dancing, and the rewards will be... plentiful."

Roy's stomach twisted. He wanted to run outside, but his legs wouldn't move.

"What do you want from me?" he managed to choke out.

The man smiled, revealing his teeth gleaming like polished ivory. "Only your loyalty."

The Devil never plays fair. He fights like a man with nothing to lose—because he already knows how his story ends.

Roy frantically glanced back and forth at the exit door. He could still leave. He could still. . .

A sparkle of silver caught his eye.

A necklace. A simple cross hanging around someone's neck. It jolted something deep within him as he looked at it, a memory buried beneath layers of sins and regret.

No matter how far I've fallen, my soul was never mine to sell. It was already paid for—in blood.

The spell shattered.

Roy stepped back, his hands trembling. "I won't let you take me."

The Shadowy Man's expression darkened with anger. His amusement was replaced with something colder and more dangerous.

"You think you can just walk away?"

"I choose life," Roy shouted at the top of his lungs.

Hell doesn't take what belongs to Heaven without a fight. And I wasn't going down without one.

Roy's conviction grew. He looked around, gathering strength from the memories of his faith. The air around him crackled as if some unseen battle was taking place—a war not of flesh but of spirit.

God doesn't abandon His own. Even when we run, He fights for us.

Roy stepped forward and ran past the Shadowy Man fearlessly. The Shadowy Man started to recoil as if burned.

"You don't own me!" Roy yelled confidently.

The warehouse blurred around him. The moment he burst through the door and stepped into the cool night air, he collapsed against the railing, gasping.

The stars shone above him, indifferent yet unwavering.

This wasn't just about escape. It was about redemption.

Chapter 9

Backroads And Fear – But Hollywood Beckons

The night before Roy Ferguson left home, an unsettling silence filled the air. It wasn't the kind of quiet that brought peace but the kind that pressed against his chest, reminding him that once he stepped out that door, there was no turning back.

He was 21 now, and the world was waiting—but so was the unknown. And the unknown had a way of sinking its claws into the unprepared.

He packed with precision, stuffing his duffel bag with the essentials: a few changes of clothes, his music tapes, and the notebook that carried his lyrics—his lifeline. As he slung the bag over his shoulder, he stole one last glance at his bedroom. Faded posters on the walls, the bed he had outgrown, the worn-out Bible his mother left on his nightstand, open to *Psalm 23*. He shut his eyes, inhaling deeply. Then, he walked out.

This had been two years earlier. Since then, Roy had moved to Connecticut in search of a future—he didn't know what kind, only that his destiny lay somewhere beyond the borders of what he'd known. But destiny, he would soon discover, has a way of testing the soul before revealing its purpose.

The early morning air in Bridgeport, Connecticut, was crisp as Roy stepped outside, the chill biting at his skin. It was 3 A.M.—a time when most people were deep in slumber, but for him, it was the start of another long day. The world was quiet except for the distant hum of traffic and the rustle of leaves. He had grown accustomed to this rhythm—waking before dawn to deliver newspapers for the *Bridgeport Post.* It was humble work, but it gave him time to think, to dream, to hope.

He had arrived in America with dreams bigger than the ocean that separated him from Jamaica. Living with Mr. Robinson and his family had given him stability amidst uncertainty. Gloria, with her warm smile, welcomed him as one of her own. Colin, his old high school buddy from Herbert Morrison Comprehensive, was a steady companion, alongside his younger brother Michael and the two girls, Drew and Sue. They became his family away from home, but as months passed, Roy's heart grew restless. He wanted more.

It was Gloria who introduced him to Carnette, her coworker at the Trumbull Nursing Home. She was radiant, her laughter carrying the warmth of the Caribbean sun. Roy, fresh from military service and dreaming of becoming a Navy pilot, was captivated. He had already aced the Navy's ASVAB test with a score of ninety-nine percent, and *Top Gun* training at Annapolis loomed on the horizon. Yet, week after week, as the brown Navy recruitment car arrived at the Robinsons' house, his certainty began to waver.

Six months later, he stood at the altar, marrying Carnette beneath a canopy of hope. She was his anchor, but also the voice of caution. "The life expectancy of pilots is only three years," she warned softly, fear threading her words. Torn between ambition and love, Roy chose her. He set aside the sky and focused on building a life on solid ground.

Their daughter Simone was born soon after—a miracle that brought joy and responsibility in equal measure. Determined to build a stable future, Roy enrolled at Sacred Heart University, majoring in premed with a double in political science and chemistry. His days were a blur of study, volunteering at Bridgeport Hospital, and delivering newspapers before dawn. Exhaustion was constant, but so was his determination.

Then came the visit to his ophthalmologist—a moment that would alter everything.

"Glaucoma," the doctor said, his voice measured, professional, but distant. "You'll need three medications to preserve your sight. The side effects may include... impotence."

The words struck harder than the diagnosis itself. Roy felt the ground disappear beneath him. How could he tell Carnette?

How could he be a husband, a father, a man, if his very treatment robbed him of the ability to love her as before?

Darkness began to creep in—not just in his eyes, but in his spirit. He sought escape in dimly lit bars and strip clubs, drowning his fears in liquor. Every glass numbed the ache; every night blurred the pain. His grades slipped, his marriage trembled, and his dream of becoming a neurosurgeon crumbled.

Carnette tried to hold on, but the weight of Roy's despair became too much. When she revoked her sponsorship for his permanent residency, it was as if the final light went out. His world collapsed into shadows.

He drifted further, haunted by his own failure, frequenting massage parlors, clinging to fleeting illusions of comfort. Yet God, even in Roy's rebellion, was not done with him.

Out of the blue, old friends from Jamaica—Mutty Lewis, Tenny Hambersly, Charles Grant, and Keith Grant—showed up. They had come chasing their own musical dreams. Their laughter stirred old memories, and for a moment, Roy glimpsed who he once was. Still, even among friends, he could not hide the redness in his eyes—the visible mark of his suffering.

Then came the morning that felt like judgment itself. He stepped outside and found his 1985 Grand Am—the car he used to deliver newspapers—gone. Stolen. It was as though the universe itself had turned its back on him.

Defeated, he met with the guys. They listened, then offered something unexpected—*a new dream*. "Come with us to Hollywood," they said. "Let's take the band to the next level."

Hope flickered, fragile but real. Roy agreed.

A week later, he stood at the Bridgeport Greyhound station, clutching a one-way ticket to Los Angeles. His friends surrounded him, their faces glowing with belief. "You're our manager now," they said, handing him a demo tape wrapped in the scent of sweat and hope. "Make it happen for us."

The air inside the terminal was thick with diesel and stale coffee. He gripped the ticket tightly, his palms slick. This was it—the beginning or the end; he couldn't tell which.

The bus doors opened with a hiss, and Roy climbed aboard. He found a window seat and set his duffel on his lap, holding it like it contained his whole life. In many ways, it did.

As the bus rumbled to life, the lights of Bridgeport flickered past. The city that had been both cradle and crucible faded into the distance. The streets of Jamaica, the chill of Connecticut, the echoes of his mother's hymns—all of it slipped away.

And now, again, he was leaving the familiarity of his past two years behind him.

But the reality was that memories didn't pay the bills; dreams did. Or at least, it was what he was counting on, because ahead lay Hollywood—bright, magnetic, and dangerous. It called to him like a siren's song, promising power, fame, and something more intoxicating than salvation: control. Deep down though, Roy felt it—the tremor of something darker, waiting just beyond the glimmering horizon.

The journey stretched endlessly, each mile dragging him further from certainty. The hard bus seats turned from stiff to unbearable, every jolt in the road sending pain up his spine. Restless sleep came in fits, interrupted by the wails of babies, the snores of strangers, and the monotonous hum of the road.

Rest stops became his only salvation. At each stop, he stretched his legs and arms and went out to get some fresh air to shake off the exhaustion. He survived on cheap vending machine snacks and greasy diner food.

At a truck stop in the middle of nowhere, he met Hank, a long-haul trucker with eyes like cracked asphalt.

“Where ya headed, kid?” Hank asked, stirring a cup of black coffee at a roadside diner.

“Hollywood,” Roy answered with a steady voice.

Hank smirked, nodding knowingly. “Ah, chasing the dream, huh? You a musician?”

Roy’s chest swelled with pride. “Yes, sir. I sent a demo tape to Capitol Records a while back.”

Hank took a slow sip of coffee before leaning in. “Listen to me, kid. That town’s got teeth. It’ll chew you up if you ain’t ready. Keep your head on straight.”

Roy wanted to laugh it off, but the weight in Hank’s voice settled deep in his bones. He didn’t need the reminder—he already knew Hollywood wouldn’t be easy. But he had no choice.

By the time the Greyhound wheezed to a stop in Los Angeles, the city greeted him not with open arms, but with an indifferent glare. The air was thick, humid, laced with exhaust fumes and desperation.

Hollywood was not what he had envisioned. The sidewalks were cracked, littered with cigarette butts and broken dreams. Neon signs flickered like dying stars. Homeless men stared through him with vacant eyes. Where were the red carpets? The flashing cameras? The golden gates to success?

He gripped his duffel bag tighter. He needed a place to stay.

He headed towards a motel named Vine Lodge. It wasn't exactly the Ritz-Carlton, but it would do. It was a cheap motel tucked away on a side street, its neon sign flickering as if unsure whether to stay lit or go dark.

Roy stepped inside after taking a deep sigh. Inside, the air was filled with the scent of old carpet and mildew. The manager, a grizzled man with tired eyes, barely looked up as Roy placed his money on the counter.

"Room's yours for a week," the man muttered, sliding a key across the chipped wood.

Roy nodded as he grabbed the key. He had seven days to figure out how to turn nothing into something.

As Roy unlocked the room's door, he realized that the room was small, with a bed, a nightstand, and a bathroom that looked like it hadn't been cleaned properly in years. However, to him, it was a palace. He dropped his bag onto the bed and exhaled deeply. He had made it. Now, the real work began.

Days blurred into each other as he walked the streets, knocking on doors that never opened. Studios ignored him. His money ran out faster than he expected. Then, one night, when he returned to the Vine Lodge, he found his room locked.

He approached the manager, who informed him that he was behind on rent.

"Your stuffs in storage," the man said flatly. "No payment, no room."

Roy swallowed hard. "I just need my medicine."

The manager didn't budge. "Rules are rules, kid."

Roy stood there for a long moment, the weight of the situation pressing down on him. He had nowhere to go.

That night, he wandered the streets of Hollywood with a heavy heart and racing thoughts. The Walk of Fame was beneath his feet, and each golden star reminded him of how far he still had to go.

At midnight, he passed the Scientology building, its blue walls looming over him like a silent giant. Outside the building, a woman sat on a nearby bench, wrapped in a headscarf, her eyes eerily knowing.

"When were you born?" she asked, her voice soft but commanding.

Roy hesitated. "November 16, 1964."

A slow smile spread across her face. "You're a comeback kid," she whispered. "You will make it."

And just like that, she was gone.

Roy stood frozen, his pulse roaring in his ears. Was she a prophet? A lunatic? Or had he just brushed against something divine?

His stomach growled, dragging him back to the present. Hunger outweighed pride and he looked for a place to fill his hunger. He walked until the sun began to rise and after finding a place for breakfast he walked door to door, asking store owners for just a dollar. Thirty doors later, he had thirty dollars—enough to buy another night off the streets.

But the tomorrow he dreamed was just that, a tomorrow that he wondered, would it ever come?

That morning, desperation led him to the Seventh-day Adventist Church on Hollywood Boulevard.

A greeter at the entrance shook his hand warmly. "Good morning, brother. Welcome."

As the choir sang, something inside him stirred. He had grown up with these hymns. Their melodies wrapped around him, unraveling the tight knots of fear.

After the service, he met MC Cole, a towering man with a deep, resonant voice. They talked for hours, laughter filling the spaces between words.

"You'll love our lunch! We have some amazing cooks here," Maddison Cole said to Roy as they walked together to join other members of the church seated at long tables adorned with colorful tablecloths and delicious food.

"We call each other brothers and sisters here," Roy thought. *"Not because we share blood, but because we share faith in Jesus Christ."*

When he sat down among the others, Roy sensed a weight slipping away, as though unseen hands were lifting his burdens. A quiet ease settled over him—gentle, freeing—like the peace that comes only when God lightens the load a man was never meant to carry alone.

"After being lost for so long, I finally felt like I belonged again."

That evening, as the sun bled gold over the city, for the first time since arriving, he felt something unexpected—

Peace.

He had survived.

And he was still standing.

And maybe—just maybe—his dreams weren't as far away as they seemed.

Chapter 10

A New Dawn

The sky was bright and cloudy over Los Angeles. Roy, now 31, stood politely on the balcony of the Hollywood Terrace Apartments, his new home.

The apartment was modest but comfortable, shared with his two roommates, Maddison and Shannon. The three of them had come to Los Angeles with dreams as big as the city itself, though their paths to get there had been very different.

Maddison, in his late forties, was the creative force of the trio. He was thoughtful and introspective. With a passion for storytelling and a knack for voiceovers, he had a way of bringing characters to life with his voice alone.

He was the kind of person who could walk into a room and instantly make everyone feel at ease with his confidence and charm infectious. Maddison had been in LA for a few years, trying to make it in the entertainment industry, and his optimism never wavered, even when the odds seemed to be against him.

Shannon, on the other hand, was in his early fifties, a seasoned musician with a wealth of experience and a heart full of wisdom. He had seen the highs and lows of the music industry for a long time and had come to LA to help Roy and Maddison navigate the treacherous waters of Hollywood.

Shannon was the steady hand, the voice of reason, and the one who always seemed to know the right thing to say. Together, the three of them made an unlikely but formidable team.

That morning, Roy and Shannon decided to explore the city. As they strolled down Hollywood Boulevard, Shannon pointed out the landmarks with the enthusiasm of a tour guide. "And over there," he said, gesturing toward a grand building, "that's the famous Grauman's Chinese Theatre. Can you believe the stars that have walked that red carpet?"

Roy nodded, forcing a smile, but his thoughts were somewhere else. His mind drifted back to the pastor's office, the weight of his predicament still heavy on his shoulders. He had come to Hollywood for a new start, but now he couldn't shake the feeling that his troubles were far from over.

"I thought I was escaping my troubles, Roy reflected, but little did I know, they were just beginning to unfold."

Later that evening, Roy lay on the couch in their apartment, scrolling through his phone. Maddison walked toward him wearing headphones and carrying a notebook. He was always working on something because his mind was constantly buzzing with ideas.

"Hey, you ready to hear my latest voiceover? It's for that documentary on Hollywood's hidden history," Maddison said.

Roy smirked. "Sure, let's hear it. Maybe you'll uncover some secrets about our new home." Roy said with sarcasm.

Then Maddison began to play the recording on full volume. Both were excited. Shannon joined in later and the trio spent the evening sharing their life stories.

The morning sun streamed through the kitchen window, casting a warm glow over the neatly arranged kitchen. Madison adjusted his tie in the mirror, a hint of a smile playing on his lips, while Shannon was waiting for everyone to get going.

"You know," Madison said, looking at his reflection, "I always look forward to Saturdays. It feels like a fresh start."

Shannon smiled back at him and said, "Especially with the new sermon series. I've heard it's going to be powerful."

Roy rushed into the room, grabbing his coat. "Let's make sure we leave on time. I want to get a good seat!"

The three shared a moment of anticipation before finishing their preparations.

Later, Madison, Shannon, and Roy pulled into the bustling parking lot filled with cars. The lively atmosphere greeted them as they stepped out. People were welcoming one another, laughter mingling with the sounds of chatter.

"Looks like it's a full house today," Madison remarked, glancing around.

As they walked toward the entrance, Madison, a close friend of Little Richard, spotted him waving at them from the entrance.

"Hey, over here!" Richard called out, a wide smile on his face.

They waved back and made their way to him.

Entering the church's lobby, Madison, Shannon, and Roy were enveloped by the lively chatter. They spotted Richard surrounded by an entourage, the atmosphere shifting slightly as people buzzed around them, eager to engage.

"There's Richard and his team," Shannon whispered to Madison. "It's going to be an interesting morning."

"Let's see what they're up to," Madison replied, intrigued.

As they approached, Richard's face lit up upon seeing them.

"Ah, Madison and Shannon, so good to see you. We could use your insights this morning. And I am guessing Madison, this must be Roy, the musician you told me about. Great to meet you Roy," he greeted warmly.

At Little Richard's comment regarding 'using their help,' Madison exchanged curious glances with Shannon and Roy, a hint of apprehension lingering in the air.

"What's the occasion?" Madison asked, smiling.

Richard's expression turned serious. "We're discussing a new community initiative. We want to rally support, and your perspectives are crucial."

The entourage nodded in agreement, some scribbling notes while others watched intently.

Later in the church's sanctuary, the congregation settled in, the atmosphere charged with excitement. Madison, Shannon, and Roy found seats together, glancing back at Richard's group, now seated near the front.

"This could be the start of something big," Shannon leaned in, whispering.

"Or something complicated" – Roy mused.

As the service began, the Pastor stepped up to the podium, his voice resonating with warmth and authority.

"Today, we gather not just in worship but in community. It's about reaching out and making a difference together," he addressed the congregation.

His message was powerful, focused and targeted, to the state of the Dead, and where do we go after we die. To Hell with Satan, or Heaven with Jesus Christ, our Lord and Savior. It was about reaching the lost.

Roy suddenly felt a nervous sensation invade his body as he realized this was a God moment. A moment when God's vision, through him, might be fulfilled by the very tape of the music he had in his possession.

Madison, Shannon, and Roy exchanged looks, the weight of the moment settling in as they considered the implications of Richard's presence.

As the church's service concluded, people began to mingle. Madison, Shannon, and Roy quickly approached Richard, who was deep in conversation with others.

"Richard," said Madison. "That was truly a great message today, wasn't it? By the way, can I introduce Roy, a church brother from Jamaica. He is a songwriter for his group and I think you would love what he has to present. Can we take a moment of your time to talk about his initiative and maybe gain your support to promote what he has? His demo tape of the music is, in my limited opinion, phenomenal."

Richard turned, his expression brightening. "Absolutely! Let's discuss it over a bite to eat. If it is worthy I can certainly have an influence on it, especially as a fellow brother. Let's eat at Aunt Kizzy's you'll love the southern cuisine. I'll give you a ride in my Limo."

Roy, beaming with pride, and just a little humble, blurted out, just a little too enthusiastically. "Wow, Thanks Sir."

Little Richard smiled knowingly. "Sounds intriguing, guys. Let's make that happen."

Soon after lunch the trio, in Little Richard's own Limousine, arrived at the Hyatt Regency, the sunset casting a warm glow over the modern architecture. They entered, the ambiance shifting to a more upscale setting.

The lobby buzzed with energy as Little Richard piloted his way to what was obviously his reserved table, a table with an impressive and commandeering view.

"Quite the location you've got here, Richard," Madison remarked, looking around.

Little Richard chuckled. "It's a hub for conversations and connections. Perfect for what we're discussing."

They sat down, and Roy pulled out his demo tape, ready to present.

"Little Richard, the music I have written is all about raising awareness of Jesus Christ to the lost. We have been doing this in our local churches and to our community in Jamaica, but, with your help Mr. Richard, I believe we can reach the world very much like what the Pastor was talking about this morning. Truly Mr. Richard, I believe this was a God ordained moment we have had today," Roy said excitedly.

As Little Richard listened to the demo tape, Shannon and Madison, with beaming smiles, watched him keenly. As he leaned in closer, he looked clearly impressed.

"This could revolutionize how we connect with our community. I can see great potential here," Little Richard said, nodding thoughtfully.

The conversation flowed effortlessly, ideas bouncing back and forth. The chemistry among them was palpable, a sense of purpose filling the air.

"If we can get more people involved, we can truly make a difference," Shannon said enthusiastically.

"Together, we can create something meaningful," Madison added, nodding in agreement.

Little Richard looked at them, a glimmer of excitement in his eyes. "Let's bring this vision to life. I can help with the resources you need."

As they left the Hyatt, the night was alive with possibilities. Madison, Shannon, and Roy walked together, reflecting on the day.

"I didn't expect today to turn out like this," Roy said, grinning. His smile was as deep and as broad as the Grand Canyon itself.

"Sometimes the best things come from unexpected meetings," Shannon replied, smiling.

Madison looked at both of them with a sense of hope and determination in his eyes. "This is just the beginning."

A few days later, Roy found himself in the opulent penthouse of the Hyatt Regency, a world away from the modest apartment he shared with Maddison and Shannon. The room was bathed in golden light, the large windows offering a breathtaking view of the city. Roy stood wide-eyed, taking in his surroundings, as Maddison chatted animatedly with Little Richard, the legendary rock and roll icon.

Little Richard, with his flamboyant personality and larger-than-life presence, was a force of nature. He greeted Roy with a warm smile and a twinkle in his eye. “You boys are gonna love it here!” he said, his melodic voice filling the room. “This is where the magic happens.”

Roy looked at Maddison, who nodded knowingly with a glimmer of excitement in his eyes. *Maddison had a way of making everything feel effortless*, Roy thought. *Like he belonged in this world. I was just a visitor, mesmerized by the spectacle.*

Danny, Richard’s adopted son, stood near them, quietly observing the interaction. He was in his early thirties, with a calm demeanor and a sharp mind. Danny had been by Richard’s side for years, helping him deal with the complexities of fame and the entertainment industry. He was the kind of person who could blend into the background but was always watching, always listening.

As the evening progressed, Richard handed Roy a stack of papers—the movie script for “Leap of Faith.” Roy’s eyes widened as he took it, feeling the weight of the moment.

“Wow, this is incredible!” Roy exclaimed.

Richard grinned. "But you're not just holding it. You're gonna read it, Roy."

Roy looked at Maddison, who gave him an encouraging nod. Roy cleared his throat and began reading the script aloud.

"Faith is a powerful thing... it can move mountains."

Richard interrupted, his voice filled with passion. "Oh, no, no! That's not how you read it, baby! You gotta feel it!"

Roy tried again, this time channeling Richard's energy. "Faith is a powerful thing... it can move mountains."

Richard nodded approvingly. "That's it! Feel every word!"

As the reading wrapped up, Richard seemed proud. "You've got a gift, my friend. With a little polish, you could shine!"

Maddison nudged Roy, encouraging him to take it in.

"You know, there's more to showbiz than just talent. It's about connections, perseverance, and sometimes... a little luck; whilst implying the importance of the casting couch," Little Richard said as he leaned back on his chair.

"I came to Hollywood hoping to get a record deal for my group. Any advice?" Roy asked.

Little Richard chuckled with a twinkle in his eye. “First, you’ve got to stand out. Show them who you are. And never let anyone tell you no.”

As the night wore on, Roy found himself drawn into Little Richard’s world, a world of glamour, creativity, and endless possibilities.

“You have to come to the studio tomorrow. Richard’s working on something big, and I think you’d fit right in,” said Danny.

Roy was in disbelief as he heard him. “Really? I would love that!”

As Roy rested quietly in his apartment, the stillness was broken by the buzz of his phone. A message from an unknown number lit the screen: “You’re in over your head. Stay away from Richard.”

Roy’s heart raced as he contemplated the ominous warning, setting the stage for the challenges and revelations that lay ahead.

Two days passed quickly and Roy and Maddison found themselves in the back of a luxurious limousine again, gliding through the vibrant streets of Hollywood. The city sparkled in the sunlight, a place where dreams were made and broken in equal measure. Sitting next to Roy was Little Richard.

Little Richard grinned, his signature charisma on full display. "I played that demo cassette you gave me on repeat! Those boys from Jamaica have got something special!"

Roy felt a rush of pride and forgot about his earlier uneasiness. "I'm glad you liked it!" he replied, a smile breaking across his face. "They've got talent, and they just need the right break."

Maddison, sitting across from them, leaned in with a smirk. "You realize that not everyone gets to ride in a limo with a legend, right?"

Roy chuckled, shaking his head. "I know! This feels surreal."

As the limousine drove past iconic Hollywood landmarks—the Hollywood Sign, the Walk of Fame, the bustling studios—Roy felt a sense of wonder wash over him. But beneath the glitz and glamour, he couldn't ignore the weight Richard seemed to carry every day. Despite his flamboyant personality and infectious energy, there was a vulnerability in Little Richard's eyes, a quiet struggle that Roy couldn't understand.

Little Richard turned to Roy, his expression shifting to something more serious. "You know," he said, his voice softer now, "I always carry these—" He reached into his bag and pulled out a stack of small books, handing them to Roy.

Roy looked down at the books and saw copies of Steps to Christ. "I give them away to fans," Little Richard explained, his tone intense. "Faith keeps me grounded in this crazy world."

Roy nodded as he was touched by Little Richard's openness. "That's... really amazing," he said, flipping through one of the books. "It's not something you'd expect from a rock and roll legend."

Little Richard smiled, but there was a hint of sadness in his eyes. "Faith is everything, Roy. Without it, this life can eat you alive."

The limousine came to a stop in front of a busy café. Little Richard stepped out, and almost immediately, fans rushed to greet him. He posed for photos, signed autographs, and exuded warmth and charm, his larger-than-life persona shining brightly. Roy watched from the car, admiring the connection Little Richard had with his fans. It was a side of fame he had never seen before—one that felt genuine and heartfelt.

Back in the limousine, Roy and Maddison sat in silence for a moment, watching the scene unfold outside. Maddison broke the quiet, his voice thoughtful. “You know, Richard’s got a lot of love to give. But he struggles with his identity.”

Roy nodded, his mind drifting back to the conversation in the car. “Yeah, he asked me to pray for him. It’s humbling, really.”

Maddison gave him a knowing look. “You are a good friend to him, Roy.”

Roy leaned back in his seat, his thoughts turning inward. *I had my own demons*, he reflected, his voice echoing in his mind. *Living in the shadows without documentation. My life felt like a series of obstacles, each one heavier than the last.*

Chapter 11

Los Angeles – Realizing the Depth of Evil

The city of Los Angeles was a powder keg, ready to erupt into war at any moment. The streets which were once bustling with life, now echoed with the sounds of shattered glass, distant sirens, and the angry cries of its people pushed to their breaking point. The Rodney King riots had erupted, and the city was engulfed in flames—both literal and metaphorical. For Roy, the chaos that was outside was relatable to the chaos inside of him. He stood on the rooftop of the Hollywood Terrace, his eyes scanning the horizon as plumes of smoke rose into the night sky. Tension was everywhere, and the weight of the moment pressed down on him like a physical force.

Maddison joined him at the rooftop with worry visible on his face. The two men stood in silence for a moment, the gravity of the situation rendering words unnecessary. Below them, the streets were alive with confusion and turmoil—looters ransacked stores, fires raged unchecked, and the cries of protestors filled the air. The city was unraveling, and Roy felt a deep sense of unease settle in his chest.

"This is getting out of hand," Maddison finally said in a dull voice.

Roy nodded, his jaw tightening. As a former Jamaican soldier fighting crime and civil unrest in the streets of his homeland, Roy had seen so much more than what he was witnessing right now. But this was Los Angeles, the home, the Stars, a window for the world to live vicariously through the eyes of make believe, of Hollywood. Where the unreal became real for a few hours on the big screen. This was real life imitating the art of make-believe, and it felt both terrifying and surreal.

The acquittal of the officers involved in Rodney King's beating had ignited a fire that had been smoldering for decades. The African American community, long marginalized and oppressed, had reached this extremity. And now the city and its people were paying a price, in many cases with their lives.

Roy's thoughts were interrupted by the arrival of two officers from Special Protective Services. The officers approached the rooftop with a tight posture.

"Is anyone interested in working security for the apartments at Masslien and 6th Street?" one of them asked, sounding urgent.

Roy exchanged a glance with Maddison. The offer was tempting—not just for the money, but for the chance to do something meaningful. He had spent so much of his life feeling like an outsider, like he didn't belong here. But now, standing on the rooftop of the Hollywood Terrace, he felt a sense of purpose stirring within him.

"I need the money," Roy said, his voice steady. "But more importantly, I want to help."

Maddison nodded with a look of pride in his eyes. "You'll be great at it. Just remember to stay safe, Roy."

The Masslien Apartments were a stark contrast to the chaos outside. The building was a modest structure, its walls weathered but sturdy. The atmosphere was tense inside. The residents, mostly families and elderly individuals, huddled together in the lobby and fear was evident on their faces. The distant sounds of the riots echoed through the halls, a constant reminder of the danger lurking just beyond their doors.

Roy patrolled the dimly lit hallways of the building and his footsteps echoed in the silence. He could feel the weight of the residents' eyes on him, their fear palpable. He had been in tense situations before—both in the military and during the riots—but this felt different to him. This wasn't just about protecting property; it was about protecting people. And that responsibility weighed heavily on him.

"I felt a sense of duty," Roy thought as he walked the halls. "Protecting those who were scared. But I was also scared... scared of what might happen next."

The tension in the air was suffocating. Every creak of the floorboards, every distant shout, sent a jolt of adrenaline through Roy's body, and he would prepare to fight. He knew that at any moment, the chaos outside could spill into the building. And if it did, he would be the only thing standing between the residents and the looters as a shield.

As the night wore on, the sounds of the riots grew louder. Roy stepped outside for a breather, the cool night air doing little to calm his nerves. In the distance, he saw a group of looters approaching a nearby store. They moved with a sense of purpose, their faces masked by bandanas and hoods. Roy did not know what to do. He was torn—on one hand, he wanted to protect the residents of the Masslien Apartments. On the other hand, he couldn't ignore the cries for justice echoing through the streets.

"This is not easy for me, I need to protect," Roy thought, his eyes fixed on the looters. "It is a reckoning. And I am in the middle of it all, trying to find my place in a world that felt chaotic and unforgiving."

Back inside the lobby, the tension was palpable. The residents huddled together, their faces filled with fear and uncertainty. One of them—a middle-aged woman with graying hair—approached Roy.

"Do you think they'll come here?" she asked with a trembling voice, her eyes wide with fear.

Roy met her gaze, and his expression was stern but reassuring. "I'll do everything I can to keep you safe."

The woman nodded, but the fear in her eyes was still evident. Roy could feel the weight of her trust, and it only strengthened his resolve. He knew that he couldn't let them down.

Suddenly, a violent crash erupted from down the street. Roy rushed to the window, his pulse hammering, as flames tore into the night sky from a nearby building. The looters were closing in, and with every passing moment the danger grew more real, more immediate.

"This is it," Roy thought, his mind racing. The moment of choice. Either stand by and watch the world burn or rise and fight for something greater.

The residents turned toward him, eyes wide with fear yet flickering with hope. One among them—a young man with a hardened gaze—broke the silence.

"You're our only line of defense," he said, urgency sharpening every word.

Roy drew a steady breath, his voice calm but resolute. *"Stay together. Stay calm. We'll make it through this."*

He no longer doubted what he had to do. Stepping outside, he faced the looters head-on, his stance unshaken, his voice carrying the weight of conviction.

"You need to leave!" he shouted, his voice cutting through the chaos. "This isn't right!"

The looters paused and were surprised by his defiance. The lead looter, who was a tall man with a menacing presence, stepped forward, sizing Roy up.

"What are you gonna do about it?" he sneered. "You think you can take us on, tough guy?"

Roy stood tall, his heart racing but his resolve unwavering. "You're not welcome here. This community is better than this!"

The standoff was tense, the air thick with anticipation. The residents watched them from the lobby, their breaths held as they waited for what would happen next. And then, just as it seemed like the situation might escalate, the sound of sirens filled the air. The looters hesitated, their bravado faltering as the police closed in.

"Looks like the party is over," the lead looter said, smirking as he and his group began to run away.

Inside the lobby, the residents cheered as the looters retreated. Roy felt a rush of adrenaline, knowing that he had made the right choice this time. He had stood up when it mattered, and in doing so, he had protected a community that needed him.

Maddison approached his friend. "I heard about how you stood up to these thugs tonight. You did good, man. You stood tall when it mattered; I'm proud of you."

Roy exhaled, the weight of the night's events settling over him. "I just. . . I want to make a difference."

As the chaos of the night began to dissolve, Roy stood on the steps of the Masslien Apartments, watching as the police restored order. The city was still in turmoil, but in that moment, he felt a renewed sense of purpose.

He had come to Hollywood to chase his dreams, but now he realized that his purpose was bigger than himself. He was ready to step up, ready to face his demons, and ready to stand for something greater.

The next morning, the city was a different place. The bus rattled down Fairfax Avenue, Roy staring out the window at the destruction. The streets were filled with debris, remnants of the night's violence. Roy walked through the aftermath and his mind was racing with thoughts of his future here in Los Angeles.

The words of Rodney King echoed in his mind: "Can't we all just get along?"

He had faced the chaos head-on, and in doing so, he had found a sense of clarity. He knew that the road ahead would be difficult, but he was ready to face all of it, unlike before.

With that, Roy was assigned to similar tasks to guard the city. He arrived at the security office along with other officers, where he turned in his mag light and later discussed the next day's assignments.

As he prepared to leave, one of the officers said to him, "Things should calm down soon. But keep your guard up, boy."

As he approached Hollywood Terrace, he paused for a moment, reflecting on his life and the choices he had made. He had spent so much of his life living in the shadows, but now he felt ready to step into the light.

Later that day, Roy met Maddison at a café on Hollywood Boulevard. The atmosphere was a stark contrast to the chaos of the night before, but the effect of it still lingered.

Maddison leaned in, his voice low. “I heard something. Richard is planning a big event to bring the community together. He wants you to be part of it.”

Roy was surprised. “Me? Why?”

Maddison smiled. “You stood up during the riots. People noticed. Richard believes you can help bridge the gap.”

Roy contemplated the offer, torn between his past struggles and the opportunity to make a real difference. Could he really be a part of something bigger? Could he help heal a community?

That night, Roy sat in his room silently. He pulled out the Steps to Christ books given to him by Little Richard and flipped through the pages. The words resonated with him, offering a sense of peace amidst the turmoil.

“Maybe this was my chance to step out of the shadows and into the light. To embrace my purpose,” Roy thought.

As he walked through the quiet streets of Hollywood, he felt a renewed sense of determination. The city may have been in turmoil, but he was ready to fight for change. He was ready to step up, ready to face his demons, ready to stand for something greater than himself.

The echoes of the riots would linger for a long time, maybe, but for Roy, they were a turning point.

And as the sun rose over the smoldering city, Roy knew that he was no longer just a man chasing dreams. He was a man with a mission. And he was ready to see it through.

Roy's journey from Jamaica to Hollywood had been fueled by dreams of stardom, but fate had other plans. After the Rodney King riots, where he had become an unexpected hero by quelling chaos in his neighborhood, his reward wasn't fame but a security job at the Sports Connection gymnasium. A far cry from the glamor of the movie industry, it was nonetheless a chance to rebuild, to find purpose. Yet, Roy couldn't know that his greatest battle was yet to come—one that would change his life forever.

His new role at the Sports Connection was deceptively simple: patrol the gym, maintain order, and navigate the peculiar dynamics of a diverse clientele. As he stood at the entrance to the locker room, his gaze swept over the chiseled bodies and determined faces.

The low hum of chatter and the rhythmic clinking of weights created a strange, almost soothing symphony. But beneath the surface, Roy felt the tension—both within himself and in the world around him. The scars from the riots were still fresh, lingering like a shadow that never quite left his side.

"I've faced the rage of a city on fire," he thought. "This should be easy."

When the Chief of Staff had offered him the position, there had been pride in the man's eyes, a recognition of Roy's courage in the face of chaos.

"You did an excellent job during the riots, Roy. We'd like to offer you a position at the Sports Connection," the Chief had said, his handshake firm and approving.

Roy had accepted without hesitation, his military discipline and sense of duty propelling him forward. Yet, as he walked the gym floor now, the irony gnawed at him. Outside, he had quelled a riot. Inside, he was on what Kim, the gym manager, had called the "penis patrol", keeping order among men who sometimes tested the boundaries of discretion.

Kim had sensed his discomfort and laughed it off. "Just be tactful," she had advised. "We don't want any lawsuits."

Tact. It was a skill Roy had mastered on the chaotic streets, but here it took on a new dimension. The clientele—mostly gay men—were polite and confident, their charm tinged with a boldness that left Roy feeling strangely vulnerable. "This job is more intimidating than the riot," he thought wryly.

In the cafeteria, as Roy shoveled chicken and brown rice into his mouth, food was no longer a pleasure but fuel. He watched the others eat, their conversations light and carefree, and felt a pang of longing for connection. He swallowed it down with another bite, unwilling to let weakness seep through his disciplined exterior.

It was during one of those quiet moments—when the gym had wound down and the last stragglers were finishing up their routines—that it hit him.

A slow, insidious blurring of his vision. His heart raced, pounding like a war drum in his chest. The world around him swirled and twisted, shadows blending into light. He gripped the counter, his knuckles white, trying to hold on to reality. The sound of his own breath roared in his ears, muffling the distant chatter of the few remaining members.

"What's happening to me?" The thought was fleeting, fragmented. Panic clawed at his mind, a beast determined to consume him. He forced himself to move, stumbling out of the cafeteria and into the hallway, where the walls seemed to tilt and sway. He leaned heavily against the cool concrete, gasping for air.

The episode passed as suddenly as it had come, leaving him shaken and drenched in sweat. Roy wiped his face with a trembling hand, the fear still sharp and unyielding. He couldn't afford to fall apart, not now, not ever. As his vision slowly cleared, he straightened himself and took a deep, steadying breath.

"Is it stress? Exhaustion? Or something more sinister?" He couldn't know then that this would become his new reality—one that would haunt him for decades to come. But in that moment, he made a silent vow: to fight through whatever demons threatened to tear him down. His mother's words echoed from a lifetime ago: "You, Roy, are going to do great things for God."

As he stepped out into the quiet West Hollywood streets, the world around him seemed vast and unforgiving. But somewhere within the turmoil, Roy found a glimmer of hope—an ember that refused to die out. And with that fragile flame guiding him, he kept moving forward, determined to face whatever fate had in store.

Chapter 12

Physical Eyes Closed & Spiritual Eyes Opened

With frequent episodes of his vision blurring and with constant headaches, Roy knew he had to get help. The next day, as Roy sat in the cold, sterile examination room at UCLA's Jules Stein Eye Clinic anxiety overcame him.

He could not comprehend what was happening and his hands clenched tightly together on his lap. The walls were bare, and the atmosphere was high with uncertainty. A single fluorescent light hummed overhead, casting a harsh glow on the ophthalmologist in front of him.

The doctor appeared to be in his mid-40s, with graying hair and observant eyes. He adjusted the overhead examination light before speaking.

He cleared his throat and said, "We're going to check your optic nerves and measure the pressure in your eyes."

Roy swallowed hard as he heard the doctor. He felt his stomach knotting due to apprehension. He had always prided himself on his independence and his ability to navigate life with confidence. But sitting in that chair, with the weight of uncertainty pressing down on him, he had never felt more vulnerable.

The ophthalmologist leaned in closer, administering numbing drops to Roy's eyes before beginning the examination. Roy focused on the blurred shapes in front of him, trying hard not to panic and practice steady breathing.

"Just relax," the doctor said, pressing a cold instrument against Roy's eye.

Minutes passed in tense silence as the doctor completed his tests. Roy, although unable to fully visualize the Doctor's expression, could feel it, the tension in the room was palpable, and even though he could not see the Doctor's expression he just knew something wasn't right. And, then, without a word, he left the room, leaving Roy uncertain and becoming more and more worried with every passing second.

He sat there motionless, his fingers gripping the armrests of the chair. A gnawing fear crept into his chest.

Something is not right. I can feel it.

Moments later, the door swung open, and the doctor returned, this time accompanied by a small group of physicians. Roy could not clearly see their faces but the heavy mood told him what that expression might be, and he braced in fear of what was coming.

The Ophthalmologist turned to Roy and said in a serious tone, "The pressure in both eyes is forty -four, and your optic nerves are almost severed."

Roy's heart sank as soon as he heard the doctor. As his breath hitched, he spoke, "What does that mean for my vision?"

He didn't hear most of what the doctor said—not at first. Just the last few words hit him like a slap to the soul.

"...Your optic nerves are nearly severed. If we don't intervene now, you'll be blind."

Blind.

The word echoed in his chest like a tolling bell. It didn't make sense. Not here. Not now. Roy blinked, hard. His heart pounded against his ribs as if trying to escape. This couldn't be real. It had to be a mistake. He was young. Healthy. Driven. He had plans. And God... well, God had plans for him too, didn't He?

But those words, "you'll be blind" made everything else fade. The future he imagined, the work he'd poured himself into, the vision—literal and spiritual—he relied on to navigate life. It all unraveled in an instant.

The doctor's voice was calm but firm, clinical. "We're referring you immediately to Harbor General. You need surgery.

Time is critical. It's our only shot at saving what little vision remains."

Roy nodded numbly, trying to hold himself together, to remain composed. But inside, a storm raged. The silent kind. The kind that slowly cracks the soul.

He left the clinic like a ghost—adrift in the bright California sun, surrounded by a world he could barely see and no longer understood. The city hadn't changed, but Roy had. Something had fractured.

He boarded the bus home, squinting to find his way. His vision was deteriorating faster than he feared. The signs blurred. He missed his stop. Nothing felt familiar. Strangers became guides. The streets felt foreign. For a man who had always prided himself on independence, the reliance stung.

Back at his apartment, Madison and Shannon met him at the door. They saw it in his face. The way his shoulders sagged. The way he didn't speak. He walked past them without a word and shut himself in his room.

It was dark. Silent. Safe.

Roy collapsed onto the floor. Not the bed. The floor. Something about being low, grounded, close to the earth—matched where he was spiritually.

He began to cry. First silently, then openly. Desperately.

“God...” he whispered into the silence. “If you just let me keep my sight... I swear I’ll serve You. I’ll give up everything else. The industry, the distractions, the pride. Just please... don’t let me go blind.”

The words came fast, tumbling out in a torrent of fear and emotion.

“I’ll be better. I’ll work harder. I’ll do Your will. Just... let me see.”

And then the room was still.

No voice thundered from heaven. No warmth wrapped around him. Just the quiet realization that he was bargaining. That this wasn’t faith. This was fear.

His thoughts drifted back to Jamaica—to his mother’s voice. Her calm, prophetic words: “You will do great things for God, Roy. But not on your terms.”

He could still see her in his mind’s eye—standing by the door, apron dusted with flour, eyes soft but fierce with conviction.

“You don’t make deals with God,” she had said once. “You surrender.”

That night, Roy didn't sleep much. But something shifted. The tears dried. The bargaining quieted. And from somewhere deep within came a question: *What if I serve Him even if I go blind?*

The next morning, after explaining to Maddison and Shannon what was happening, Roy made his way to Harbor General. He could barely read the bus numbers. He asked strangers for help. Something he never would've done before.

At Harbor, the chief retinologist examined him and made the same call. "You need emergency surgery. USC Hospital has specialists and you need the surgery now. We will make arrangements for you to be admitted immediately.

He arrived at the hospital disoriented, exhausted, and unsure of what awaited him. The receptionist greeted him kindly. "They're expecting you."

Within an hour, Roy was seated before Dr. Shodogie and Dr. Chow. They examined his file, then him.

"Your optic nerve is still intact—but only barely," Dr. Chow said. "We need to operate immediately. But Roy... do you have insurance?"

Roy lowered his eyes. "No."

A pause.

"We can still do the surgery," Dr. Shodogie said. "If you're willing to sign a teaching waiver, we can cover it. You'll be part of a case study. We're training surgeons, and your situation is rare."

Roy didn't hesitate. "I'll sign."

It wasn't a deal. It wasn't a bargain. It was a surrender.

The night before surgery, Roy lay alone in the pre-op room, draped in a thin hospital blanket. The quiet buzz of medical monitors was the only sound. He stared at the ceiling, eyes raw from strain.

This time, he didn't ask for healing.

He asked for peace.

"God," he whispered, "if I wake up blind, let me still see You. If I walk in darkness, let it be with You. I'm Yours. Whatever that means."

He exhaled, long and deep.

The next morning, the OR was buzzing with hushed urgency. The anesthesiologist leaned over him. "We're going to begin the procedure. You'll feel pressure—but we'll manage the pain."

Midway through, the pressure turned to pain. Roy gasped. “It hurts!”

Dr. Chow didn’t stop. “We’re almost there. Stay with us.”

He gripped the edge of the table. A nurse placed a hand on his shoulder. “You’re not alone.”

Then blackness.

When Roy woke, everything was blurry. Bandages covered his left eye. The right was fogged and hypersensitive. He blinked, slowly adjusting to the dim light.

Dr. Shodogie appeared at his side.

“The surgery was a success. We stabilized the pressure. The right eye may last you five years. The left eye... I’m sorry, Roy.”

Roy nodded. No tears. No despair. Just quiet acceptance.

He had surrendered. This was the road now. And God would walk it with him.

The weeks that followed were filled with follow-ups, medications, and injections. Roy learned to navigate differently. He moved slowly, more carefully. But he also moved with a new purpose.

He began journaling—not goals, not dreams, but prayers.

Each day started with the same line: "God, I trust You."

He visited a church again—not as a guest, but as a seeker. He began speaking. At youth centers. At churches. At recovery programs. He told them what happened—not that he almost went blind, but that God had opened his eyes.

He spoke of control. Of fear. Of surrender. Of grace.

He told them about the floor of his apartment. About the bargain. And about the moment he let go.

And he quoted his mother often.

"She said I'd do great things for God. And she was right. But not because I was strong. Because I was broken. And He used me anyway."

Twenty-seven years later, Roy would still have vision in that right eye.

But it was never about the sight.

It was always about the surrender.

Whenever someone asked him how he made it through, Roy would smile and say, "I stopped trying to trade with God and started trusting Him."

And when the moments of fear returned as they always do, he'd whisper the words that changed everything:

"God, I trust You."

But the transformation didn't stop after surgery. Roy wasn't just recovering from trauma — he was being rebuilt.

The man who once believed in control, who thought faith meant action and reward, began to understand something deeper: that faith meant trust without proof, love without condition, and obedience without guarantees.

Recovery wasn't linear. There were days of doubt, fear, and silence. Roy would wake up with blurry vision and panic. The world still didn't look the way it used to, and neither did he.

There were headaches that lingered like ghosts, light that stabbed at his skull, and moments when everything faded into a haze so deep he wondered if the doctors had been wrong.

But he no longer reached for the bargaining table. He reached for God.

He stopped asking *why* and started asking *what now?*

He filled journals — not with complaints or goals — but with prayers. Honest ones. Ugly ones. Hopeful ones. "Use me." "Change me." "Help me see in the dark." "Take whatever You must but give me Your presence."

One morning, a passage from Scripture caught his attention and refused to let go: *"My grace is sufficient for you, for my power is made perfect in weakness."* Roy stared at the page through squinted eyes; the words were blurry but the message razor sharp.

He began to believe that maybe, just maybe, his story wasn't one of loss but one of calling. A different kind of calling. Not to stage or screen, but to souls.

He remembered his mother's voice again.

"You'll do great things for God."

He had once assumed she meant influence. Recognition. Lights and stages. But now... now he heard it differently.

"Great things" didn't always look like triumph. Sometimes, they looked like service. Humility. The quiet faithfulness of a man who could no longer rely on what he saw, but only on whom he trusted.

Roy began speaking again — but this time, not as a performer as a witness.

At shelters, he told his story to men who'd lost their families and didn't believe in second chances. At youth prisons, he told boys who'd never known a father that there was still a future written by the Author of grace. At churches, he stood behind pulpits not to preach, but to testify.

He shared about that night on the floor. The bargain. The silence. The dream of his mother. The surgery. The surrender.

People wept. They saw themselves in his pain. And more importantly, they saw what God could do with someone broken but willing.

Roy never pretended to be whole. That was the power of it. He let his weakness become his platform. His testimony wasn't about how he escaped blindness. It was about how God made him see.

One day, years later, Roy visited his old neighborhood in Jamaica.

He stood outside the church where his mother used to pray, where he used to sit with his arms crossed, pretending not to listen. The roof had rusted. The paint had peeled. But the spirit of the place hadn't changed.

He stepped inside and knelt at the front pew.

"Thank You," he whispered. "For not giving me what I asked for. For giving me what I needed."

He thought of all the people he'd spoken to. The lives he'd touched. The souls who'd come to Christ because of his honesty — not his vision.

He thought of the boy he used to be. Arrogant. Focused on achievement. Afraid of failure. Always trying to control outcomes.

And he thought of the man he had become. Scarred. Dependent. Devoted. Peaceful.

Not because God had spared his sight, but because God had restored his heart.

When Roy finally returned to his apartment in Los Angeles, he opened his journal to the last page and wrote only one sentence:

"God, I trust You — even in the dark."

That night, he slept more soundly than he had in years. He was ready to do God's work, whatever that meant and wherever that may be. No longer bargaining, no longer tormented by his lack of clear sight, but now with a vision that comes to him daily in prayer, in his fellowship with God. A vision that is more clear than anything he had experienced in the past. He was ready for God's plan to be fulfilled, no matter where it took him.

Chapter 13

Realization - Shattered Dreams/Spiritual Potential

Roy faced difficulty adjusting to life with this new challenge. Everywhere he went, he would stumble, leaving him with minor injuries every day. But he couldn't stop himself when the producer called him to visit his office; he had something important to talk about.

On his arrival, Roy was ushered into the producer's office. Though his sight was slowly improving, the room around him remained hazy and indistinct. Yet he did not need clarity of vision to sense the opulence—the gleam of marble beneath his feet, the glossy portraits of stars lining the walls. To most, these might have seemed symbols of success.

To Roy, they stood as reminders that whatever this meeting promised, it was never likely to be the Lord's plan for him. His blurred vision, far from being a curse, had become a truth he could not escape: God intended him to lean on faith, not on his own strength. So, he waited, quietly, in that assurance. The door swung open and a sharply dressed man entered, a leather-bound folder under his arm. He crossed the room with confidence, extending his hand and clasped Roy's warmly.

Then, with a practiced flourish, he slid the folder across the desk, his smile wide and persuasive. “We want you, Roy. This could be your big break. And as a token of our commitment...” He placed a shining set of keys for a brand-new Mercedes-Benz Convertible in front of him.

Roy looked down and slowly picked them up, feeling the power in his hands. Then, with a quiet determination he placed them on the leather folder that he intuitively knew contained a substantial contract. And despite knowing this would secure his future and his dreams; almost in a whisper he said “no”.

Roy shook his head, cutting him off as he rose to his feet. “Thank you. But no.” His tone was firmer now, carrying the weight of conviction. He turned and walked toward the door before the man could press him further.

Each step away from the desk felt heavier than the last, yet somehow freer too. His pulse pounded in his ears, matching the echo of his footsteps across the marble floor. In his chest a storm raged, part of him grieved the dream he had once held, but a deeper part knew this was victory, not loss. He could almost hear the whisper of scripture threading through his heart: *“What does it profit a man to gain the whole world, yet forfeit his soul?”*

His hand gripped the door handle, slick with the sweat of choice. Behind him, the polished office—its portraits of smiling stars and marble floors—seemed to fade into something shallow, almost hollow. For a flicker of a moment, he thought of the Mercedes keys on that desk, gleaming like false treasure. Then he breathed a prayer under his breath, steady and sure: *"Lord, my life is Yours. Keep me on Your path, not mine."*

As the door clicked shut behind him, the muffled voice of the producer followed, dismissive and sharp. "What's up with this guy? People would leave everything for an opportunity like this. Anyway—call the other guy. I've got too much work today."

Roy kept walking, not slowing, not looking back. The corridor stretched before him, dim compared to the dazzling light of the office, but in that dimness there was a strange peace. For the first time in a long time, he felt the strength that comes only from surrender. The world had offered him its glittering prize, but he had chosen instead the unseen treasure of obedience.

And though the pit of uncertainty still lay before him, he knew he was not walking it alone.

The Los Angeles sun blazed mercilessly overhead, yet Roy felt as though he was moving through shadows. Each step carried the echo of what he had lost—and the haunting uncertainty of what might never return. *Everything I dreamed of was within reach, but the cost was too high.*

That night felt darker than usual. He sat on his bed, surrounded by posters of bodybuilding champions and Hollywood legends. He felt like he was abandoned by everyone.

Why me, God?

His fingers traced the spine of his Bible before flipping it open. The pages fell to a verse about perseverance.

"I will not lose faith," he whispered.

Across the room, Maddison glanced up from his script. "You good, man?" he said loud enough for Roy to listen, but his tone was gentle.

Roy exhaled. "Just... wondering if I made the right choice today."

Maddison set down his papers. "Turning down the car?"

"Turning down the life that came with it," Roy added further.

Maddison was quiet for a moment, then shrugged. "Maybe you didn't turn it down. Maybe you just chose a different path."

Roy smirked. "Since when did you get so philosophical?"

"Haha, I'm a bit of an all-rounder, my boy. Oh man, you won't believe what happened today," he said, dropping onto the couch beside Roy. "So, I'm in this meeting with the producers, right? And they try to lowball me on the rate for this new animation gig."

Roy turned his head toward Maddison's voice, a small smile forming. "Umm, let me guess - you walked out?"

Maddison snapped his fingers. "Better. I leaned forward, looked him dead in the eye, and said—." He paused dramatically before delivering the line with perfect timing: "You can't put a price on talent!"

Roy laughed. "No way. And what'd they say?"

"The room got so quiet you could hear a pin drop," Maddison said, smirking. "Then the lead producer started laughing and said, 'Damn right we can't.' They doubled the offer on the spot."

Roy clapped while smiling. "Only you can have such talent."

"Hey, someone's got to keep Hollywood honest," Maddison said, stretching his arms behind his head. "Besides, now I can afford to keep up for another month."

Roy felt grateful for the friendship that had blossomed despite his challenges.

"You always know how to lighten the mood, Maddison."

"I know I'm the best," Maddison said, walking toward his room.

The next morning, Roy walked toward the kitchen to make himself some breakfast. His vision, though far from sharp, had been improving bit by bit. He still moved with care, sometimes brushing a shoulder against the wall or reaching a hand out to steady himself, but he managed. Opening the fridge, he found only eggs and sausages waiting for him.

As he began cooking, the silence pressed in—broken only by the ticking of the clock, the gurgle of water beginning to boil, and the faint hum of LA traffic. Roy worked deliberately, relying on both sight and the habits of muscle memory. His knife moved slower than it once had but steady all the same.

"Need any help?" Shannon's voice came from the doorway, warm but without pity.

Roy shook his head with a faint smile. "I've got this. Just... maybe let me know if I'm about to set something on fire."

Shannon chuckled. "No fires. Though Maddison left his protein shake on the counter again. Try not to knock it over."

"Noted," Roy said, reaching for the spice rack where everything was kept in its usual order. His mother Gloria had taught him to cook as a teenager, and the lessons came back naturally now. Soon, the smell of vegetables and eggs filled the kitchen, bringing comfort with their sizzle.

When he finished, Shannon quietly slid a plate within reach, and Maddison wandered in to set the table. The city lights flickered faintly beyond the window, but inside that warm kitchen, Roy felt a different kind of brightness—one that came not from eyes, but from belonging.

That afternoon, Roy attended church. He sat quietly among the congregation, head slightly bowed, hands resting on his lap. His eyesight still qualified as legally blind, but he could make out shapes and light enough to orient himself. More than that, he sensed the atmosphere—the closeness of people around him, the rustle of Bible pages, the quiet rhythm of voices in prayer.

The pastor's voice rang out: *"In our weakness, God's strength is made perfect!"*

The words pierced Roy deeply. He couldn't clearly read expressions, but he could feel the hunger for hope that filled the room. For the first time in a long while, he nodded—not out of routine, but with conviction.

Later that day, Roy met with an agent at a buzzing Hollywood coffee shop. The place was alive with chatter—actors pitching, writers bent over laptops, producers holding court at corner tables. Roy sat across from a sharply dressed woman who leaned in with intent.

"It wasn't about what I lost," Roy explained. "It was about what I found in the process."

She studied him. "Most people would have walked away. But you? You adapted. Reinvented yourself. That's a story people need."

Roy allowed himself to smile a small smile. "Life doesn't end with a setback. Sometimes, it's the start of something greater."

She tapped her pen thoughtfully. "We'll arrange a meeting with our development team. Your voice could resonate with a lot of people." Then she added, "And Roy? Don't downplay your vision loss. It's not weakness—it's part of your strength."

Roy left the café with his chest a little higher. He hadn't imagined this path for himself, but God had been shaping it all along, just as his mother had once told him.

Outside, LA moved with its usual chaos. Roy walked at his own pace—cautious but unaided, confident enough to navigate the sidewalks. Suddenly, a cry cut through the noise: *"Help! Someone call an ambulance!"*

Roy turned instinctively toward the sound. The energy of the crowd shifted, tense and urgent. He stepped forward without hesitation.

A young woman lay on the pavement, her breathing uneven. Roy knelt beside her and gently found her wrist. Her pulse fluttered beneath his fingers, quick but steady.

"Stay calm," he told her. "Help is on the way. What happened?"

"I—I tripped," she gasped. "My leg... I can't move it."

"Don't try," Roy said softly. "Just breathe. You're not alone."

The crowd hovered—some filming, others genuinely worried—but Roy's attention never wavered until the ambulance arrived.

"Thank you," one EMT said, clapping his shoulder. "You kept her calm. That mattered more than you think."

Roy nodded quietly. *In my weakness, I found strength—not just for me, but for others.*

That night, Roy sat at his desk, the glow of a lamp spilling over his journal. He wrote slowly: *I used to think faith meant knowing the path ahead. Now I know it means trusting the ground beneath your feet—even when you can't see it clearly.*

From the living room came Maddison's laughter, followed by Shannon's teasing reply. The sound reminded Roy of something more precious than sight: he wasn't alone.

Later that week, the agent called with news. Roy had been invited to share his story at a community event on Saturday. When he told his roommates, they immediately decided to go with him.

The day arrived quickly. The community center was packed, every chair taken and people standing in the back. Roy stood at the front, the microphone cool beneath his fingers.

"Life may have dealt me a hard hand," he began, "but I refuse to be a victim. I am a survivor. And if my story helps even one person find their footing in the dark, then every struggle was worth it."

The applause thundered. A middle-aged man clasped Roy's hand afterward. "My son was just diagnosed with retinitis pigmentosa. You gave him hope tonight."

Roy swallowed hard. "Tell him to call me. Anytime."

Backstage at a talent showcase soon after, Roy's heart pounded as the emcee's voice rang out: *"Please welcome Roy Ferguson."*

The lights onstage blurred his vision, but it didn't matter. He could feel the presence of the audience, hear the anticipation, and sense the moment.

He drew in a deep breath. "I stand before you not as someone defined by sight, but as proof that what feels like the end can also be the beginning of a new journey."

When he finished, Maddison swept him into a bear hug. "You were incredible! You have a gift, my friend.

Roy laughed, the adrenaline still coursing through him. "Yeah?"

"Yeah," Maddison said, grinning. "Now, let's get tacos. You've earned like twelve of them."

"I couldn't have done it without the support of friends like you," he said emotionally.

"You forgot me?" Shannon said sarcastically.

"No, bud. You guys have been there for me always," Roy replied.

The walk home was so different this time. Roy had never felt this sense of fulfillment in his life; however, little did he know that God had something more for him to test him and make him strong.

That night, as they were entering the apartment, Maddison saw a letter lying outside the door. He opened it and was left speechless.

"What is it?" Roy asked, concerned.

"It's an eviction notice, Roy."

"Hey, what?" Shannon and Roy said together.

The trio went inside with a look on their faces. Nobody said anything, and everyone went into their rooms.

As Roy lay on his bed, he thought, *My newfound faith was about to be tested. I was out of a job and facing eviction from my apartment—a situation that couldn't come at a worse time. What plans do you have for me, God?*

With every sleepless night, Roy's faith was tested. He clung to the hope that something would change.

The eviction day came. Roy stood at the entrance, watching as officials prepared to forcefully evict tenants. Suddenly, a woman with a media name tag around her neck, and wearing a turban head wrap, appeared in front of him—an African American woman. She recognized Roy from a distance.

"Hi, I'm Monica. I remember you from the day you saved my life."

Roy stood flabbergasted. “I’m sorry. I don’t understand. What do you mean saved you?”

“I tripped on the road. You were there for me by my side till the paramedics arrived,” she replied.

“Oh, Hi, how is your leg now?” Roy asked as he remembered her.

“I’m better now. Thanks to you. More importantly, I happen to be a journalist who is investigating and advocating for people who have been given notice unfairly, and they are being evicted. So, I guess Sir, Karma has followed you, because I have in my hand a court injunction to delay this eviction. Your goodness Sir, has been rewarded.” Roy’s eyes widened in disbelief as an ‘Amen’ exited his mouth followed by a loud “Praise God!” Sometimes, the universe sends help when we least expect it,” she replied, smiling.

When she left, Roy thanked God for making things a little easier.

Weeks later, Roy was overjoyed to hear the news of getting a new apartment from the Government via a Section 8 voucher. He shared it with his roommates, who were so excited for him to start fresh.

"You guys don't worry. God has plans for everyone. You too will get a new place soon," Roy said, reassuring his roommates.

They shared a hug, and Roy started packing for his new place.

Two days later, Roy stood in front of the Wolfe Apartments on Rosewood Avenue. His heart was racing with anticipation. He walked inside, greeted by the fresh scent of new beginnings. The apartment was modest but welcoming. Roy put down his belongings, taking a moment to breathe in the fresh start.

By the grace of God, I found a new place to call home.

He walked out to see the neighborhood and met Kim and Greg from Sports Connection.

We're glad to have you back, Roy. You're a valuable part of our team," said Kim.

"Just hang tight while we sort out your immigration situation," Greg added.

"Thank you! I won't let you down," Roy replied.

A few days later, with sleeves rolled up and jaw clenched, Roy unfolded a portable massage table in the living room, locking each leg into place with quick, practiced movements. He took out the calendar and marked a circle on Thursday. It was a deadline for placing the LA Weekly advertisement.

I need to make this work.

Later that night, Roy sat at his messy desk. Determination furrowed his brow as he tapped away at the keyboard. Words didn't come easily, especially with blurred vision—and certainly not when your future depended on a few lines of text.

"Professional massage services—discreet and personal."

The next day, the phone rang.

Roy lunged for it, catching it just before the third ring. His voice, bright with excitement, almost betrayed how badly he needed this to go right.

"Hello? Yes, I have openings available for massages," he said.

And the hustle had officially begun.

When the doorbell rang that afternoon, Roy took a deep breath before opening the door. A man stood on the other side—well-dressed, confident, and carrying an air of something unspoken. He looked Roy up and down with an amused smirk.

"I heard you give the best massages in town," the man said, stepping inside.

“I’ll do my best to meet your expectations,” Roy replied confidently.

The session was awkward. Professional, technically—but the client’s comments and demeanor hinted at something else. Roy kept his distance, both physically and mentally, but as the days went on and more calls came through, he started to notice a pattern. Many of these clients weren’t just looking for a massage. They were looking for something... else.

I quickly learned that this hustle came with its own set of complications.

He needed a new plan.

Back at his desk, he pulled up the LA Weekly ad form again.

“Seeking female models for massage therapy sessions. Must be comfortable and professional.”

The new ad was a hit.

Within days, his apartment saw a steady stream of women arriving—some nervous, others confident, all curious. Roy greeted each one with a handshake and an open mind, asking about their experience, their comfort levels, and their goals.

The energy in the apartment shifted. Once a quiet, solitary space, it now hummed with activity. Women prepped in the back room, chatted in the kitchen, and prepared for their sessions as Roy coordinated the schedule.

"Alright, ladies! Let's keep it professional and respectful," Roy said boldly.

"You know I've got your backs, girls. If anyone tries to mess with you, you call me. No hesitation."

The day was long. That night, he lay peacefully on his bed.

I had turned my life around, finding a way to support myself, even in the face of adversity.

Through every trial, I learned to lean on my faith. Every good thing that happened was a reminder of the strong women who had supported me, from my mother to the mysterious woman in the head wrap.

He wore a look of pride mixed with something heavier—an uneasiness. He smiled when the girls laughed. He nodded when they waved. But inside?

Deep inside, I felt a sense of uneasiness about making money this way. But desperation had a way of clouding judgment.

One usual day, he arrived at Gold's Gym like he always did—punctual and determined. There, under the clang of metal and thump of bass music, he pushed his body harder than ever. Bench presses, curls, pull-ups—each rep was a declaration that he was still in control.

In Hollywood, looks can take you far. I had to keep up with the competition, especially when everything else was slowly slipping away.

He then walked into the Greens Studio. The camera flash popped as Roy shifted his stance in front of a white backdrop. He flexed a little, offering a confident half-smile to the lens.

“Alright, let’s see that confidence!” the photographer called out, moving around him.

Roy posed for the picture in confidence. Only after he noticed a few of the layout boards lying on a side table did he realize—this was for TORSO, a gay magazine. His heart skipped. For a second, he considered backing out.

But then he reminded himself of his own promise. He wasn’t going to compromise his integrity—not even for comfort.

That night, he returned to his apartment. He joined some of the girls who were just ending their shift. He sat with them, sharing stories from the shoot. Then, almost nervously, he opened a small cardboard box and placed it on the coffee table. He then pulled out “Steps to Christ.”

"Little Richard gave me this," he said. "Figured they might help someone."

One of the girls picked it up, turning it over.

"I don't know, Roy..." she said gently. "This doesn't really fit the vibe here."

Another girl chimed in, "Yeah, it feels... conflicting, y'know?"

Roy tried to smile, but the rejection stung. He pushed the box aside, nodding. "Yeah, I get it."

The night deepened, and silence crept through his apartment.

Roy lay on his bed, unable to sleep. He stared at the ceiling, recounting his life. Suddenly, something got his attention. Footsteps echoed faintly outside his door as if someone was spying. He started sweating, thinking, *What if the cops were watching? What if they were pretending to be clients?*

The following morning, he decided to talk to the neighbors and convince them there was nothing serious going on in his apartment in case cops investigated. However, the neighbors seemed to have noticed the number of women entering and leaving his apartment during the day. Hence, they were unconvinced when Roy tried to pretend that it was just a movie script he was working on with the girls since they knew he was a part of Hollywood.

He went back to his apartment, pacing inside anxiously. He considered the implications of his operation and the risks involved. He couldn't wait any longer. He rushed to the apartment's manager with something on his mind.

He slipped a few bills into the manager's hand, his expression urgent.

"Just keep quiet about the girls coming and going, okay?" Roy explained.

The manager nodded, gesturing 'zip-the-lips' and then pocketed the cash.

He felt some relief, but soon, his paranoia escalated when he overheard the neighbors talking about his suspicious operations inside.

He shut the door quickly and thought, "*I couldn't risk it anymore; the cops were watching. I had to get out before it all came crashing down.*"

He looked around his apartment. His eyes were at the massage table folded in the corner and the box of Steps to Christ gathering dust.

It was time.

Time to shut it all down.

Time to disappear before the lights went out for good.

He packed all his belongings within a day and headed toward Stephanie's apartment, his favorite girl among the workers.

When Roy arrived at the Saint James Apartments, Stephanie greeted him with a warm smile. "You're safe here. I've got your back."

Roy felt a sense of relief. "Thank you, Stephanie. I really appreciate this."

That night, Roy slept in broken fragments, waking again and again until the hours bled into morning. By 8 a.m. he rose tired and with a heaviness about him, the weight of the previous day still pressing hard on his shoulders.

Stephanie greeted him with quiet tenderness, setting down a cup of mint tea and a plate of biscuits as though offering more than just food—offering care. They sat together at the table, the soft murmur of a drama serial filling the background like a faint reminder that ordinary life still carried on somewhere beyond the walls.

When he finished the last sip of tea, Roy closed his eyes and let the warmth settle within him. He knew he had hit rock bottom—there was no denying that. Yet for the first time in a long time, he wasn't facing the darkness alone. Stephanie's presence, steady and unspoken, was a small light in the pit, and that light was enough to remind him that hope had not been extinguished.

Later that night, Roy opened up to Stephanie, recounting the recent events. She listened patiently without saying a word.

"I just want to find a way to make a living without living in fear," he said. His voice was barely audible, but she heard him.

"You're stronger than you think. We'll figure this out together," she said politely, trying to reassure him.

In the days that followed, Roy stayed indoors more. The world outside still felt like it could collapse at any moment, but inside the apartment, he began to plan. A spiral-bound notebook became his new companion, its pages slowly filling with scribbles, bullet points, and half-formed dreams. Ideas came in fragments, but they were his ideas that were untainted by fear or shame. He was trying to think long-term, to build something real.

I had to find a way to survive in this unforgiving city, but I needed a new plan.

One evening, he invited a few of the women from his former studio to the apartment. The gathering was casual—some laughter, some food—but there was an unspoken understanding that something needed to change. Roy sat on the couch and opened his notebook.

"What if we start a wellness center instead?" he asked. "Something that emphasizes health, healing—something we can be proud of?"

Everyone's attention shifted to Roy. The girls were excited and curious. The idea was still raw, but it had potential. Most importantly, it had integrity.

They began tossing out ideas with their own areas of expertise. The energy became infectious.

"Maybe this was my chance," Roy thought as he watched the girls talk and laugh, "to turn my life around. To create something positive out of the chaos."

CHAPTER 14

ECHOES OF HOLLYWOOD: REDEMPTION IN SHADOWS

The spark of the wellness center still lingered in Roy's chest like the last ember of a once-roaring fire. That night with the girls had felt like a turning point—laughter, dreams, and purpose flickering into life. For a brief moment, hope breathed through him again. After all, he'd lost—his vision, his footing, the dreams he once gripped so tightly—here was a chance to build something new, something real. But like so many dreams in Hollywood, it began to dissolve without ceremony.

One girl got a full-time job and disappeared. Another had to return home to care for her sick mother. Stephanie, the one Roy trusted most, moved when the rent spiked again. Life's demands didn't ask for permission. And just like that, the dream faded—not with a crash, but like mist in the morning sun.

Roy found himself alone again. Vision failing, rent overdue, sleeping on borrowed couches and scrambling for meals. The streets of Los Angeles, once symbols of promise, now mocked him with every step. Neon signs and red carpets gave way to fast-food wrappers on cracked sidewalks, their glow replaced by the flicker of police lights down alleyways.

“I used to walk these streets like I belonged here,” he thought bitterly. “Now, I barely know where I am.”

On a night when he could no longer pretend he was okay, Roy went to see an old friend from Jamaica—a woman who once supplied him with marijuana, a connection from a darker time.

She lived in a weathered building off Crenshaw Blvd in Inglewood. Her apartment was immersed in perfumes of incense and shadowed by silence.

He hoped, maybe, she'd have a couch or floor space to offer.

She opened the door, her eyes narrowing in recognition.

“Roy,” she said flatly. “You look rough.”

“I need a place for a night or two,” he said, eyes cast low.

She leaned against the frame, her arms crossed. “I got too much going on here, brother. Can’t do it. Not now.”

Roy nodded slowly. He didn’t argue. Just turned and walked away.

His feet carried him toward an intersection he hadn’t consciously chosen.

Hollywood and Van Nuys.

The old Seventh-day Adventist Church stood there, unchanged in its faded dignity. Its weather-worn sign seemed to call to something deeper in him—something nearly lost.

Without thinking, Roy walked through its doors.

Inside, laughter and warmth swelled through the fellowship hall. Folding tables overflowed with trays of food. The scent of macaroni and greens, of bread and kindness, wrapped around him like a forgotten blanket. For the first time in months, he felt human again.

Mary, the program coordinator, spotted him.

"Roy! Is that you? You here to help?"

His voice cracked as he replied, "Yeah... yeah, I'd love to."

He rolled up his sleeves and scrubbed pans until his fingers ached. He passed out water, stacked chairs, and served meals. And in the middle of that humble labor, he found something he hadn't felt in ages—purpose.

Later, during the sermon, the pastor's words pierced through Roy's armor.

"Let us remember those who are suffering," he said. "And seek strength in our faith."

Roy bowed his head, but inside, he wasn't sure he believed it anymore. Still, the warmth of the community stirred something fragile in him.

As he walked into the parking lot afterward, the night air was cool on his skin and a young woman named Lisa called out to him.

"Hey, you alright?" she asked.

Roy hesitated. "Honestly? I'm homeless. It's been rough."

Lisa didn't flinch. "I've got a place. Sure, it's not much, but it's safe."

Roy blinked, stunned. "Thank you... I mean it."

The apartment was small and bare, cluttered with the ghosts of others who'd passed through, people escaping demons, many not far from the ones Roy knew. The air was thick with the scent of stale cigarettes and something harder. He laid his gym bag in a corner and took the blanket she offered.

That night, curled up on the floor, Roy whispered, "Thank You, God... for this floor. For this roof. I don't know what tomorrow looks like, but tonight, I'm not outside."

The next day, he returned to Gold's Gym, where he'd begun training clients again. The clang of weights, the pulse of upbeat music, the ambition in the air—all of it energized him. Sometimes, he spotted celebrities like Jennifer Lopez or Fabio, and their drive became his own.

Gold's Gym became my sanctuary, he mused. *Seeing people chase their dreams kept my spirit alive.*

However, over the next few days at Lisa's apartment, reality came crashing in. The apartment, while safe from the streets, was a revolving door for addicts. Over time, everyone disappeared—even Lisa. Roy found himself alone again, in silence, in a shell of a home filled only with discarded syringes and roaches.

When the sheriffs arrived with the eviction notice, Roy didn't flinch.

"I'm not leaving," he told them, arms limp at his sides.

They brought in LAPD backup. A young Korean officer crouched beside him, voice low.

"You know this could put you in jail."

"I know," Roy replied. "I'm tired. I don't care anymore."

And he meant it. Every rejection, every betrayal, every loss had hollowed him out.

He was taken to Parker Center and placed in a holding cell. No phone calls. No visitors. Just fluorescent lights and the cold, metallic smell of despair.

When he finally stood before the judge, he looked like a ghost of himself—unkempt, thin, eyes sunken not just from hunger but from hopelessness.

"You're being charged with trespassing," the judge said. "Anything you want to say?"

Roy's voice was a whisper, but it echoed in the courtroom like thunder.

"I just want to go back home to Jamaica."

The judge stared at him for a moment—silent, then sighed.

"You haven't committed a felony. You're free to go."

Free. The word felt like a joke.

Back on the street, Roy walked slowly, his vision improved but still uncertain. The city around him was blurred, yet he moved forward with deliberate care, trusting that where his eyes faltered, God would guide his steps.

The city bustled as if it didn't see him. Bright billboards loomed over the skyline, flashing new movie releases and new dreams—dreams that once seemed within his grasp.

"From Hollywood studios to a sidewalk bench," he muttered. "What happened to me?"

A passerby, noticing Roy's worn face, suggested a mission on Skid Row. Roy didn't argue. He followed the directions like a man following his own shadow.

The streets near Skid Row were a graveyard of dreams. Tents stacked like tombstones, sidewalks slick with waste, and the smell of urine, sweat, and suffering heavy in the air. Sirens wailed in the distance. People muttered to themselves, staggered from curb to curb, searching for something they couldn't name.

Once, he was rubbing shoulders with Little Richard. Now, he was standing shoulder to shoulder with forgotten souls, waiting for a cup of soup and a mat on the floor.

Inside the mission, there was noise—so much noise. Coughing. Weeping. Snoring. Whispered prayers. But beneath it all, a strange calm settled into Roy's bones.

He curled up in the corner of the common room, head resting against a concrete wall, and listened to the sounds of men and women whose lives had unraveled just like his.

And for the first time in a long time, Roy didn't pray for a breakthrough.

He didn't beg for sight.

He didn't plead for escape.

He simply whispered, "God... I'm still here."

And somehow, that was enough.

Chapter 15

A Vision Of Hope Revealed

Roy found some peace volunteering at Skid Row. When he looked at the people there, fighting for their miserable lives, he realized that God had blessed him more than he deserved.

As usual, he moved carefully toward Skid Row, his vision still clouded, but it was the clarity of its broken streets that hit him hardest, reminding him again of the work God had set before him. The streets were a harsh reflection of life's brokenness. Tents lined the sidewalks like a patchwork of desperation, and the air carried the weight of unspoken struggles. Roy was able to identify that some of the people there were addicts because of its smell. Since his vision had become impaired, his other senses had developed far more sensitivity to all that was around him; another blessing he realized God had given him. Roy walked among them, his heart heavy yet determined. He had spent years chasing dreams in Hollywood, only to realize how empty they felt without something deeper.

"This is where I need to be," he thought. "After years of chasing my dreams in Hollywood, I felt compelled to give back. Volunteering at the mission was my way of confronting the reality of my own life."

The Saint Vincent House Mission stood like a beacon in chaos. Inside the house, Roy could feel the energy. The clatter of the dishes and the sound of the conversations made the area alive. Volunteers moved swiftly, serving meals to those who had nowhere else to go. Roy joined them, handing out food trays, meeting with a blur, the eyes that held stories of pain and resilience.

"This was a place of refuge for many, but it was also a reminder of what could happen if I strayed too far from my faith," he realized as he saw with straining eyes, the worn faces of the customers who were battling with challenges that, with God's help, could be more easily overcome.

In the mission dining hall, hundreds of men, women, and even children gathered each day. They were not only given meals, but also a fleeting taste of normality in a world of chaos—a table to sit at, a companion to talk to, and a hope they had missed while sleeping on cardboard boxes. For some, there was even the fragile possibility of being granted a bed in the overcrowded dormitories of the mission.

For Roy, the hall stood as a constant reminder of the hope that still pulsed within the mission walls. As he served, his eyes moved from face to face, absorbing the quiet dignity and desperate gratitude that filled the room. That day, one man in particular drew his attention—an older gentleman with wild, unkempt hair and a presence that seemed both quiet and unsettling. He accepted the food without a word and settled alone in the corner, watching Roy with calm intensity.

He was different—almost magnetic. There was something in his stillness; the way he received the meal, without demand or complaint, stirred something deep inside Roy.

Drawn to him, Roy moved toward the corner. He walked with practiced caution, the world around him still softened by the milky blur that had become his daily companion.

Yet even through the haze, the man stood out in sharp relief, as though God Himself were urging Roy to notice him. As he walked towards him the overhead lights fractured in his eyes like watercolors left too long in the rain and as he neared the table, just a few steps away from this mysterious man, a strange sensation swept over him.

The noise of the dining hall softened. The air felt still.

And then—clarity.

It wasn't the kind that glasses or surgery could bring. No, this was deeper. A sudden shift, as if another lens had overlaid his failing vision. Roy could see. Not perfectly—not in the way he once had—but with startling purpose. Faces lit from within.

Shadows stripped away. In place of the man's disheveled appearance, Roy saw something eternal flickering behind his eyes. A deep sorrow, yes, but also a glimmer of unbroken dignity.

Roy drew in breath, the world pausing around him for a moment.

This was not an ordinary sight. This was his God eye—opening. A glimpse into the realm where heaven touches earth and the veil thins just enough for the heart to see what the body cannot.

He stepped closer. The man's eyes did not waver.

"Mind if I sit?" Roy asked.

The man nodded once, slow and deliberate, and Roy knew before another word passed between them that this moment had been appointed. Not a coincidence. A calling.

The man smiled and said, "Greetings, my friend."

His voice was gentle yet carried authority. Roy hesitated before speaking again. "I've seen you here before. You're not like the others."

The man chuckled, "I suppose not. I'm a Nazarite."

Roy frowned. "A Nazarite? What's that?"

The man leaned forward with his eyes gleaming with wisdom. “A vow of dedication to God. It comes from the Book of Numbers—chapter six. A calling to separate oneself for a time, to abstain from certain things, and to live solely for the Lord’s purpose.”

Roy’s pulse quickened. *A vow?* The idea stirred something deep within him.

“I want to become a Nazarite!” Roy said impulsively, almost too quickly. The Nazarite smiled at Roy’s quick response and he studied him carefully before speaking. “This is not a light decision. It requires sacrifice. No wine, no cutting of the hair, no contact with the dead. It is a vow of holiness.”

Roy swallowed. “I need this, man. My life has been... directionless. I need something to anchor me.”

“You need to think clearly and make up your mind,” the man replied, placing a comforting hand on Roy’s shoulder.

That night, Roy sat on the floor of his room at the St Vincent House, his Bible open to Numbers 6. He fervently read the passage over and over, underlining words that leaped out at him:

"When a man or woman makes a special vow, the vow of a Nazarite, to separate himself to the Lord..."

He exhaled sharply and reached for his laptop. With practiced keystrokes, he activated the screen reader, its robotic voice filling the small room:

"Search results for 'Nazarite vow.'"

He looked for more details, and the findings made his spine tingle. Ancient Jewish traditions. Modern-day practitioners. Stories of men and women who'd given up wine, who'd let their hair grow wild as a sign of surrender. Reading about all of this ignited a fire in his gut.

But suddenly, a doubt crept in. How could he, a vision impaired man who'd spent years drowning in self-pity, take on something so sacred?

Then, the screen reader continued: "The Nazarite vow is not about physical sight, but spiritual vision."

Roy's heart skipped a beat.

The next morning, after meeting with a friend for breakfast, he returned to the mission, navigating the blurred edges of the world with steady resolve. He found the Nazarite sitting in the common room reading his bible. As he approached him the Nazarite's gaze met his, and his features eased into a warm, knowing smile that needed no words. "Good to see you Roy" he exclaimed. They shook hands and Roy sat, eager to tell him his news.

"I've been researching," Roy said excitedly. "And I want to tell you that I'm ready for the vow."

The Nazarite asked Roy to move closer, and in a quiet but firm tone, asked him to think about it again before saying, in a serious but enquiring manner. "Tell me Roy, what draws you to this?"

Roy exhaled. "I've lived for myself for too long. I've made mistakes—big ones. I need... purpose. Not just for a season, but for my life."

The Nazarite nodded. "The vow is a mirror. It shows you who you are—and who God calls you to be. But it is not easy. The world will not understand."

Roy clenched his fists. "I'm not here to be understood by people, so I don't care. My mother always wanted me to be close to God. I let her down many times, straying away from my path, but not anymore."

The Nazarite smiled. "Good. Then let us begin."

As they left the mission together and walked the streets of the homeless in downtown LA, Roy's inquisitive nature came to the fore. He asked the Nazarite directly, a question that had lingered in his mind from the moment he had met him.

"What was your journey like before you took the vow?"

The man sighed, "Ahh, well, I was the same as those you see every day at the mission. I wandered here, lost in my desires and the temptations of the world. The vow gave me purpose and strength."

Roy somehow felt relieved hearing the answer, knowing that everyone sometimes goes astray before they find God again and he knew he was ready.

Over the next few days, Roy absorbed himself in preparation. He fasted and prayed. He studied Scripture late into the night, scribbling notes on scraps of paper, on napkins, and even on a brown paper bag when inspiration struck.

One evening, as he knelt in prayer, a melody drifted into his mind—soft at first, then growing stronger. It was a song, but not one he had ever heard before.

Is this... from God?

He grabbed the nearest thing he could write on— the brown paper bag containing goods from the store and began scribbling lyrics as they flowed through him.

“Take my life, let it be consecrated, Lord, to Thee...”

His eyes filled with tears.

Soon, the day of the vow arrived, a day Roy had been waiting so desperately for. Inside a quiet room at the mission, the Nazarite stood before Roy, his hands raised in blessing.

“Are you ready?”

Roy took a deep breath. "Yes."

The prayer that followed, although not the official vow, was simple but powerful and a representation but no less impactful, both spiritually and emotionally, of the vow he would officially embrace and express to his fellow parishioners in the weeks that followed, at the Ephesus Seventh Day Adventist Church in South Los Angeles.

The ‘vow’ was a dedication, of separation, of a life no longer his own. As the final “Amen” was spoken, Roy felt something shift inside him—a weight lifted, a chain broken.

The vow marked a profound turning point for Roy—a commitment to live a life set apart, no longer guided by his own desires but wholly dedicated to a higher purpose. As the final “Amen” echoed through the quiet room, he felt an unmistakable transformation within. A sense of freedom washed over him, as if a heavy burden had finally been lifted and the shackles that once held him back were broken. This act of separation was not just ritual; it was an inward release, a redefinition of his very existence.

When he stepped back outside Skid Row, the world looked different. The same broken people were there, but now he saw them with new eyes.

"I was no longer just a spectator in this world; I was committed to making a difference," he thought.

This is my mission now.

No longer lost. No longer afraid.

He knew he would become a Nazarite.

The following morning, Roy attended the Ephesus Seventh-Day Adventist Church to learn more about this vow. He sat in the front row with his hands resting on the smooth braille hymnal in his lap. He had picked it up without realizing he no longer needed it; a smile for God forming on his lips. 'Oh, how he loved the Lord' he thought.

The familiar scent of polished wood and faint candle wax filled the air, mingling with the soft rustle of clothing as the congregation settled into their seats. The Pastor then started speaking.

"The Nazarite vow is rarely practiced today, but in ancient times, it was a sacred commitment—a total surrender to God's will. No wine. No cutting of the hair. No defilement from the dead. It was a path of holiness, a separation from the world for a divine purpose."

Then, a soft shuffle of footsteps approached. The familiar scent of lavender and peppermint—Mother Lucas's signature blend—reached him before her voice did.

The Nazarite Call "Roy," she murmured, her voice soft yet steady. "You've been quiet today. What's stirring in that heart of yours?"

Roy hesitated. Mother Lucas had known him since his first day at the mission — back when he was still reeling from the streets, blind both in sight and in spirit. She had prayed with him, fed him, and reminded him that God's plans weren't bound by human limitation. If anyone could understand what he was feeling now, it was her.

"I think..." He swallowed hard. "I think God is calling me to take the Nazarite vow."

Her silence lingered before she answered, her tone gentle yet edged with holy gravity. "Roy, do you understand the weight of what you're saying? This isn't just a promise — it's a life set apart unto God."

Roy nodded slowly, emotion rising in his voice. "I know. But I've spent too long running — from my past, from my blindness, from Him. I don't want to run anymore. When the Nazarite at the mission prayed with me yesterday, I felt something break inside me — and something new awaken. It was as if God Himself whispered, *This is the way — walk in it.*"

Mother Lucas exhaled deeply, her spirit discerning truth in his words. "Then let us pray," she said softly.

The Church seemed to fall silent as her prayer filled the air: "Lord, You see this child's heart. You know his fears, his failings, and his faith. Prepare him for the path of consecration. Strengthen him for what lies ahead. And if this vow be of You, make it plain — clear as the morning light."

When the prayer ended, she held his hand. "You'll need guidance," she said. "Pastor Dawson at our Church studied the Nazarite tradition. He'll walk with you. And that Nazarite you met — he wasn't a wanderer, Roy. He was sent."

Roy's eyes widened. "How do you know about him?"

A soft chuckle escaped her lips. "Roy, you think the Lord only speaks to you in whispers?" She patted his hand gently.

"Now come. Service is starting. And you've got a journey ahead of you."

As the congregation rose to sing, Roy stood with them. His voice joined the others — strong, humble, renewed. For the first time in years, the darkness behind his eyes no longer felt like confinement; it felt like calling.

The Path of the Vow In the weeks that followed, under the guidance of Pastor Dawson at Ephesus Church, Roy began to study the vow of the Nazarite. Together they opened the scroll to *Numbers 6*, and the pastor read aloud the ancient charge:

"When either man or woman shall separate themselves to vow a vow of a Nazarite, to separate themselves unto the Lord:
He shall separate himself from wine and strong drink, and shall drink no vinegar of wine, or vinegar of strong drink, neither shall he drink any liquor of grapes, nor eat moist grapes, or dried.
All the days of his separation shall he eat nothing that is made of the vine tree, from the kernels even to the husk.
All the days of the vow of his separation there shall no razor come upon his head: until the days be fulfilled, in the which he separateth himself unto the Lord, he shall be holy, and shall let

the locks of the hair of his head grow.
All the days that he separateth himself unto the Lord he shall come at no dead body.
He shall not make himself unclean for his father, or for his mother, for his brother, or for his sister, when they die: because the consecration of his God is upon his head.
All the days of his separation he is holy unto the Lord.” (*Numbers 6:2–8, KJV*).

Roy listened intently, his heart stirred by the sacred weight of each word. Pastor Dawson closed the scroll and looked at him. “Roy, this vow isn’t about ritual. It’s about surrender. It’s a declaration that every breath, every moment, belongs to God.”

Days turned into weeks as Roy studied and prayed. He meditated often on *Ecclesiastes 5*, which Pastor Dawson urged him to memorize before taking the vow:

“Keep thy foot when thou goest to the house of God, and be more ready to hear, than to give the sacrifice of fools: for they consider not that they do evil.
Be not rash with thy mouth, and let not thine heart be hasty to utter anything before God: for God is in heaven, and thou upon earth: therefore let thy words be few.
For a dream cometh through the multitude of business; and a fool’s voice is known by multitude of words.

When thou vowest a vow unto God, defer not to pay it; for he hath no pleasure in fools: pay that which thou hast vowed. Better is it that thou shouldest not vow, than that thou shouldest vow and not pay.
Suffer not thy mouth to cause thy flesh to sin; neither say thou before the angel, that it was an error: wherefore should God be angry at thy voice, and destroy the work of thine hands?" (*Ecclesiastes 5:1–6, KJV*)

Those words pierced Roy deeply. He realized this vow was not a gesture of zeal, but a covenant of consecration — a binding promise before a holy God. Each verse reminded him that *obedience was greater than emotion*, and that to make such a vow required a heart both steady and surrendered.

Under Pastor Dawson's tutelage, Roy began to live the principles of the vow even before it was formalized — abstaining from strong drink, devoting himself to fasting and prayer, and setting apart his thoughts and speech for holiness. Each morning, he rose early to meet God in quiet devotion, whispering, "Let my separation be unto You, O Lord."

At last, the day came when Roy stood before the congregation of Ephesus Church. His hair had begun to grow long, a visible sign of inner consecration. Pastor Dawson placed a hand upon his shoulder and prayed:

"Lord, this son has heard Your voice and answered Your call. Consecrate him by Your Spirit. Let his life be a living testimony that holiness still matters — and that surrender opens heaven."

The congregation responded softly, *"Amen."*

And as Roy lifted his face toward the altar, he felt no fear — only peace. The vow he once spoke in trembling had now become his path. He was no longer a man who had lost his sight; he was a man who had found his vision – his spiritual vision.

It felt like the veil before a revelation—lifting. And God was beginning to paint.

Chapter 16

The Making of the Epic

Roy's encounter with the Nazarite during his short stay at Saint Vincent's House lingered in his spirit like incense rising in a temple. It had been more than a meeting—it was a divine stirring, a quiet reminder of who he was meant to become.

Memories surged forward in the aftermath: his mother's prophetic words spoken long ago, that he would one day do great things for God; the solemn promises he had whispered into the darkness during seasons of despair; and the fragile hope that those vows had not been forgotten in heaven.

As he stepped into the shower that evening, fragments of his childhood returned with surprising clarity. He could almost hear his mother's voice once more—putting music to Scripture, making the Word come alive in melody and rhythm. She had planted seeds of faith in him through song, and now, after all these years, those seeds were stirring again.

Then it happened.

A flood of music rushed into his soul—joyful, holy, unlike anything he had ever known. His lips parted, not in English, but in Hebrew, singing a melody he had never learned yet somehow knew.

The song flowed from somewhere deep within him, ancient and sacred. He fumbled to finish washing, barely drying his hands before he raced out to find a pen and scrap of paper. He had to capture it before it vanished like a dream at dawn.

The walls of Roy's room seemed to press closer with each passing night as he wrestled with the words. His room was messed up with crumbled papers everywhere, indicating fragments of lyrics that never quite captured the vision burning in his soul.

He stayed up late every night, hovering his fingers over the notebook with great determination to write the lyrics. There were days when the doubt threatened to swallow him whole, when the weight of what he was attempting made him want to quit. But then the words from Ecclesiastes would echo in his mind: “When thou vowest a vow unto God, defer not to pay it...” (5:4-5)

He pushed back for a little while to straighten his back, which ached from sitting for long hours. As he stood to walk outside his room, something shifted inside him - a sudden rush of clarity like a dam breaking.

His pen flew across the page with new urgency, ink bleeding into the paper as the verses poured forth fully formed. "The Epic Seven-Fold Doxology... The Song of Moses and the Song of the Lamb." The words carried so much weight because the song proclaims the greatness, majesty, power and dominion of God. It is a song that extols the mighty works of God on behalf of his people. After completing the writing, Roy's hand trembled and he felt a rush of inspiration.

As he was winding up, a sudden sound of rushing wind from outside the window sent papers flying. Roy froze for a moment, his skin prickling with goosebumps. "What was that?" he whispered as he stumbled outside, only to find the street eerily calm in the nighttime. Yet, the air seemed to be charged with something holy that Roy couldn't understand.

The sacred text that Roy had written was the beginning of the arrangement for the Song of the Lamb with the Seven-Fold Doxology. It was the beginning of an arrangement that could only come from God; Roy despite not knowing Hebrew, was writing it in freehand Hebrew and English and in an arrangement that only God could orchestrate.

Some days later, Roy found himself sitting across from Pastor Holman in the quiet of the church office. Sunlight streamed through stained glass windows, painting colorful patterns across the desk where his lyrics lay exposed. The pastor held the notebook in his hands and started reading. His lips moved silently as he absorbed every single word.

When he finished reading, he looked up at Roy with his eyes gleaming with pride. "Take this to the Voice of Prophecy," he said, his voice carrying a weight of certainty that made Roy's breath catch.

The next day, Roy arrived at the ministry offices, where he found the doors locked with a handwritten notice on the door announcing their temporary closure. Disappointment settled heavily in his chest until another possibility occurred to him. The Jews for Jesus organization might understand the significance of what he'd created - a bridge between covenants, a song meant to unite. It's a place that serves to engage Jewish people with the message of Jesus as the Messiah, provide them with resources and spiritual care, and equip them to live meaningful lives of faith.

At the representative's office, Roy sat confidently, though a thread of uncertainty tugged at him as the man read what Roy believed to be his "*masterpiece*" with growing intensity.

Roy watched as the man read through the words once, then twice, his expression shifting from curiosity to something approaching awe. As the man finished reading, he said bluntly, "This could be the song the world is waiting for."

In that very moment, Roy saw it clearly - a vision of 144,000 voices from all the 12 tribes of Israel raised in perfect harmony, singing his song at the end of days. The Epic had taken on a life of its own, becoming something far greater than he'd imagined. As he stepped back out into the sunlight, his heart swelled with hope and he finally understood that this was just the beginning of the Epic.

Chapter 17

A Meeting by Chance

The Monday morning sun poured through the window of Roy's modest apartment at the Boyd House illuminating the dusty corners that had become familiar over the past year. His heart raced with anticipation as he recalled his conversation with Pastor Walker the previous Sabbath. The pastor had been captivated by the sacred text of the Epic Song of the Lamb, and under his guidance, Roy's path had taken an unexpected turn.

"Roy," Pastor Walker had said, his eyes sparkling with enthusiasm. "You need to take this to the next level. The LA Philharmonic Orchestra might be good, but have you considered Oakwood College? Their Aeolians choir is world-renowned, and Dr. Eurydice Osterman runs a remarkable music department."

The pastor's words echoed in Roy's mind as he prepared for the journey ahead. After a brief conference, Pastor Walker cashed a check and gave him some money to cover his Greyhound bus ticket and purchase a few necessities. With excitement and trepidation about the trip to Huntsville, Alabama, Roy purchased his ticket at the Greyhound bus station and boarded his ride to Oakwood College.

The journey was long, three and a half days on the Greyhound bus, but every mile brought him closer to his dream. As he stepped off the bus at the Greyhound station in Huntsville, Roy was greeted by a friendly face. A young woman stood waiting, her smile warm and inviting.

"Hi! You must be Roy," she said, extending her hand. "I'm Janet. Pastor Walker told me to expect you."

Roy felt a sense of relief wash over him. Janet had never met him before, yet here she was, ready to help him transition into this new chapter of his life. They exchanged pleasantries as they made their way to Peterson Hall, where Roy would be staying.

Once settled into his dorm room, Roy wasted no time. He reached out to Dr. Delbert Baker, the president of Oakwood College, who welcomed him with open arms. "You're just in time, Roy. I've heard great things about your work. Dr. Osterman is expecting you."

With a heart full of prayer and purpose, Roy made his way to the music department. As he entered Dr. Osterman's office, he was struck by her presence—her passion for music radiated like the sun spilling into the room. She greeted him warmly, eager to hear about the Epic Song of the Lamb.

"Before we dive into the orchestration, let's pray," she suggested, her voice soothing. Roy nodded, feeling a sense of peace enveloping him. They prayed together, asking for guidance and inspiration.

As Dr. Osterman began to work on the orchestral score, Dr. Baker was busy behind the scenes, ensuring everything fell into place. He approached Mr. Brathwaite in the accounts department, requesting a $200 payment to Dr. Jacques Doukhan at Andrews University for a Hebrew translation and transliteration of the song. "It's crucial we get this right," Dr. Baker insisted, his voice steady with determination.

Amidst the whirlwind of activities, Roy enrolled at Oakwood College, majoring in theology with a minor in music. However, the lack of documentation for financial assistance became a major hurdle; his former wife had cancelled all support she had previously given for his immigration application. So, to support himself through college, he took on the role of a literature evangelist, selling books in the neighborhoods around Huntsville.

During one summer break, Roy and a group of students organized a trip to Gary, Indiana, where they would stay at one of their classmates' homes. Each day, they ventured into the neighborhoods, selling books and sharing their faith. One day,

Roy and a teammate found themselves hopelessly lost in an upscale Michiana neighborhood. The sun was beginning to set, casting a golden hue over the meticulously manicured lawns and grand mansions that lined the streets. Instead of panicking, he wandered in awe, allowing the beauty of his surroundings to fill him with wonder.

Each house appeared more lavish than the last, but one estate took his breath away—a sprawling mansion that seemed to be plucked from the pages of a magazine.

"That's Oprah's summer home," he murmured to himself, his heart racing at the thought. He stood frozen, staring at the property, awash in a mix of disbelief and curiosity. Before he could talk himself out of it, an impulsive thrill surged through him, and he found himself walking up the long, winding driveway—just as a sleek black Mercedes glided in.

The car came to a stop, and an elegant woman stepped out, her demeanor busy and purposeful. Roy's pitch died in his throat as she waved him off, her tone dismissive. "Not today, young man. My son needs me."

Feeling a mix of respect and disappointment, Roy nodded. "No problem, ma'am," he replied, pivoting to leave.

“Wait!” she called suddenly, her tone shifting. “You can join us if you’d like.”

Intrigued, Roy followed her inside, and the moment he crossed the threshold, he was engulfed in a world of luxury. The mansion was breathtaking—vaulted ceilings, contemporary art adorning the walls, and floor-to-ceiling windows that framed a stunning view of Lake Michigan.

“I’m Jenelle,” she introduced herself, pouring him a vibrant green health drink from a crystal decanter. The drink sparkled in the light, and Roy hesitated for just a moment before taking a sip. The tangy, refreshing flavor danced on his tongue, and he struggled to focus on anything other than the opulence around him.

As they walked through the home, Roy couldn’t help but glance at the framed photos lining the walls—Jenelle with celebrities, politicians, and even one with Steven Spielberg on what looked like a movie set. His mind raced with questions, but before he could voice any, Jenelle casually remarked, “I train dolphins in Hawaii.”

Roy’s eyes widened in surprise. “Dolphins? That sounds incredible!”

"Come meet my son, Brandon," she said, leading him into a sunlit playroom filled with colorful toys and laughter. A lively nine-year-old bounded toward them, his energy infectious. He immediately launched into questions about marine life, and for the first time in days, Roy felt the weight of his responsibilities lift as they shared stories of dolphins and dreams.

Just as Roy was beginning to forget about selling books, Jenelle stunned him with her next words. "I'll take your entire inventory," she announced, pulling out a checkbook.

Roy's jaw dropped. "All of them? But I haven't even—"

"Trust me," she interrupted, her confidence unwavering. "I know quality when I see it. And Brandon likes you."

Time slipped away as laughter filled the room, and Roy found himself immersed in this unexpected encounter. They swapped stories about dreams, ambitions, and the challenges that lay ahead. He felt a sense of belonging that he hadn't anticipated, a connection that transcended their different worlds.

When he finally rejoined his group that evening, his bag was empty, but his heart was full. Isaiah, one of his teammates, looked at him with curiosity. "Where have you been? And where are all your books?"

Roy simply smiled, the memory of Brandon's parting words warming him: "When you're in that movie, send me tickets!"

Weeks later, as the van carried the fellow students back to Oakwood College in Huntsville, Alabama, Roy remained with a team of evangelists he had met while selling books in Michiana, and they were captivated by the story behind the Epic Song of the Lamb. They took him to Berrien Springs, Michigan, for the performance of the Song of the Lamb at Pioneer Memorial Church at Andrews University.

As they drove to Berrien Springs, Roy felt a surge of optimism. The journey ahead was uncertain, but he was ready to embrace every twist and turn, armed with new friendships, inspiration, and a powerful story waiting to be told. The echoes of laughter, the promise of his music, and the warmth of unexpected connections fueled his determination to make the Epic Song of the Lamb resonate far beyond its original vision.

Chapter 18
It Begins

As the van entered Berrien Springs, Roy sat by the window in quiet reflection, watching the rows of trees and wide fields drift by. The landscape felt different here—almost holy. There was a quiet reverence in the air, as if the earth itself knew the battles he had fought to get here. Every mile was a memory, every field, a field of sacrifice. And yet, every breath now felt like grace.

Soon, they reached Andrews University. It stood beneath the twilight sky like a sanctuary—its buildings glowing faintly, neither grand nor imposing, but quietly majestic, as if heaven itself had traced its silhouette. Roy stepped out of the van, breathing deeply. He had made it. But so had something else.

Mama Florence had arranged for him to stay in a small white trailer just off campus. Locals affectionately called it "The White House," which made Roy laugh when he saw the modest structure with its leaning screen door and chipped paint.

"This is it?" he asked, half-smiling.

"Don't let the size fool you," Mama Florence replied, placing a gentle hand on his shoulder. "Plenty of history's been made in this little house."

Inside, the trailer was simple, furnished with care, clean linens, and the soft aroma of sage and cinnamon. There was peace in the air. A kind of sanctuary. As Mama Florence handed him a plate of food and the keys, she spoke words he hadn't heard in a long time: "You're welcome here, Roy. You'll be safe here. And inspired, too."

That night, at the small kitchen table, Roy opened his laptop and returned to his life's work—*The Epic Song of the Lamb*. The words poured out like a river unblocked. For the first time in years, he didn't feel the weight of his past—only the gravity of his calling.

This isn't just a documentary, he thought. It's a testimony.

But as he stared out the window into the stillness, a flicker of unease brushed his spirit. That old feeling crept in—like something was watching.

The next morning energized and focused, Roy walked across campus to the Department of Religion and Biblical Languages. There he met Dr. Jacques Doukhan, a scholar of great depth and quiet strength.

"Thank you for meeting me, Dr. Doukhan," Roy said with a humble nod.

"I've heard about your project," the professor replied, his eyes searching Roy's face.

"Dr. Delbert Baker of Oakwood College must've told you about my project. I believe it holds the key to redemption—personally, historically, prophetically. I need your help translating the sacred text for The Epic Song of the Lamb from English to Hebrew. It's crucial for my project, I believe it holds the key to redemption—personally, historically, prophetically." Roy said.

"I need the text to sing in the language it was born in." he continued. Dr. Doukhan leaned in. "This is no small task, Roy. The Song you speak of—if it's what I suspect—echoes the ceaseless praise of the Lamb slain before the foundation of the world. Are you ready for what that calls forth?" "The Epic Song of the Lamb? This is a powerful undertaking with such a sacred text. What's your intention?" Dr Doukhan said with a raised brow.

"I believe it holds the key to understanding our past—and can inspire hope for the future. But I need the sacred text written in its original Hebrew language to capture the true essence." Roy replied confidently. Dr Doukhan nodded thoughtfully before speaking. "Very well." He stated firmly; and cautioned wisely "This is no easy task. Be conscious of the fact, that this song echoes the awe throughout the ceaseless ages of eternity of Jesus Christ the Lamb slain before the foundation of the world to be Savior of those who are lost."

"Sir, with God's help, I believe we can bring this to light. That we can make a huge difference in the world working on this project together." Roy said.

Over the next few days, Roy kept in close contact with Dr. Doukhan, who worked intently on the translation and transliteration of the sacred texts of *The Epic* in his office at the Old Testament Seminary. Roy spent much of that time in the campus library, surrounded by scrolls and commentaries. Dust particles danced in the sunbeams filtering through the tall arched windows as he pored over the pages, his brow furrowed in concentration. Ancient phrases seemed to whisper across the centuries, drawing him deeper into their mystery.

It was during one of those quiet afternoons that Dr. Doukhan stepped into the library, carrying a stack of manuscripts under his arm. Spotting Roy at a corner table, he approached with a knowing smile. Lowering his voice, he said, "Look at this," and pointed to a passage that shimmered with revelation.

"The phrasing here—it doesn't just speak of deliverance. It hints at a deeper liberation. Redemption that's personal."

Doukhan peered over his glasses. "Yes. In Hebrew, the verbs are layered with nuance. This isn't just a song—it's a call to action."

One afternoon, as they sat together talking about the weight Hebrew verbs can carry, and as if summoned by the discussion itself, a chill swept through the room. Both men turned as a dark figure passed the threshold. But no one was there. Just a shadow that vanished as quickly as it came.

Roy's face paled.

"That wasn't the first time," he said quietly. "He's followed me before. A man—tall, intense. Cold eyes. I used to call him Evil. I saw him in an airport restroom years ago, whispering promises. I saw him when I first touched a Ouija board. He's the voice behind every shortcut, every temptation."

Doukhan closed the book slowly. "The adversary doesn't let go of those who once listened."

Roy's chest tightened at the words. They struck deeper than he expected, stirring memories he thought he had left behind—the glittering seductions of Hollywood, the whispered promises of fame, the subtle pull of pride and compromise. He had walked away from that world, but in that moment he realized the truth: leaving the stage didn't silence the enemy's song.

Evil had learned his name.

It wasn't bound to geography or distance; it followed those who had once opened their hearts to its voice. The war for his soul had not ended when he fled Los Angeles—it had only changed its battleground.

A chill moved through him as Doukhan continued softly, "Satan doesn't surrender what he believes is his. But, Roy... he only pursues what heaven already has plans for."

Roy lowered his head, the weight of it sinking in. He understood now that his calling came with a shadow—the constant pursuit of an adversary who would not rest. Yet in that same realization was peace, for the battle only proved that he was no longer the enemy's possession but God's reclamation.

He whispered to himself, half in prayer, half in revelation:

"The farther I run toward the light, the harder the darkness will try to follow. But the Lord is my keeper; the enemy cannot claim what Christ has redeemed."

Later that evening, as Roy stepped from the library into the dim hallway, the air changed. It wasn't a drop in temperature, it was the sudden heaviness, as if the very oxygen had been drawn from the corridor. The lights flickered. Shadows thickened at the edges. Then, without footsteps or sound, a presence emerged—not walking but becoming.

He wasn't a man. He had the shape of one, but none of the warmth. No heartbeat echoed from his chest. His eyes, though set in a human face, held the kind of knowledge that shouldn't exist outside the veil. Ancient. Predatory. Smiling, but not with joy.

"You've come far, Roy," the figure said, voice silked in false admiration. "You've worked so hard to climb out. And now you think this... this song... will save you?" His tone lingered on the word like a mockery.

Roy didn't speak. He couldn't. His hands gripped the papers at his side like a lifeline.

The figure stepped closer, though no footsteps were heard. "Why strain toward the Light when the dark has always known your name? I was there in the airport... remember? When no one else saw you. I was with you at the Ouija board. I whispered when no one answered your prayers."

His breath wasn't breath at all—but a presence pushing against Roy's soul. "You want truth?" he hissed. "Then let me give it to you: The world isn't changed by prophets. It's ruled by those who dare *own* the truth, bend it, shape it. I can give you words that shake nations. I can make your 'Epic' echo from halls of power to stages of fame. Just stop running from what you are."

It wasn't a threat. It was an invitation. A contract unspoken but offered again.

Roy felt it—that ancient lure. The same voice from his past, now in sharper focus. The seduction was not in violence, but in relevance. Power. Escape. Fame. And he knew: this was no man.

This was Satan.

Roy's knees buckled—but not in surrender. In resistance. He clutched the papers he held to his chest, like a breastplate of armor for protection.

"I don't belong to you," he whispered. The shadow smiled wider. "Not yet."

And then, like vapor beneath a sudden breeze, he vanished.

He knew that presence. It had been with him before, many times, in struggles and also in success, always tempting, always promising.

Satan. The deceiver. The one who had chased him through the darkest chapters of his life.

Roy ran straight to Dr. Doukhan's office. Breathless, he spilled his history—witchcraft, false paths, occult games that once fascinated him but now chained him.

Doukhan stood without hesitation. "Let us pray."

In that quiet room, surrounded by sacred texts and Hebrew scrolls, the two men knelt. The prayer was not polished—but it was powerful.

"Father, this man is Yours," Dr. Doukhan declared. "Cover him with the blood of the Lamb. Break every chain. Rebuke the enemy. Let this project be not just a work of art—but a weapon of truth."

Roy wept.

And something within him broke.

Later that night, Roy returned to his trailer under the watch of a moonlit sky. Clutching his notes, he passed the chapel and the whispering trees of Andrews' campus. At last, inside his room beneath Dr. Economou's house, he locked the door, exhaled, and sank into silence.

The Sabbath was coming.

That evening, after worship and a quiet supper with Mama Florence, Roy at last felt the weight lift from his spirit. As he lay in bed, peace began to settle over him like a gentle tide.

For the first time in decades, he had not run. He had stood his ground.

But he knew the battle was not over, and possibly never would be.

Yet Roy knew he no longer stood alone.

The next day, Roy went to Mama Florence for Sabbath preparation and as the sun set that Friday evening and after supper and worship to welcome the Sabbath, Roy went to bed while Mama Florence stayed up a little later reading her Bible.

The following morning through the windows of the trailer, sunbeams cast a warm, golden hue across the wooden table where Roy sat sipping mint tea on his usual visit with Mama Florence. The silence of the early hour was comforting, filled only with the occasional chirping of birds outside and the faint rustling of wind through the trees.

Mama Florence entered the room wearing a brightly patterned African garb. There was something timeless about her—her presence calm and yet commanding, as though she carried generations of wisdom in her bones.

"So," she said teasingly, as she poured herself a cup of herbal mint tea, "did you dream of grand palaces or presidents last night?"

Roy smiled, setting his cup down. "Neither. Just a trailer park with a cozy vibe."

She laughed, the sound full and rich. "Well, then you're in the right place for your epic journey."

Later that morning, the two of them gathered for devotion, a small Bible resting respectfully between them on the table. A hush settled in the space as they bowed their heads in prayer.

"How was your sleep?" Mama Florence asked, her voice soft and sincere.

"Quite well, thank you," Roy replied.

"Good. Let's give thanks for this day and the journey ahead."

Their whispered prayers rose into the quiet, and Roy felt a sense of peace take root in his chest. Mama Florence's trailer radiated a kind of energy that Roy never felt.

Afterward, breakfast was served in the kitchen—an array of fresh fruit, grains, and nuts arranged beautifully on ceramic dishes. Roy was grateful and savored every bite.

Mama Florence's dedication to health and her faith were inspiring, Roy thought. It felt like a nurturing environment, perfect for my new beginning.

That afternoon, a gentle knock on the trailer's door broke the quietness of the day. Roy opened it to find Pastor Tait,

Michael, and Dr. Cerna standing there, each with a warm smile and a palpable sense of purpose.

“We’re here to pray and counsel you on this epic journey God has called you to fulfill,” Pastor Tait said.

Roy’s heart swelled with gratitude. “Thank you all for your support. It means a lot to me.”

They settled into the living room, surrounded by open Bibles, notepads, and spiritual books. For the next hour, they discussed The Epic—Roy’s vision, the theological implications, and the spiritual warfare it might awaken. Then, together, they bowed their heads and lifted their voices in a heartfelt prayer. It was a sound of unity and strength; voices braided with conviction and compassion.

They were investing their time and energy into my success, Roy thought as he stopped and looked at them with a glimmer in his eyes while they were still working, and he felt the weight of that responsibility.

Over the next three months, Roy's life became a rhythm of intense preparation and spiritual refinement. Each morning began with devotion and study. Each day brought meetings with the pastors, who shared ideas, prayed fervently, and challenged him to go deeper.

Saturdays were spent in the echoing halls of Pioneer Memorial Church, where the sermons stirred his spirit. On other weekends, he visited the Philippine Seventh-day Adventist Church and learned about fellowship, humility, and what it meant to truly serve.

The night air was still and heavy as Roy sat with Mama Florence in the small trailer kitchen. The faint hum of a distant generator pulsed beneath the silence, while the aroma of steeping mint tea wrapped the room in warmth. Shadows flickered across the walls from the soft light above, casting gentle halos around her worn features.

Roy had come to speak with her again about the strange woman he had once met in Michiana—Jenelle, the beautiful and mysterious figure who lingered in his mind like an echo. There had been something otherworldly about her, something that shimmered between charm and danger.

"Mama Florence," he began quietly, "I can't shake the feeling that Jenelle wasn't just another woman. There was something about her—something dark."

Mama Florence looked up from her cup, her expression unreadable. The overhead light caught the contours of her face, accentuating the calm weight of a life deeply lived; etching wisdom and pain in equal measure. "The Queen of the Coast," she murmured finally. "That's the name some give her kind."

Roy frowned. "Her kind?"

"She is not of this world," Mama Florence said softly, as though speaking more to the air than to him. "There are powers that dwell in deep waters—spirits that promise beauty, wealth, and knowledge, but take the soul in return. Some call her Jenelle. Some call her Jezebel of the Deep. But it's the same spirit, child. Always the same."

A chill ran through Roy. "You sound as though you've seen her before."

For a moment, silence fell. Mama Florence's eyes drifted toward the small window, where the moonlight traced the outline of her weathered hands. Her lips parted slightly, then closed again. When she finally spoke, her tone was distant, almost sorrowful.

"There was a time," she said slowly, "when I thought I could pull one such soul back from the deep. But once they've tasted power, they no longer hear the voice of the Shepherd. They only hear the tide."

Her voice trembled just slightly, and Roy felt the words lodge deep in his spirit. He didn't press her further, but something in her tone—a faint, haunted note between confession and lament—told him she was speaking of more than a story.

Mama Florence rose slowly, her eyes distant—as though she'd known this moment was coming long before she arrived. From the worn satchel she always kept close, she drew out a small bundle wrapped in linen and bound with a red cord. Setting it gently on the table between them, she said quietly, "The Lord impressed on me to bring this tonight. I didn't know why then... but I do now."

The air in the trailer thickened, a sacred hush settling over them. It was as if truth itself hovered at the edge of revelation—ready to speak yet restrained by divine timing.

"This belonged to a woman who once served those spirits," she said. "Inside are prayers written by her own hand. Prayers of deliverance... and of regret."

Roy hesitated. "Was she saved?"

Mama Florence met his gaze, her eyes shadowed and reflective. "Only God knows, Roy. But she was given a chance. We all are."

He unwrapped the cloth carefully. Inside lay a faded leather-bound journal, the edges water-stained, its pages filled with cramped handwriting. Across one torn page, a line stood out in trembling ink: *'I heard them calling from beneath the sea. I thought it was love. But it was hunger.'*

Roy's breath caught. He looked up, but Mama Florence had already turned away, staring into the flame of the lamp.

"She was beautiful," she said quietly, almost to herself. "Beautiful and broken. Some wounds run so deep they call to others like them."

Roy's chest tightened. He didn't need to ask—something in his spirit already knew. Mama Florence had not merely heard of Jenelle. She had known her. Perhaps she had even tried to save her.

"Watch and pray," she said suddenly, breaking the silence. "Because the same spirit that tempted her will not easily leave you alone. You've been marked since the day you opened that door."

Roy's throat went dry. "Marked?"

She nodded slowly. "The enemy remembers those who once listened."

He sat back, sensing the weight of her words—truths he would only later hear echoed by Dr. Doukhan, on a night when both men would face a shadowed figure at the edge of the road.

In that moment, though, he already felt it: an unseen thread binding every dark encounter he had ever faced.

Mama Florence reached across the table, her hand resting lightly on his wrist. "The Lord brought you here for a reason, Roy. You've walked too close to the fire not to carry the smell of smoke. But God is still calling you out of it."

Tears pricked his eyes. "What if it's too late?"

Her gaze softened. "It's never too late for those who choose light over shadow. But you must decide. The sea has claimed many who thought they could swim against its pull."

Outside, the wind stirred, rattling the metal siding of the trailer. Somewhere far off, thunder rolled across the horizon.

Roy looked down at the journal again. Near the bottom of the page was another faint line, written in a different hand—perhaps later, perhaps desperate: *'If ever you find this, pray for me. The Queen will not let me go.'*

He closed the cover and whispered, "God help her."

Mama Florence's eyes glistened as she nodded slowly. "And God help you too, child. Because her story and yours are not as far apart as you think."

The lamp flickered, casting her face half in shadow. Roy didn't speak again, but he felt the truth pressing on his heart as Mama Florance quietly left the trailer: Mama Florence had once walked through that same darkness—and perhaps, somehow, Jenelle's fate had been bound to hers.

Outside, the storm broke, and the rain began to fall.

The rain came harder now, drumming against the thin metal roof of the trailer as Roy stepped outside to reflect on all that he had learned. The air was cool and electric, charged with the scent of dust and ozone. He tilted his face upward, letting the drops sting his skin.

For a long moment, he stood still, the journal pressed to his chest. The rhythmic patter of rain became a kind of music—a reminder that even in storms, heaven still spoke.

Mama Florence's words echoed in his mind: *"The enemy remembers those who once listened."*

He felt the truth of it. No matter how far he had traveled—across islands, cities, and years—the darkness had followed, whispering promises of power and control. And now, for the first time, he saw the pattern clearly: every door he had opened in curiosity had become a threshold for something unseen.

Through the rain-streaked window in Mama Florance residence beyond his trailer, he could see her kneeling in prayer, her lips moving in silent intercession. Even from where he stood, Roy could sense her communion with something holy and eternal.

A tremor of realization moved through him. *She knew Jenelle. I'm sure of it.* She had tried to save her, maybe even loved her as a lost soul—and still carried that burden in prayer.

The thought pierced him deeply. This wasn't just about one woman, or one choice—it was about the war. The eternal struggle between heaven and hell that had shadowed his every step since Jamaica.

Lightning cracked across the sky, lighting up the horizon. The brilliance lingered for an instant, then fell away, leaving only darkness and rain.

He gripped the journal tighter, feeling the weight of it like a cross in his hands. He had been spared too many times to believe in coincidence. His blindness, his deliverance, his calling—they were all threads in a greater design.

A scripture stirred in his mind:

"For we wrestle not against flesh and blood, but against principalities, against powers, against the rulers of the darkness of this world..." (*Ephesians 6:12*)

He whispered the words into the storm, and they seemed to take life in the air around him.

Opening the journal one last time, he read the final line again: *"If you read this, know that light and darkness both wait for your choice."*

Roy closed it gently, his pulse steady now. Somewhere deep within, a decision had begun to form—not out of fear, but out of faith.

He looked toward the horizon where streaks of gold broke through the clouds. And in that brief silence between thunder and dawn, he whispered, "Lord, show me what to do next."

The rain softened to a whisper. The night no longer felt like confinement—it felt like consecration. Something had ended, but something greater had just begun.

He spent the evening alone, the trailer dimly lit as shadows danced across the walls. On-screen, the documentary was unlike anything he had seen before—startling, raw, spiritual in its terror and truth.

The weight of what I was learning began to settle in, Roy thought. This was more than just an epic tale; it was a battle of good and evil.

When the screen finally faded to black, he sat in silence for a long while because something had changed.

He had felt it within him.

The Epic was no longer just a project; it was a calling, he thought.

I was on a path that could change everything—not just for me, but for the world.

The next morning crept in quietly, pale light filtering through the blinds and spilling across the cluttered desk in Roy's small dorm room at Drew Economu's house. The folder Mama Florence had handed him the night before sat partially open beside his Bible and notes, its linen wrapping a silent reminder of secrets half-revealed. He barely slept. Every time he closed his eyes, her words echoed — about darkness, redemption, and the price of truth.

He rubbed his temples, staring blankly at the papers before him. His mind wasn't on his work; it was still back in that trailer, replaying the strange weight that had filled the air when she placed the bundle before him. There had been power there — the kind that hums just beneath the skin of reality.

A thought whispered in the back of his mind: *Was this just another one of those dark moments?*
Those moments that had followed him for years — since that night by the door, since the creak of the floorboards announced his presence, since the spirit world had taken notice of him. Try as he might to walk away, the shadow always found a way back into his path.

The sudden ring of the phone shattered the quiet. Roy jumped, his pulse quickening. For a second, he thought the sound came from *inside* the dream that still clung to him. But it was real. The shrill insistence of the call pulled him back into the tangible world.

"Hello?" His voice was groggy, uncertain.

"Mr. Ferguson? This is Lisa from the International Monetary Fund. We received your proposal regarding *The Epic.*"

Roy straightened, his breath catching. "Oh—thank you for calling," he said, fumbling for composure.

"We find your proposal intriguing," she continued. "We'd like to discuss possible funding. However, we'll need more information before proceeding."

Her voice was crisp and professional, but the words carried a strange resonance in Roy's mind — *We find your proposal intriguing*. A flicker of unease stirred in his chest. Was this divine favor or another seduction dressed in opportunity?

As he hung up, his eyes drifted back to the bundle on the desk. For a moment, it seemed almost to breathe, its presence heavy and alive.

Light and darkness, he thought. *They never stop circling each other.*
And as the morning sun rose higher, Roy couldn't shake the sense that both forces had once again found him — and that this call might be more than it seemed.

He sat for a long while after the call ended, staring at the silent phone as if it might ring again and confirm what he wanted to believe. His heart still beat fast — part excitement, part warning. *The IMF*. It sounded almost impossible, like the sort of miracle preachers spoke about when they said, *"God will make a way."*

A trembling smile crossed his lips. "Maybe this is it," he whispered to himself. "Maybe this is God's favor after all — His way of redeeming my past."

It was easier to think that way, easier to believe that the very thing he had dreamed of — recognition, impact, purpose — was now unfolding by divine design. He rose from his chair, pacing the room with restless energy. The doubt began to fade, replaced by a growing fire of determination.

He reached for his notes, spreading them across the desk — plans, timelines, calculations. The rational world was a comfort; it gave him something solid to hold onto. *If God had opened this door,* he thought, *then it was his duty to walk through it.*

Yet somewhere in the back of his mind, Mama Florence's voice whispered faintly:
"Not every open door leads to heaven, child. Some lead straight into the lion's den."

Roy shook his head, trying to push the thought away. There was no time for fear now. The world was waiting. The Epic was calling. And he — despite everything that lingered from the shadows of his past — was ready to step forward.

Later, as he walked through the campus, Roy felt lighter and heavier all at once. His steps were purposeful, his heart full. The support was flooding in—from professors, churches, spiritual elders, and now possibly international organizations. He could see the fruits of his labor. The massive support was overwhelming, each response fueling his passion for The Epic.

That afternoon, he met with Dr. James Lee III at the campus, the renowned composer who had supported his vision from the beginning. Dr. Lee and Roy strolled together from Pioneer Memorial Church to the music department at Andrews University as they discussed the importance of The Epic, which Roy was commissioning him to compose the music for the Hebrew translation.

"Dr Lee" Roy said with genuine appreciation, "I'm so grateful for your help. Your orchestral score is going to be a game-changer."

Dr. Lee smiled, tapping his pencil against the desk. "It's your vision, Roy. I'm just helping you make the heavens sing."

And with that, the foundation of The Epic grew stronger—deeply rooted in prayer, lifted by purpose, and carried on the shoulders of those who believed in Roy and the impossible.

As the sun dipped low behind the chapel spires, its golden light spilled across the campus lawns like a benediction. For the first time in a long while, the shadows that had trailed Roy seemed to retreat, dissolving into the horizon as though banished by the brilliance of new hope. The air felt clean again, almost holy, and his spirit rose with the fading light.

It was as if the darkness had lost its hold—receding quietly, almost into oblivion.
But somewhere beyond the glow of the evening sky, unseen and patient, it waited still.

Chapter 19

Reflections of the Heart – The Weight of Dreams

The walls of the mission room felt smaller that night, pressing in like judgment. Roy sat on the edge of his narrow bed, the hum of the city bleeding through the single cracked window. On his bed lay a worn script titled *Signed in Blood*. The pages were smudged with edits, half-finished thoughts, and dreams that once blazed like fire. Now they looked like ashes.

He rubbed his eyes and leaned back, staring at the ceiling fan that circled aimlessly above him. The rhythm reminded him of his own life—turning, turning, never quite moving forward. His breakup with Tara had reopened old wounds he thought time and ministry had sealed. The silence left in her absence was unbearable, an echo chamber of every failure he had carried since boyhood.

He whispered to the room, “There’s got to be more than this.”

The words barely left his mouth before a memory rose uninvited: Tara laughing on the beach, sunlight catching her hair; the smell of salt and coconut oil clinging to the air; the warmth of her hand in his. For a moment, it felt real again. But the scene dissolved as quickly as it came, replaced by the cold glow of his computer screen and the realization that he was back where he started—alone, surrounded by unfinished dreams.

His gaze fell again on the title page. *Signed in Blood.* The name had come to him years ago after his moment of deception and release to a force greater than anything he had ever experienced. The story was about choice, covenant, and redemption. He had once believed his experience, if told in the right way, might change the world, maybe even change him. Now it felt like a reminder of promises, dreams never quite fulfilled.

He rose and paced the small room, the thin carpet muffling his steps. "How did I get here?" he murmured. He thought of his younger self—the boy who had left Jamaica with fire in his chest and a duffel bag full of faith. He had faced demons, both real and imagined, survived Hollywood's glimmering deceit, and wrestled with the darkness of his own making. And yet here he was, years later, staring at the wreckage of what could have been.

He sat again, head in his hands. The mission around him stirred with the noises of the night: distant coughing, footsteps in the hall, a snore from the next room. The faint smell of disinfectant mingled with the old wood of the floorboards. It wasn't the life he'd envisioned, but it was the life he had; and he started to remember.

He had nowhere to go when he returned from Israel, so he sought out the URM a place he remembered from the past. And as he sat in a small room, now cluttered with his meagre possessions; old movie posters and dusty film reels, he started to recall his journey from the moment he signed his allegiance to Satan in blood on the Sangster Airport terminal bathroom mirror.

In his late fifties now and feeling just a little lost, he couldn't help being drawn again to the unfinished screenplay and as he reached for it frustration clouded his eyes. "There's got to be more to this... something bigger," he whispered to himself. And the memories returned like a flood, raw and emotional. His return from Israel to a life without Tara, the date etched in his mind 'Feb 12, 2024', was like falling back into a vacuum of nothingness, the loneliness and devastation consuming him; a feeling of abandonment enveloping him with an awareness that he must move on from.

Suddenly, inspiration struck. He grabbed a notepad and began to write, with purpose. And as he wrote, he 'Remembered':

It was 2005 when he presented to a group of Men at the URM in downtown LA. A representative of a foundation named Concerned for Others, who were strong financial supporters of the mission, approached him with an offer of $3200 to help him with his project. At the time he did not know who or what prompted this display of support; it would be revealed to him later. It wasn't enough to achieve very much, but a small acknowledgement that they thought he had something important going down. Later, at the Union Rescue Mission, Roy remembered standing in front of a group of men and women. A projector behind him showed images of Jerusalem and Hollywood.

"What if I told you that together, we can create something monumental?" Roy had said passionately; emboldened with a check for 3200 dollars in his pocket. What if we could produce a docudrama that tells the story, 'Connecting Hollywood and Jerusalem."

A homeless man raised an eyebrow. "And what makes you think we can do it?"

Roy smiled. "Because every story matters. Our stories matter. Together, we can make Jerusalem WON a reality."

He reflected on his trip to Jerusalem in 2023. He recalled standing on the Mount of Olives in Jerusalem, holding his dreams, his beliefs and his passion for what his mother had told him decades before, in his heart. The sunset bathed the city in a golden light and he was filled with a sense of purpose.

From Hollywood's streets to Jerusalem's ancient stones, Roy believed his vision was taking shape.

He believed he stood at the precipice of something monumental, surrounded by the cacophony of a world on edge. The tension in the Middle East was palpable, with whispers of war growing louder by the day and Iran, Russia, China, and a formidable Muslim confederacy were aligning against Israel, threatening to unleash chaos in the Jezreel Valley that would become in his vision, apocalyptic scenario. Yet, amidst the storm, Roy's vision for "Jerusalem WON" remained steadfast—a docudrama that would capture the essence of faith, hope, and divine intervention.

He remembered clearly, as he stood on the sun-drenched Mount of Olives, holding tightly to his screenplay, praying for God to show him the way, the weight of prophecy hanging heavy in the air, echoing the words of Ezekiel 38 and 39. And he pictured a time when the armies of the world would gather against Israel. But he also envisioned something greater: the 144,000 singers rising to sing the Song of Moses and the Song of the Lamb in Hebrew, their harmonies piercing the darkness of impending war. And he murmured to himself at the time "This isn't just a film script I am holding, it's a battle cry."

As he continued to write, Roy remembered his plan for his project to win over the believers in Hollywood; the producers, the writers and the actors of renown, 'He Wrote the Script In His Mind'. He had dreamed that when he returned to Los Angeles, the buzz surrounding 'Jerusalem WON' would be palpable. Hollywood insiders, influencers would be intrigued, armed with ambition and with the thoughts of a crossover of faith, prophecy, and the raw stories of redemption, they would be lining up to talk to Roy and his team. He would organize, panels of prominent investors and producers at renowned film festivals, to share the vision.

"Ladies and gentlemen," he would begin, before packed audiences, "We're at a crossroads. The world is in turmoil, and our stories can bridge the gaps." He would gesture to a montage of images showing the stark contrasts between the glamour of Hollywood and the struggles faced by those in Jerusalem. "We are telling a story that transcends borders, one that speaks to our shared humanity." he would tell them.

He envisioned the audience falling silent, captivated. Producers, trying to be noticed, would raise their hands to reveal, not wisdom, but a clear lack of understanding of the connection between Jerusalem WON and the current tensions in the Middle East.

Roy's heart raced as he continued to write, he remembered verses in the Bible like 'Ezekiel' that prophesied a time when nations would rise against Israel. And he would announce to the world, his desire to sow the seeds of peace; the armies will come, but God will fight for Israel, he would announce. And we will be there to reveal the ambushment of those who threaten His people by exposing the truth through Jerusalem WON.

The crowd would nod knowingly and applaud the boldness of his vision.

In his imagination he continued to describe to the audience 144,000 singers standing before the Israeli Defense Forces, their voices rising in unison, drowning out the sounds of war. They will sing the Song of Moses and the Song of the Lamb, reminding us all that in the face of annihilation, there is a call for faith and resilience." He would say.

A few days later, as he pulled his small team together Roy discussed how they might fulfill their mission.

He described his belief to all that would listen, saying "We will do this by empowering the voices of those who have lived through conflict, those who have faced despair and found hope.

Their narratives will not only resonate with the audience but will also showcase the resilience of the human spirit." And as the discussions continued, Roy felt a surge of determination. He had a vision, and it was gaining traction. He began reaching out to musicians and artists, hoping to gather the 144,000 singers from the children of Israel, to create a powerful soundtrack that would resonate deeply with the themes of the film.

In the weeks that followed, Roy's team grew. He met with directors, actors, and musicians who believed in the mission. They all shared a common goal: to create a docudrama that wouldn't just entertain but would also inspire and educate, that would change the world and bring forth a global revival.

And then he remembered, the moment he was changed, the moment in 2005 when he was first at the mission, that he met David, a fellow program member.

David's smile was genuine, his spirit unbroken and he introduced Roy to someone new.

"Meet Tara," David said warmly. "She's my fiancée's friend. You two might get along."

Roy turned and saw her—Tara, a woman whose eyes held gentleness and quiet strength.

"Hi, Tara," he greeted her with a hopeful smile.

Their conversation started simply, but something profound stirred in Roy. For years he had dreamed of a love as radiant as Halle Berry's image on a movie screen—but now, standing before him, Tara was real, present, and soon, she would steal his heart.

Roy remembered as this new relationship blossomed, another door opening. Some time earlier Dr. George Bell, director of the Mission, gave Roy a rare opportunity—to submit a grant proposal.

Roy's voice trembled slightly, but his conviction was firm. "I believe this project can make an immediate difference here in our community—and even extend hope to Israel and the world."

Dr. Bell's response was swift and supportive. "I'll do everything I can to help you." He had already encouraged a foundation to donate to Roy's project at an earlier event and that night, again, he felt he was back in control, receiving support from numerous quarters. And he began to believe the wheels of the project had begun to turn, slowly, but heading in the right direction. And the presence of Tara, surrounding him like a warm shawl of encouragement gave him hope for his vision for 'The Epic', but also his future with someone, Tara, who would come to believe in him.

Hope surged. "The Epic is becoming a reality," he thought, tears threatening to rise.

Later that evening, from the top floor of the Mission, Roy gazed out over the shimmering city. Dreams and fears wrestled within him—but above all, he felt resolve and he continued to remember.

"This is only the beginning," he whispered into the night. "And I'm ready to give it everything I have—for the sake of The Epic."

He recalled, gathering his team in a dimly lit conference room. They spread out maps of Jerusalem and the surrounding regions, highlighting areas affected by conflict. "This is not just a story of war; it's a story of faith under fire. We must be authentic. We must show the world the beauty in the struggle and the hope that arises from it."

The team nodded, their enthusiasm palpable. An actress spoke up; her voice filled with conviction. "Let's create something that will resonate beyond the screen. Let's invite audiences to join us in this quest for peace."

As the months rolled on, news of Roy's project reached beyond Hollywood. It sparked conversations in universities, churches, and community centers. People from various backgrounds began to engage with the themes of the film, sharing their own stories of struggle and hope.

Roy's heart swelled with pride; the vision was becoming a reality. He could almost hear the harmonies of the 144,000 rising through the air, a divine soundtrack echoing through the ages.

In reflecting on his fact-finding mission to Israel he was reminded of a scene in a bustling café in Jerusalem. He had overheard two tourists discussing the film. "I heard they're using the Song of Moses in the soundtrack. That's powerful," one said.

The other replied, "It's like they're bringing the past into the present. We need to see more of that."

On another day, he recalled, he was walking through Jerusalem again, taking in its history. He recorded a video on his phone. He had stood at the Western Wall in Jerusalem again. He placed a piece of paper between the stones. On it was a quote he had written: "Every story is a thread in the tapestry of humanity." "Thank you for this journey," he had whispered.

Late one night, Roy recalls he found himself back in his office, staring at the screenplay. "This is bigger than us," he murmured. "This is about the world." But amidst the excitement, Roy couldn't shake the feeling of urgency. The tensions in the Middle East were escalating. Reports of military buildup and threats loomed large. He knew that his film had to be released at a pivotal moment, and it was crucial to capture the essence of their message before the situation spiraled further out of control.

With renewed determination, he began to write an open letter to the world, urging unity and understanding. He wanted to remind everyone that in the face of adversity, stories hold the power to heal, to unite, and to inspire action.

As dawn broke over Hollywood, Roy stepped outside, breathing in the crisp morning air. He looked up at the sky, feeling the weight of his mission. "Let's make Jerusalem WON a beacon of hope," he whispered. "Let's change the narrative."

With that he remembered that he had set out to rally the troops, ready to film a docudrama that would not only entertain but also challenge the world to consider the power of stories—stories that could transform pain into purpose, and division into unity.

However, as the months rolled by, enthusiasm waned and money became tight, the project faltered, the screenplay remained unfinished and the book of the same name had not even started.

Roy's ideas on a film's release went nowhere, 'my gosh, the film did not even have a full screenplay' He thought, and certainly the money was not forthcoming. Roy had envisioned the climactic scenes: the armies gathering, the tension building, and then the resounding voices of the 144,000 filling the air with praise. In a moment of divine intervention, the enemy would turn upon itself, and the sea of blood would rise to the bridles of horses, a testament to the power of faith and divine justice. And now the imagination was fading.

The truth is, the journey had only just begun and the roadblocks ahead often looked insurmountable. But, Roy believed, in his heart of hearts, that in the face of the brewing storm, he had a message that could resonate far beyond the silver screen; indeed, he believed it could be told in real time.. This was more than just a film, it was real life; it was a call to arms—spiritual arms of faith, hope, and love against the backdrop of a world in crisis. And as he contemplated this and as he stared at photos of Jerusalem and quotes on the wall he quietly whispered, "This isn't just a film, it's a movement."

And then Roy stopped writing, stopped describing his vision, his desires; his own reality, the reality of life began to possess him. He could not fulfill God's plan by imagining or reflecting on the past; he was a doer and he feared, the work ahead to get this done, was so monumental and such a heavy burden that he and his team might not be ready to carry… and he prayed.

That night, back in the real world, Roy retired with a heavy heart, but an unrelenting spirit of truth, and a belief that God's plan will be revealed. He will make a way, and as he fell into a deep sleep exhausted from everything that was happening, he dreamed of the words of his friend, from 2002, a respected composer, Dr. James Lee III, known, world renowned, for his transcendent orchestral and choral works.

"It's an honor to be part of this project," he had said earnestly. "I believe I can create an orchestral score that surpasses even your expectations—something that draws deeply from Hebrew musical traditions."

Encouraged by his dream, a dream that had been over 20 years in the making, Roy prayed for understanding. "Lord, it has been so long since I started this journey and I have not always released my 'whole' to you. Please give me direction, for I am lost and I just feel that my life is at a turning point. I have met with executives, producers, Hollywood elites and given my story of the vision I have, but nothing has been forthcoming. Lord as I approach this next juncture in my life, the corner I am approaching, I need you, I want you to be with me. Lord, deal after deal have come to nothing again." And as Roy stepped out into the glare of a Los Angeles morning, weary but not broken, his spirit ached, but his mission endured.

As he consumed breakfast in the mission, he thought of *The Epic*—the project that had once united scholars, musicians, and believers from around the world. He remembered again Dr. James Lee III walking beside him on the campus of Andrews University, speaking with conviction about the score he would compose. "It's your vision, Roy," Dr. Lee had said. "I'm just helping you make the heavens sing."

The dream had reminded Roy that there was a time when he felt the project was unstoppable. Roy could still hear the echo of Dr Lee's words, and with it came the sting of everything that followed—the funding that never materialized, the promises that slipped through his fingers like sand, the weariness that had settled into his bones.

Back in the present, he lifted his script again, thumbing through pages covered in notes. A faint whisper crossed his mind: *Maybe it isn't finished because neither are you.*

The thought startled him. He exhaled slowly, leaning back as a deep ache filled his chest. He missed Tara, yes—but more than that, he missed purpose. The kind that used to keep him awake at night, scribbling words and prayers in equal measure.

He turned to his Bible on the nightstand; the one Mama Florence had given him years before. Its cover was frayed, its pages soft from use. He opened to Ecclesiastes 5, the words staring back like a mirror of his heart:

Keep thy foot when thou goest to the house of God, and be more ready to hear than to give the sacrifice of fools.

He read on, letting each verse cut through the fog:

When thou vowest a vow unto God, defer not to pay it... Better is it that thou shouldest not vow, than that thou shouldest vow and not pay.

Roy closed the book slowly. He had made vows—many of them. To God. To people. To himself. And he had broken everyone. The weight of it pressed against his chest until he couldn't breathe.

He knelt by his bed. No eloquent prayer came, just a whispered plea: "Lord... if there's still something You want from me, show me."

The silence stretched, but in that stillness a memory rose—Mama Florence's face, lined with wisdom and light. He remembered her words years earlier in the trailer when she had prayed over him: *"Roy, you may stumble, but the Lord never loses sight of His own."*

A quiet conviction stirred within him. It had been years since he last spoke with her, yet something in his spirit told him it was time. She would understand what this emptiness meant—what it was trying to tell him.

He reached for his phone, thumb hovering over her number.

"Maybe," he whispered, "this story isn't finished after all."

"Mama Florence," he said, his voice tinged with desperation, "I need your guidance."

Her reply, soft but unwavering: "My son, believe in the vision. God's plan hasn't changed, but sometimes we only see the ending, an ending that we have imagined, and the journey is forgotten. Roy, my child, look at the journey God has taken you on, remember every part of it, the highs and the lows, the victories and the failures. They were planned by God an eternity ago; again, I will say to you, accept that God's plan has not changed and the journey he has had you on is very much integral to the destiny He has for you.

Those words reignited the flame inside him. This wasn't just a creative endeavor—it was a divine calling and this was a divine call that he had just made. Roy knew he would go to any length to fulfill the promise of that call. But what was going to change was that never again would he step forth onto the battlefield without the Holy Spirit leading the charge.

Roy thought deeply about what Mama Florance said. He was alone after coming back from Israel, in a mission for men's recovery, a place of struggles and hope and he remembered Mama Florance words: "This is your journey Roy, that God had planned for you, and one that your Mama foreshadowed when you were just a small child."

It all began quietly, almost imperceptibly, beneath the soft glow of evening light. Tara had met Roy at the Union Rescue Mission—two souls whose paths had been battered by life but drawn together by grace. What started as a conversation over shared faith and weariness soon became something deeper—a sense of purpose neither had expected.

One evening, as the sun sank beyond the city skyline and the sky turned a tender shade of amber, Tara found Roy sitting at the kitchen table. The light from the window painted his face in gold, his eyes distant yet alive with thought.

"What's on your mind?" she asked softly, resting her hand on his shoulder.

Roy looked up, his voice calm but certain. “God’s plan is so magnificent,” he said. “Through His church, He’s putting the forces of hell to open shame.”

Tara smiled faintly. There was something in the way he spoke—an assurance that felt like peace after a long storm.

Later that week, Roy walked through the neighborhood, the evening wind brushing against him with an edge of mystery. He could feel something shifting, not in the air but in the unseen. The world seemed restless—its spiritual pulse quickening.

“The winds of war and strife are rising,” he thought, watching the lights flicker across the city. “The enemy knows his time is short. But God is awakening His people.”

Back home, he lingered before an old photograph—his family frozen in a moment of joy. A weight settled on him, not of despair but of calling. “Jesus said greater works will be done through His church,” he whispered. “We are the church. And this... this is our hour.”

Tara joined him quietly. She didn’t speak—she simply placed her hand over his. Her touch was steady, a reminder that he wasn’t alone in the mission that stirred his soul.

That night, they stood on the small balcony overlooking the city lights. The hum of traffic below seemed distant, irrelevant.

Roy opened his Bible and read from Revelation, his voice low but resolute.

"The sealing of God's servants," he said, eyes tracing the passage. "It's not just protection—it's purpose."

Tara listened, her heart swelling with reverence. She saw in him not just conviction, but a tenderness that faith had refined. They prayed together—hands intertwined, words rising like incense. "Lord," Roy prayed, "prepare us. Use us for Your glory in this late hour."

Under the starlit sky, the night held a stillness that felt sacred. Roy lifted his hands heavenward. "We know the hour is near," he whispered. "And we trust You with what's coming."

The days that followed were alive with motion. Roy spoke with anyone willing to listen—on sidewalks, at the mission, in small gatherings. "We're living in prophetic times," he told a young man near the corner store. "God is waking His people."

Back home, Tara sometimes watched him with quiet concern. "What of the enemy?" she asked one evening. "Won't he respond to what God is doing?"

Roy's expression hardened slightly, though not with fear. "He'll counterfeit it," he said. "Through systems of deception—a false peace, a false savior. The world will see the Antichrist before it recognizes the King."

Later, by the shoreline, Roy's heart wrestled with heaven's weight. The waves mirrored his thoughts—chaotic yet rhythmic. "The millennium will be in heaven," he murmured. "But Jesus will reign on earth again."

At home, the lamp cast a soft glow on his open Bible. Tara sat beside him as he read from 1 Thessalonians: *"When they say, 'Peace and safety,' sudden destruction comes."*

"So... until He returns," Tara asked softly, "there won't be real peace?"

Roy shook his head, his eyes distant. "No. For when they say, *'Peace and safety,'* then sudden destruction comes upon them, as labor pains upon a pregnant woman—and they shall not escape." *(1 Thessalonians 5:3, KJV)*

He paused, his voice quiet but steady. "In His plan, even waiting is action. Our patience is obedience; our watchfulness is faith."

His voice grew firm, almost reverent. "Our waiting is not stillness—it is readiness. Every breath is obedience until He comes."

Roy shook his head. "Not in Jerusalem. Not until the trumpet sounds, and the Kingdom is restored."

They knelt together on the living room floor, their voices woven into one prayer: "Lord, bring peace to Jerusalem, and salvation to Your people."

When Roy stepped outside later, the stars shimmered above him like ancient witnesses. "Armageddon will come," he thought, "but it won't have the final word."

Inside, Tara's voice broke the stillness: "That's what the angels promised when He was born—peace on earth." Her simple faith rekindled his smile, and in that moment he called the family together. They joined hands, their circle small but full of heaven's gravity.

"May we be faithful until that day," Roy prayed. "And help us share Your hope with everyone we meet."

As the night deepened, Roy sat alone, surrounded by notes, maps of Israel, and Scripture pages pinned to the wall. His Bible lay open to Daniel and Thessalonians—each verse pulsing with prophetic urgency. "We're standing at the brink," he whispered. "The choices we make now will echo into eternity."

Tara entered softly, sensing his burden. "What weighs so heavy tonight?"

Roy met her gaze. "Jerusalem," he said simply. "It's the center of God's covenant—and the enemy knows it."

They stood together at the balcony once more. The city glimmered below, unaware of the spiritual conflict hovering over it. "One day," Roy said quietly, "Jerusalem will be the capital of the universe, when Christ sits on David's throne."

The fire in his eyes met the gentleness in hers. "Then we'll stand," she said. "Together."

Roy nodded, the conviction settling deep. "We must be light in this darkening world."

That night, they knelt again, joined in prayer—partners in faith, bound by purpose. "Lord," Roy prayed fervently, "make us ready. Let us be Your voice and Your truth. Until You return."

Outside, the wind whispered through the streets of Long Beach, but within that small apartment, heaven felt close.
A flame had been rekindled.
A mission reborn.
And in the hush that followed, Roy's voice—quiet yet resolute—carried into eternity:

"We must prepare ourselves and others for the return of the Prince of Peace."

Years later, when Roy looked back on those nights—the whispered prayers, the flickering lamplight, the city humming beyond their balcony—he realized it had been a season of holy beginnings. The world around them had been restless, trembling beneath the weight of prophecy, yet inside that small apartment, heaven had drawn near. It wasn't grand or dramatic. It was simple. Two people who had once wandered through their own deserts now found themselves walking together toward the same horizon.

He would often remember the way Tara's hand felt in his—warm, steady, unshaken by fear. She had been his calm in the storm, his reminder that faith was not found in understanding every mystery but in trusting the One who held the plan.

What began at the Union Rescue Mission—a meeting born of brokenness and grace—became the seed of something far greater. They were not merely rebuilding their lives; they were being drafted into God's unfolding story. Their kitchen became an altar, their prayers the foundation of a calling neither had foreseen. Through tears and laughter, through prophecy and promise, they learned that ministry was not about speaking to crowds—it was about surrendering to God's whispers in the quiet hours of the night.

Roy would later write in his journal, *"That was the beginning of our awakening. The moment when faith turned from words into fire."*

And though the world grew darker with each passing year, he never forgot those first nights with Tara—when heaven felt close enough to touch, and the Spirit moved through the cracks of their ordinary days.

"In that season," Roy would tell others, "God taught us that redemption often begins not in noise, but in stillness. That the greatest revivals start at the kitchen table, in prayer, with a heart willing to say, 'Yes, Lord—use me.'"

CHAPTER 20

THE LOUD CRY BEGINS

Not long after meeting, Roy and Tara moved in together, but ever present was Mama Florence's words:

"This is your Journey Roy, that God had planned for you, and one that your Mama foreshadowed when you were just a small child."

The night air in Long Beach had a way of quieting the noise inside a soul—cool, salt-scented, and expectant. In those hours when traffic thinned and porch lights clicked on one by one, Roy often felt the veil thin. He would sit at the kitchen table with his notes fanned like wings across the laminate, a large map of Jerusalem pinned by his Bible on one side and a cup of mint tea cooling on the other. Roads ribboned toward the Temple Mount beneath his fingertips. Lines became stories; intersections, prophecies; and a city anointed by Scripture's breath seemed to rise from the paper and hover in the lamplight.

He did not think of himself as a prophet. He was, at best, a watchman—an ordinary man with an extraordinary burden, listening for the footfall of God on the edge of history. And lately, that sound had grown nearer.

"Something is shifting," he murmured, not to start a debate but to steady his own spirit. "All roads... to Jerusalem."

Tara would find him there sometimes, midnight collecting on his shoulders like dew, eyes alive as if he'd just returned from a far country. She never startled the moment. She simply set a hand on his and waited, a practiced patience that felt like shelter.

"What's stirring in you?" she would ask, and the question was never small.

He would answer without drama, only gravity. "The tensions between Muslims and Jews are straining toward a tear. I believe another intifada is near." Then he'd flip through clippings and notes, underline place names, circle temple routes. "A false messiah will promise a peace that is not peace. He will sit where he ought not sit."

Tara did not recoil from the weight. She leaned into it with him—Bible open, heart steady—like someone helping to shoulder a stretcher on a long road.

When words became too dense to breathe around, Roy walked. The nighttime sidewalks offered a kind of listening—palm fronds hushing over rooftops, a train moaning low in the distance, the ocean breathing in long, patient sighs. He took the same route so the street knew his footprints and he knew the street's silences.

At the shore, he would stand until wind lacquered his hair to his forehead and the waves hammered his thoughts clean. That was where certain phrases came back to him like tides: *The hour is near. The church must be awake. The remnant will rise.* Sometimes he spoke to anyone who would pause long enough to hear: a teenager on a bike, a man with a grocery sack, a woman walking a dog. He never raised his voice, but urgency sharpened his vowels.

"When the abomination of desolation happens," he told a small cluster one night, "a false messiah will seat himself in the temple and claim what belongs only to God. Do not mistake spectacle for truth." He was the Watchman; the Shore was his stage; and the ocean seemed to answer with thunder that was not thunder.

Inside the apartment, their kitchen became a war room without anger—a sanctuary of ink and prayer. Notes multiplied. Maps overlapped. Headings appeared in the margins: *Three Angels' Messages*; *Petra*; *Sunday Law*; *144,000*. Their Bibles were worn at the edges, the way a carpenter's tape is smoothed by use. Children's artwork still clung to the fridge, and next to it Roy tacked a printed headline: **"Jerusalem: A Cup of**

Trembling." He read the old line aloud in a new room—*a burdensome stone among the nations*—and heard the present answer the past.

"Is it happening faster?" Tara asked one evening, eyes moving from headline to Scripture.

"Yes," Roy said, not to frighten but to anchor. "And soon restraint will be lifted. Deceptions will swarm like summer frogs—out of the mouth of the dragon, the beast, the false prophet. We must learn to recognize truth by the cadence of God's voice, not by the volume of the world."

Tara nodded, absorbing the shape of it. "Then this is more than dates and charts. It's faithfulness."

"It's always been faithfulness," he said, and reached for her hand.

They gathered the children more frequently then. The living room became a circle—fingers laced, heads bowed—and their prayers braided into one rope they could all hold. Some nights they simply read the commandments slowly, as if each word carried water they needed to sip. Other nights, they spoke plainly about counterfeit worship and costly obedience, not to grind fear into young hearts but to plant courage.

"The Sabbath is not a technicality," Roy told them, kneeling so his eyes met theirs. "It's a window that opens to show us who God is. When the world tries to board it shut, we will need to remember where the light comes from; there are always signs and summits that reveal truth.

News found them, as it finds anyone with a heartbeat and an internet connection. Roy scanned, highlighted, sifted. A climate summit at Sinai. "Ten Spiritual Principles" invoked with a piety that felt like theater. Sunday lifted as a solution disguised as devotion.

"They don't realize whom they flatter," Roy said, weariness at the edges of his voice.

"Ra?" Tara asked softly, reading his notes.

"Call it what you will," Roy answered. "The old sun dressed in modern language. A day switched by decree as though heaven were a committee. Daniel told us such hands would try to change times and law. The real Sabbath is not fragile. But people are."

They did not turn bitter. They turned outward. Roy's steps lengthened along neighborhood sidewalks, and his sentences grew simpler, kinder, plainer.

“God’s commandments aren’t shackles,” he told a neighbor who worked nights and kept his cigarettes in his shirt sleeve. “They’re the architecture of love.”

The man stared at his shoes and said he was tired. Roy nodded. “So is the world. Rest was given as medicine.”

Like hooks in the jaws of a hungry fish, prophecy stitched ancient names to modern headlines in Roy’s mind—Gog, Magog, alliances rising and dissolving like sandbars, an economy propped on oil while denouncing it, seventy-one byproducts in toothbrushes and tires and IV tubing. The irony didn’t amuse him; it sobered him.

“The nations accuse, and yet the lifeblood they deny is the bait that draws them,” he said one night, tracing pipework on a Middle East map with his finger. “Hooks in the jaws,” he whispered, remembering Ezekiel’s cadence. “Not because God is cruel, but because history is a river with a mouth, and judgment is the sea beyond it.”

Tara listened and placed a fresh sheet under his hand, the gesture quiet and generous. “If the current is carrying us there, then we must be a lighthouse on the cliff.”

“Or a lantern in a small kitchen,” Roy said, smiling.

Roy spoke soberly about Petra a place of refuge for the weary, the Remnant—caves and crimson rock, a wilderness of refuge. He did not turn it into legend. He treated it as Scripture treated it: a waypoint in a longer obedience. *The 144,000 sealed... first fruits.* He imagined their faces not as heroes for posters but as brothers and sisters marked by humility and fire. He prayed for them as if praying for neighbors.

"The accusation will be as old as Eden and as new as tomorrow's headline," he told Tara. "They will be blamed for refusing a counterfeit worship day. Accused of stalling climate peace. Cast as enemies of the human family because they remain loyal to the Family Name."

"And the martyrs?" Tara asked, the word holy in her mouth.

"Some will be laid to rest by mercy," Roy answered. "Others will fall by sword or policy. All of them will stand."

They taught these truths to their children without theatrics. Suffering was never romanticized; it was merely named, like weather on the horizon.

Roy and Tara's small apartment was where their loud cry resonated. And if a revival is measured only by stadium noise, you would have missed theirs. It pulsed through living rooms, on park benches, around kitchen tables sticky with jam and open Bibles. Roy's voice found a register that carried across thresholds without breaking windows.

"The everlasting gospel doesn't age," he told a group wedged onto mismatched chairs, reading Revelation 14 in a voice gentle enough to be heard. "Fear God. Give Him glory. Worship Him who made heaven and earth. This is not a slogan; it is the spine of reality. Babylon will fall. Do not drink her cup, no matter how golden it looks."

Afterward, he stacked chairs, wiped crumbs, folded the sheet of notes that had trembled when he first spoke. Tara caught his hand as he passed. "They heard," she said.

"I pray they did," he replied. "I pray I did."

Tara's Reflection: *I learned to measure peace in smaller units—breath to breath, prayer to prayer. The world was tilting, yes, but I watched my husband tilt toward God faster than the world could tilt toward fear. Our apartment began to feel like a lighthouse because he kept the lamp trimmed. I was not blind to cost. I counted it while I folded laundry, while I wrote verses on index cards for the children, while I fell asleep with maps under my pillow. But I also counted grace. It kept arriving before I ran out.*

There were nights when Roy's message sounded like a shout even though he never raised his voice. Streetlight sermons urging those who would listen to "Prepare your hearts," he would say to a circle outside the corner store. "The Prince of Peace is near." And then he would leave space for silence to do its work.

A small resistance began to form—not a political caucus, not a faction—but a people who kept finding one another wherever Scripture and conscience tugged them in the same direction. They were teachers and dock workers, nurses and retirees, teenagers who had made a habit of honesty. They adapted to life as exiles, citizens of a declining city rather than a rising power. They learned to rest on the seventh day like fugitives under a tree with deep roots.

"Faith will soon cost," Roy told them, never with menace, always with mercy. "It always did, when it was honest."

Obedience can be hostile and as its call sharpened, with it came a private ache Roy had never penciled into his charts. Obedience has its clean lines in a notebook; it has shadows in a home. He and Tara had braided seventeen years of life—children, laughter, private covenants kept in quiet rooms. She had steadied him through rejection, through midnights, through long corridors in which only a single door at the end was marked "prayer."

But the call grew insistent, narrowing like a canyon path. He wrestled with God over it, not to escape obedience but to comprehend its price. *Is this something we shoulder together, Lord, or a crossing that requires me to walk alone for a season?* The question itself felt like blasphemy and yet also like truth. There is no clean way to speak of heartbreak that happens in obedience; there is only reverence.

In the end, the marriage broke. Not from contempt, not from scandal, but from a weight that even love could not balance. Papers were signed with hands that trembled and then steadied. Roy carried grief as one carries a folded flag—pressed to the chest, not shaken as a banner. He did not make the ministry an alibi; he made lament a discipline. And still, beneath the ache, the same conviction burned: *Israel. The map that would not stop pulling. The call that would not untie its knot.*

Tara did not become his enemy; she remained a co-keeper of the children's faith, a woman who had once helped him measure the size of prophecy and now helped their family measure the size of grace. In quieter seasons, they could even speak of those nights without bitterness—like veterans tracing old scars in the shape of a cross.

As headlines darkened—treaties and troop movements, economies buckling, laws drafted with smiles and teeth—Roy found his sentences getting simpler. His road became narrower; "Christ first." "Truth at any cost." "Rest where God rests." He taught the children to pack light, not only in closets but in conscience. He reminded them that persecution never gets the last word; resurrection does.

He read Ezekiel again: hooks in jaws, nations drawn. He traced routes toward Petra again, not to romanticize escape but to sanctify endurance. He stood at the shore until the repeated crash of waves taught him the advantage of the patient over the loud. And when the night pressed in, he recited to himself a liturgy he had constructed across years: **God is not late. God is not loud to prove He is God. God is faithful to the end.**

Roy and Tara's kitchen table had become their stage. One evening, dusk gathering in the corners of the room like a congregation, Roy closed his Bible and did not open his laptop. He simply looked at the map and then at his children. He spoke not as a pundit, not as a strategist, but as a father.

"God's law is not a fence to keep you from joy," he said. "It is the frame that keeps joy from collapsing. If you ever must choose between comfort and command, choose command; joy will catch up. If you must lose to be faithful, lose cleanly and sleep well."

They prayed, not for exemption but for endurance. Then they ate, and laughter managed to thread itself through the room as if laughter had heard the prayer and wanted to agree with it.

Later, under the same steady lamp, Roy whispered to the God who had been teaching him to walk by stars he could not name: "Make me faithful when I am visible and when I am not. Let me be truthful without being cruel, brave without being hard."

And so the Loud Cry did not begin with a trumpet blast in a stadium. It began with a husband and wife at a table, a circle of children holding hands, notes scrawled beside headlines, scriptures read until their music memorized the room. It began on sidewalks and at shorelines, in borrowed living rooms and around coffee-stained tables where strangers became family. It began with a man who mourned the cost and did not excuse the pain, who still lifted his eyes to a city that had been promised a future sharper than any present.

He kept saying it in different ways because truth loves repetition:

Worship the Maker, not the moment.

Rest where God rests; do not trade it for a counterfeit sunrise.

Do not fear the noise; history belongs to a whisper that became a Word and then a world.

When he grew tired, he remembered the promise that once sent him to the balcony with Tara at his side: the Prince of Peace would return, not to negotiate but to reign. Jerusalem would not always tremble; it would one day shine. Armageddon would not always threaten; it would one day end. The saints would not always scatter; they would one day descend with a City. And the map on his table would be folded, not because it was wrong, but because the geography had been fulfilled.

That night, Long Beach breathed its cool benediction. Roy stepped to the balcony and let the air find his face. He thought of Tara, of the children, of the neighbors whose eyes had softened over Scripture, of the watchmen he had not met yet and the remnant he would one day recognize by the way they carried joy under siege. He thought of Petra and of oilfields, of policies and plagues, of hooks and stone cups, of Sinai pronouncements and golden rhetoric, of saints whose rest would be mercy and of others whose witness would be flame.

He did not feel large beneath all that. He felt small and kept. He lifted his hands.

"Lord," he said, and the word held the whole room, "make us faithful. Make us true. Teach us to keep Sabbath in a restless world, to keep love in a violent one, to keep our eyes on Jerusalem without losing sight of the person in front of us. If the road narrows, make our hearts wide. If the cost rises, make our joy rise higher. And when the Loud Cry must crest, let it sound like Your voice through ours—steady, clean, and full of hope. Amen."

The apartment returned to its soft hum. The waves did what waves do. And somewhere, beyond what he could name, the City that would not tremble forever drew a fraction nearer.

Yet even as the vision of Jerusalem grew sharper in his heart, another struggle rose within him. The call of God stirred powerfully, insistent and unrelenting, but it pressed against the life he had built at home. For seventeen years, Tara had been his rock—the steady hand that calmed his storms, the mother of the three children they had raised together. She had stood faithfully by his side through every rejection, every vision, every night of prayer.

Still, Roy knew that obedience to God's calling sometimes demanded painful sacrifice. Was this cost one they were meant to bear together, or was it the path that would part their ways? In the end, despite the years of shared devotion, they became divorced. Still, he carried with him both the grief of what was lost and the conviction that Israel was the place where God's plan for him would unfold.

Chapter 21

Return From The Holy Land

Roy lay on his bed in the dimly lit apartment, staring at the ceiling. His mind replayed images from Israel, fifty-three unforgettable days that had reshaped his soul. Everything felt different now. More real.

"As I lie here, I can't shake the feeling," he thought. "Walking where Jesus walked made the Bible come alive. I see it all so clearly now."

Just weeks earlier, he had stood in line at LAX, his heart beating with excitement and nerves. The EL AL security checks were serious, far more intense than he expected.

The Israeli security officer stared at him, sharp and focused. "What is the purpose of your trip to Israel?"

Roy hesitated for a moment, then answered with quiet conviction. "I'm going to explore the holy sites and deepen my faith."

Even though the officer's tone reminded him of the tough process of becoming an American citizen, Roy felt no regret. This journey was necessary.

When he finally landed at Ben Gurion Airport in Tel Aviv, relief washed over him. Though the nation was at war, the airport moved with an almost defiant rhythm of normal life.

"It's like the people here live with conflict all the time," he thought. "But they carry on with hope."

A friendly Israeli Arab taxi driver picked him up for the ride to Jerusalem. As they drove, the man pointed out ancient sites and shared stories about the land.

"That's the old city of Jerusalem," the driver said, smiling. "Where every stone holds history."

Roy looked out the window, his eyes wide with awe. "This isn't just a trip," he thought. "This is an awakening."

He checked into the Jerusalem Gate Hotel; a place steeped in the hum of both history and modern life. From there, he moved into the Adventist Center, just steps from the Temple Mount. The sight of it left him breathless.

Pastor Daniel Stojsnovic and his wife, Sister Slavi, greeted him warmly. "Welcome to Jerusalem, Roy," the pastor said, placing a hand on his shoulder. "We're excited to show you the heart of our faith."

The days that followed were filled with holy encounters. Roy prayed at the Western Wall, walked the Via Dolorosa, the path

Jesus took to the cross and knelt silently in the Garden of Gethsemane.

"Every step," he reflected, "connected me more deeply to the roots of my faith. I wasn't just reading the Bible anymore. I was living it."

But the peace of Israel didn't follow him home. Back in California, Roy found himself sleeping on a cot at the Union Rescue Mission on Skid Row in downtown Los Angeles. The divorce from Tara had left him not just heartbroken, but homeless.

"The warmth of Israel felt so far away," he thought. "And now... this."

"Almost 18 months later, Roy was reminded of the conversations that had first stirred his spirit at the Mission. Malcolm—the Australian gentleman he had first encountered there—had remained by his side during those days. Now, after a short absence, Roy sought out Malcolm again, this time not only as a fellow resident but as a friend and guide. What had once lived only as a memory now grew into a living partnership.

Through Malcolm's encouragement, Roy found hope again and the courage to take a decisive step of faith: launching his own 501(c)(3) nonprofit organization called Jerusalem WON

Inc." "Together," Malcolm said, "we can make a difference. This project could be what the world needs to resolve the Middle East crisis and usher in the return of Jesus Christ, who is the Prince of Peace."

The fascination with the project drew the two men ever closer together as they both worked on a grant proposal back in Room 366, where they normally conducted servant leadership meetings at the Union Rescue Mission.

Roy and Malcolm worked diligently, pouring every detail of The Epic vision into notebooks and spreadsheets. Even more so, the time that Roy spent in Israel had lit a fire in him that no struggle could extinguish.

"This isn't just a project," he said. "It's a divine calling. A mission to bring hope and healing."

Finally, Roy and Malcolm had masterfully crafted The Epic grant proposal for the project, hoping to solicit funding for a docudrama filmed in real time, with the Song of Moses and the Song of the Lamb in Hebrew as the soundtrack, where praise would evoke divine intervention.

Later that night, Roy knelt in prayer and recited "The Prayer of Jabez" found in 1 Chronicles 4:9-10. Roy was calling on the God of Israel like Jabez:

"And Jabez was more honorable than his brethren: and his mother called his name Jabez, saying, Because I bare him with sorrow. And Jabez called on the God of Israel, saying, Oh that thou wouldest bless me indeed, and enlarge my coast, and that thine hand might be with me, and that thou wouldest keep me from evil, that it may not grieve me! And God granted him that which he requested."

"I won't back down," he whispered to himself. "This is my calling. I will fight for it until the end."

The following morning, Roy met Malcolm to finish drafting the grant proposal. As Roy entered, Malcolm looked up and smiled. "Roy, thanks for coming. I've been reading through the grant proposal that we wrote yesterday, and I want to ask you a few questions."

"Roy, tell me more about how you will incorporate neuro-linguistic programming with voice modulation interface in this project?"

Roy placed his laptop on the desk and opened the file. "We want to create a transformative experience," he explained. "By using voice modulation and neuro-linguistic programming, we can make the performance interactive—something that stirs the heart and soul."

Malcolm scrolled through the proposal, stopping at the section outlining the budget. "Two hundred million dollars," he said. "That's a substantial ask. Help me understand why that's necessary."

Roy leaned in, passionate and focused. "The money won't just go to the music," he said. "We need advanced tech for real-time voice modulation. We want the audience to feel like they're inside the story, hearing voices that shift, echo, and speak directly to them through scripture and prophecy."

He pointed at a graph on the screen. "Each element of the orchestra, the NLP integration, and the immersive design needs precision and expertise. We can't afford to cut corners on this."

Malcolm nodded thoughtfully, clearly impressed by Roy's conviction. "And what about outreach?" he asked. "How do you plan to ensure that this message goes beyond a performance hall?"

Roy's eyes lit up. "That's the heart of it," he said. "We'll run workshops in schools, churches, and community centers. We'll teach people how music can be a tool for spiritual warfare and emotional healing. This is about creating a movement, not just an event."

Malcolm sat back in his chair, silent for a moment. He looked at Roy, then back at the screen. "You're connecting liberation, identity, and divine purpose through music and tech," he said. "That's rare."

Roy nodded. "This project is called Jerusalem WON for a reason," he said. "It's about victory, spiritual victory in a world full of deception and despair."

Malcolm stood and extended his hand. "I'll be honest," he said. "I believe this project has merit. And I'm willing to help you accommodate the proposal. Let's work out the next steps together."

Roy shook his hand, feeling a weight lift off his chest. For the first time in weeks, hope was rising again.

That night, back at his room at the Union Rescue Mission, Roy stared at his notebook, flipping past scribbles, verses, and outlines until he reached a blank page. He wrote two words at the top: Next Phase.

The vision is becoming reality," he thought. "God sent me to Israel to wake me up—and to remind me that this dream has slept too long. Almost twenty years it's lain dormant, waiting for faith to breathe life into it again. "Now it's time to wake others." Malcolm said thoughtfully but in a determined and purposeful tone. Roy smiled. "Yes. And I believe this could change everything."

"Then we'll walk forward in faith," Malcolm said softly.

Together, they bowed their heads, surrendering the moment to God and praying for the journey ahead. A quiet stillness filled the room—yet within that stillness, Roy sensed something stirring. It was more than emotion; it was divine assurance, a spark of renewal kindling deep within his spirit. He could feel the gentle hand of Providence turning another page, guiding him toward healing, hope, and a fresh beginning.

And it was not lost on either Roy or Malcolm, that on **June 24, 2025**, the nations of **Iran and Israel** had agreed to a cease-fire after a brief but fierce exchange—a truce that seemed impossible only weeks earlier. That fragile peace became the seedbed for something even greater: the historic summit in Sharm el-Sheikh, Egypt, held on October 13, 2025. There, under the weight of centuries of division, the leaders of the world—led by President Trump and President el-Sisi—gathered to sign what became known as the Gaza Peace Plan.

Roy had watched the events unfold with both awe and apprehension. In the delicate hands of diplomats, he saw mirrored the fragile hopes of humanity. The world seemed to be reaching for peace, even as the echoes of ancient prophecy whispered warnings beneath the surface. In that convergence of faith, politics, and destiny, Roy sensed that both the mission before him and the world itself were standing on the edge of a divine reckoning—a line between renewal and ruin.

For him, Jerusalem WON was not just a project reborn; it was a symbol of God's mercy still extended to a restless world. And as he reflected on all that had transpired, he felt the Spirit whisper: *The story is not over; it is beginning again.*

Chapter 22
The Covenant of Illusion

Because it conveys that what the world hails as peace is in fact deception — a counterfeit covenant preparing the stage for prophecy's next act.

Roy remembered watching the summit unfold on the large screen in the Mission's community hall. The camera panned across a sea of dignitaries, their faces solemn beneath the weight of expectation. Flags of once-hostile nations stood side by side — a tableau of forced optimism. President Trump stood at the podium, his familiar cadence tempered by age and gravity.

"Today," he declared, "we turn a page written three thousand years ago. Today, we claim peace — not as a dream, but as destiny."

Applause rippled across the hall in Egypt, echoed faintly by the small group at the Mission watching the live feed. Yet behind every smile on that stage, Roy sensed calculation. Hope and suspicion mingled in the air like oil and water. The leaders' words were polished, but their eyes betrayed unease — the unspoken knowledge that peace, once declared, must still be defended in the chaos of human ambition.

He leaned forward, elbows on his knees, studying the faces on screen: American advisers, Israeli ministers, Arab envoys, European intermediaries. Some looked relieved, others simply weary. *Was this peace born of conviction — or exhaustion?*

Roy had walked those same streets of tension months earlier in Jerusalem, where soldiers stood at every gate and mothers whispered prayers before sending their children to school. He had spoken with young men who dreamed of normalcy but knew only the rhythm of alert sirens. Now, to see those same nations clasp hands on international television felt both miraculous and fragile — as though the world itself was holding its breath.

Trump's closing words stirred the crowd: "This peace will endure because the people demand it — and because God wills it."

The hall erupted in applause. But Roy couldn't shake a quiet unease. Something about invoking divine permanence in a human treaty felt precarious, almost presumptuous. He had learned, through his own life, that promises made under pressure often wither in the sun of reality.

That night, political commentators flooded the airwaves. Analysts called it *"the Sharm el-Sheikh Miracle."* Stock markets surged, oil prices dipped, and diplomats toasted "the end of the old Middle East." For a fleeting moment, the world exhaled. Roy wanted to believe it. He longed for the endless cycle of war and vengeance to finally break.

But as days turned to weeks, subtle fractures appeared. Iran refused to endorse the deal outright, calling it "temporary appeasement." Militias along northern borders ignored the cease-fire. A truck bomb in Damascus killed civilians, reigniting rhetoric. The same networks that once celebrated "peace in our time" now whispered caution: *Tensions Simmer Despite Historic Accord.*

Roy clipped one of those headlines and taped it into his notebook beneath the words *Next Phase.*
Below it he wrote: *Peace must be lived, not signed.*

Still, he could not escape the prophetic weight pressing on his spirit.

He recalled again the moment President Trump spoke at the summit, his voice resonating with conviction, promising a new dawn for the region. Yet beneath the applause and polished diplomacy, Roy sensed a tension ripe for conflict. Would this peace endure, or was it destined to crumble under the weight of unhealed wounds and unspoken ambition?

With each eloquent phrase, a shiver ran down his spine. The very act of declaring peace felt like a ticking time bomb. As he watched the gathered leaders sign their names with solemn pride, he couldn't shake the thought that history had a way of repeating itself — often with devastating precision. Could this be the calm before the storm, a brief lull in a cycle of violence as old as civilization itself? The world had turned its pages, but the story felt all too familiar — as if its ending had already been written in God's Word.

World leaders had come together for an historic summit — a bold attempt to quell bloodshed and usher peace into a region long defined by conflict. It was a moment of hope, a promise the President declared had been three thousand years in the making. Yet as the ink dried upon the agreement, a chilling echo from Scripture reverberated through Roy's mind: "For when they shall say, Peace and safety! then sudden destruction cometh upon them..." (1 Thessalonians 5:3).

Amid the glittering backdrop of diplomacy, Roy felt an unsettling irony. The world was proclaiming peace with its lips even as its heart trembled with unrest. He remembered the words of Jesus:

"But as the days of Noah were, so shall also the coming of the Son of man be." (Matthew 24:37).

The parallels were haunting. Corruption and violence had once filled the earth, and humanity seemed to be walking that same road again:

"The earth also was corrupt before God; and the earth was filled with violence." (Genesis 6:11).

Tracing the word *violence* back to its Hebrew root — *chamas* — Roy couldn't ignore the eerie resonance with *Hamas,* the very name of the group igniting the latest conflict. Was it coincidence, or divine foreshadowing, that chaos itself bore the same name?

The peace plan, he thought, might not be a cure at all — it might be a mirror, reflecting humanity's illusion of control. Deep within, Roy understood that some prophecies were not warnings to prevent, but declarations destined to unfold.

When the dust of diplomacy settled, the world exhaled in relief. Treaties were signed, speeches celebrated, and nations congratulated themselves on progress. Yet beneath the headlines, something deeper stirred — an unease no press release could contain.

Governments began to speak not only of peace and security but of *stability through unity*. Economic councils drafted global rest initiatives — policies to "restore the planet's rhythm" and "preserve humanity's mental health." On paper, they appeared humanitarian and environmental. But as new decrees emerged from the European Parliament and the United Nations — calling for a *Universal Day of Rest* — the language grew more theological than practical.

Religious leaders applauded, calling it a moral turning point for civilization. Politicians embraced it as social progress. What began as an appeal to conscience was quietly transforming into mandate — the *Global Rest and Renewal Act,* declaring Sunday as the official day of rest, worship, and environmental observance.

To the watching world, it felt like unity at last — peace institutionalized, morality restored.
To Roy, it felt eerily familiar.

He had read of such things in prophecy — in Daniel, in Revelation — and he knew how subtle deception often arrived dressed in virtue. *When man tries to legislate God's peace,* he thought, *he builds a kingdom that cannot stand.*

In his journal, he underlined the words with quiet certainty:
Man's peace is imposed. God's peace is invited.

Leaning back, Roy listened to the faint hum of his computer. The world was moving toward something irreversible —

something wrapped in the language of unity but rooted in control. The verse from Jeremiah echoed in his mind:

"They have healed also the hurt of my people slightly, saying, 'Peace, peace'; when there is no peace." (Jeremiah 6:14)

Outside his window, the city lights glimmered like distant fires — beautiful, but uncertain. Somewhere in the hum of the streets, he felt the pulse of a world trying to convince itself that unity still held. Yet deep down, Roy sensed something shifting — a slow, quiet descent toward the reckoning Scripture had long described, though he dared not speak it yet.

For now, he watched, waited, and wrote — determined that *Jerusalem WON* would not be merely a story of collapse, but a record of faith enduring through the coming storm.

Beyond the haze, Los Angeles shimmered beneath a restless sky. Somewhere past its noise, Roy felt the tremor of what was coming — the collision between God's Sabbath and man's decree, between divine order and human ambition.

The headlines soon faded, but the conversation did not. Across the nation, the idea of a "Universal Day of Rest" began seeping from government chambers into pulpits, workplaces, and homes. What had been hailed as a diplomatic triumph was now being preached as a moral duty. The world's definition of peace had changed — no longer the absence of war, but the presence of uniformity.

Roy noticed it first in the streets around the Mission. Flyers appeared in shop windows; local broadcasts spoke of "spiritual unity" and "planetary renewal." Sunday gatherings multiplied, drawing both believers and skeptics into the same refrain: *Rest brings peace. Compliance brings harmony.*

But beneath the hopeful slogans, Roy sensed a familiar unease — the subtle merging of faith and force.
The storm he had long felt approaching was now taking form, not in missiles or markets, but in minds and mandates. Across pulpits and parliaments, a new message was rising — one that sounded holy but carried the weight of control.
The world was preparing to test the boundary between conviction and compliance. Roy knew that soon he would stand upon that very line — the one that would separate tradition from truth and reveal the biblical day of rest.

Chapter 23

Lines in the Sand – The Day of Rest

The topic of a global day of rest first surfaced one morning at the Mission, in the small dining hall where conversation often drifted between faith, politics, and prophecy. A group of men huddled around the television as world leaders once again praised the new *Day of Global Rest* initiative. The news anchors spoke with reverence, calling it "a moral victory for humanity."

One of the men turned toward Roy, smirking over his coffee mug. This is exactly what you wanted; a world that finally honors the Sabbath?"

Roy's fork paused midair. "Depends which Sabbath you're talking about," he said softly.

Laughter rippled around the table, but Roy's eyes stayed serious. "The seventh day—the one God sanctified at creation—that's the Sabbath. Not the one man has chosen for convenience or consensus."

Another man shrugged. "What's the difference? A day's a day if it keeps people peaceful."

Roy leaned forward, his voice calm but firm. "It's not about the day," he said. "It's about obedience. If the world legislates a rest that replaces what God established, then peace becomes compulsion—and faith becomes conformity."

His words hung in the air. Some nodded; others looked away.

He reached into his worn Bible and turned to Exodus 20, tracing the familiar lines with his finger to vs 8-11:

"Remember the Sabbath day, to keep it holy. Six days shalt thou labor and do all thy work:
But the seventh day is the Sabbath of the Lord thy God."

He let the verse speak for itself. "This commandment wasn't given to a denomination," he said quietly. "It was written by God's own hand. If the world trades that away for a counterfeit peace, we're not moving toward salvation—we're walking into deception."

The room fell silent. Even the clatter of dishes seemed to pause.

That morning marked the beginning of a much larger conversation—one that would soon spill beyond the Mission's walls into churches, governments, and newsrooms around the world. As the proposed Sunday Law gained momentum, so did the unease of those who saw beyond its promises. Once again, the lines between politics, religion, and prophecy began to blur.

Roy's thumb hovered over the glowing rectangle, as if that small screen held the weight of the world. Angeles House murmured with the ordinary sounds of a Sunday evening — distant laughter down the hall, the clatter of dishes in the communal kitchen, the faint hum of traffic outside. Alone in his narrow room, curtains half-drawn, Roy sat bathed in the cold blue light of his phone, the world beyond his window unaware that its next deception had already begun.

The video began with grainy footage of darkened skyscrapers, emergency lights flickering, then a sudden, all-encompassing blackout. A caption crawled across the bottom: Project Blue Beam — The Greatest Hoax. The narrator's voice was calm, conspiratorial, and Roy felt his pulse quicken not from fear but from the peculiar, magnetic curiosity that always came before a plunge.

They spoke of artisans and technicians — teams so skilled they could stitch light into faith. When the internet fails and the power dies, these craftsmen would orchestrate a spectacle so convincing, so universal, that the world would lift its face and see God. Or gods. A second coming tailored to every tongue and creed: Christ in one district, Krishna in another, Allah in a cloud that shimmered with Arabic script, Buddha in meditative light

— a bespoke divinity for every person who looked up and searched for an answer.

Roy swallowed. The words from his Sabbath School lessons slipped into his mind like a jagged stone into still water. "And for this cause God shall send them strong delusion, that they should believe a lie" (2 Thessalonians 2:11). He had always thought of delusion as something private, a whispered lie in the recesses of a person's heart. This video made deceit feel industrial, global, engineered.

He paused the footage and stared at the ceiling. Outside, the evening deepened, normal and indifferent. But a thin thread of dread had been tugged. The idea that sight could be commandeered, that light could dress itself as truth — felt like a violation of something sacred and primal. How much of faith depended on sight? How many souls had anchored their certainty to the evidence of their eyes rather than to the quiet commandments laid down on stone tablets?

Roy's thoughts drifted to the Sabbath — to that simple, defiant rhythm of rest and reverence written in Exodus, the fourth commandment that had burnt in his young mind like a lantern. He remembered the words about remembering the Sabbath day and keeping it holy, the cadence of Creation echoing in the instruction. Somewhere along the way the world had shifted its worship to another day, “church” had been scheduled to fit convenience, and the Sabbath had retreated to the margins for many. Those decisions, he’d been taught were not merely liturgical; they were moral signposts, markers of allegiance.

If a spectacle in the sky could simulate the second coming, what else could be used to move hearts? The narrator in the video didn’t talk about theology; he talked about leverage. He spoke of a future moment when a law would be passed; a Sunday decree; and how such a law could become the pressure point that revealed men’s hearts. Roy had read the pamphlets in the church foyer about the Sunday Law, about conscience and compulsion, that many had dismissed them as alarmist. Now, though, the pieces felt less like hyperbole and more like a map.

The next morning, Roy shared what he’d seen with Malcolm over coffee in the small Angeles House kitchen. "Hey, Malcolm," Roy said, "the second coming of Jesus Christ will come through the Orion Nebula at a speed a hundred times faster than the speed of light. As He approaches Earth's atmosphere, a visible dark cloud the size of a man's fist will appear, and as He draws closer every eye will see Him as the lightning shining from the east to the west. Thus, we shall see the Son of Man come with billions of angels; a fiery stream will issue before Him to slay the wicked, the trumpet shall sound, and the dead in Christ shall rise from their graves after a massive earthquake rocks the earth like a drunkard. 'For the Lord himself shall descend from heaven with a shout, with the voice of the archangel, and with the trump of God: and the dead in Christ shall rise first: Then we which are alive and remain shall be caught up together with them in the clouds, to meet the Lord in the air: and so shall we ever be with the Lord' (1 Thessalonians 4:16–17 KJV). No Project Blue Beam, Roy told Malcolm, will be able to duplicate the spectacular return of Jesus Christ."

Roy and Malcolm had recently enrolled in **The Urban Ministry Institute (TUMI),** and the subject of the Day of Global Rest entering the discourse of the weekly lessons was not unexpected. The sixteen-week Mission program shaped future leaders for the streets of Los Angeles—where faith had to walk as well as speak. Its lessons blended theology with social justice, and present duty with end-time prophecy. So, when talk turned to the coming Day of Global Rest, it felt less like a shock and more like a confirmation. At one of the classes the discussion on days of rest, Sunday worship and the Sabbath became the center of debate. For men who had survived hardship, it was more than education — it was a calling, a way to find purpose again and although discussions such as these were sometimes uncomfortable, Roy, and to a lesser extent, Malcolm, were able to articulate their importance, and their central meaning to what was transpiring both in America and around the world.

On one particular afternoon, during a module on Revelation and the Sabbath, the atmosphere in the classroom grew charged. The instructor's lesson turned toward prophecy and the final conflict between truth and deception. The timing felt uncanny: media outlets everywhere were debating the **National Sunday Law**, a bill said to promote "unity, moral renewal, and ecological balance."

Roy listened intently, sensing tension ripple through the room. The question pressing on every heart was unspoken but heavy: *What if prophecy is unfolding before our eyes?*

For Roy, this wasn't abstract theology. It was a living truth that intersected with his own vision for *Jerusalem WON* — a vision about faith under fire. Malcolm, sitting a few rows back, caught Roy's glance. Both men knew this discussion was about more than doctrine; it was a glimpse into battles that would soon leave the classroom behind.

Roy sat forward, his eyes bright with conviction. The air seemed to hum. Around him were men and women who had walked through Skid Row with scars and hope in equal measure. Across the room sat Chaplain Ray, a calm figure in his sixties whose weathered hands and gentle eyes had steadied many storms. His open Bible rested before him like an anchor.

Unable to hold back, Roy rose. His voice rang clear — not angry, but urgent. “The National Sunday Sabbath law is more than legislation,” he said. “It’s a direct attack on faith — on us who keep the seventh day holy! This isn’t just politics; this is prophecy unfolding!”

Uneasy murmurs spread. A man with a tattooed cross on his forearm nodded slowly. Another whispered a prayer.

Chaplain Ray folded his hands and met Roy’s gaze. “Roy,” he said gently, “I understand your concern. The Bible warns of trials, yes — but it also speaks of redemption, of peace, of love casting out fear.”

From the back, a younger voice trembled. “But what about Revelation 13? It says those who refuse the mark of the beast will suffer. Isn’t that what’s happening now?”

The room went still. Even the traffic outside seemed to hush.

Chairs creaked. Pages rustled. Anxiety spread like wind before a storm. Roy could feel it — the same tension that had filled the airwaves since the proposal of a Sunday day of rest was first mentioned. He stepped forward, pacing before the whiteboard.

"This isn't about choosing a *day*," he said, his voice rising. "It's about choosing allegiance. The mark isn't just a number — it's loyalty to man's authority over God's. When we accept Sunday as law, we're accepting deception dressed as peace!"

Gasps followed. Someone muttered, "Lord, have mercy."

Chaplain Ray lifted his hand, calm but firm. "Roy, fear cannot lead us. If we serve through fear, we lose the heart of the Gospel. Christ called us to love, even in the face of persecution."

Roy's voice softened, but his conviction did not. "Love doesn't exempt us from truth, Chaplain. The law of God hasn't changed. The world is shifting fast, and the mark isn't just coming — it's forming in the minds of men even now. We have to be awake."

Ray looked at him for a long moment, then said quietly, "Faith without love becomes judgment. But love without faith becomes compromise. Perhaps our task is to hold to both."

The words lingered.

Roy drew a slow breath. "When that law becomes universal — when obedience to government conflicts with obedience to God — we'll all have to decide where we stand. That choice is coming sooner than we think."

From the corner, a whisper slipped out: “I don’t want to die.”

The phrase struck the room like a bell.

Roy turned toward the voice. “It’s not just about dying,” he said softly. “It’s about living — for truth, for the ones who come after us. If we yield now, what will our children inherit? If we stand firm, they’ll remember faith, not fear.”

Chaplain Ray nodded slowly. “Then let’s prepare,” he said. “Not with anger, but with prayer. Let every heart be ready and let every act be born of peace.”

The class ended not with debate but with silence — a holy kind of stillness that drives men to introspection and prayer.

Roy lingered as the others filed out. At the front of the room, a wooden cross hung above the whiteboard, its shadow stretching long across the floor, dividing light from darkness.

He stared at it for a long time. The flickering fluorescent bulb overhead buzzed faintly, the sound of a weary world on the edge of change. He didn’t have all the answers, but one truth burned within him like fire:

‘The battle lines were being drawn.’

Chapter 24

Decree and Defiance

Far from the Mission classroom, storm clouds gathered over Washington, D.C. The skyline shimmered beneath a churning sky as lightning flashed over the White House. Inside the Oval Office, the tension was just as heavy.

President Trump, now in his mid-seventies, sat behind the historic Resolute Desk. His posture was confident, but his eyes carried something deeper — a fusion of determination and destiny. Around him stood his closest advisors, faces half-lit by the glow of storm light through the windows.

"This is our moment," Trump said, leaning forward, his voice low and firm. "We have the chance to reshape this nation — to fulfill the vision."

One advisor hesitated. "But sir, the backlash from the public..."

Trump cut him off. "The public doesn't see what we see. They don't understand prophecy."

Across town, in a dimly lit church, a group of Christian nationalists gathered in fervent prayer. The air was thick with candle smoke and conviction. At the pulpit stood a man in his fifties, his voice ringing through the sanctuary.

"We are on the brink!" he declared. "The signs are clear! The time has come for the faithful to rise and fulfill prophecy!"

The congregation roared in unison, "Amen!" Their voices rose like a wave.

Outside, in the streets of D.C., protests erupted. Hundreds marched — young and old, black and white — carrying signs, chanting, demanding answers. Across the avenue, supporters of **Project 2025** raised their own banners, their shouts matching the oppositions with equal fervor. The two crowds clashed not yet with violence, but with raw emotion.

In a secure government operations center not far from the Capitol, intelligence officers watched the chaos unfold across multiple screens. Reports poured in by the minute — from churches, protests, and encrypted online channels. A digital map flickered with heat points marking unrest.

"If this keeps up," one officer warned, "we could be looking at civil unrest like we haven't seen in decades."

His colleague nodded grimly. "And how do we stop a movement that believes it's divinely ordained?"

Back in the Oval Office, Trump stood at the window, watching the lights of police cruisers flash against the storm. His reflection started back older, grayer, but resolute.

“I think,” he said quietly, “we are very much near the end of time.”

Lightning cracked.

Thousands of miles away, Jerusalem lay under a calm night sky. The ancient walls glowed softly beneath the moon. In a quiet study, a circle of rabbis gathered around sacred scrolls.

“The signs are all around us,” one said. “Nations are aligning, as foretold.”

Another nodded gravely. “We must prepare for what’s coming.”

Back in Washington, Trump turned from the window, eyes blazing. “We will lead them,” he said. “They may not understand now, but history will. This is prophecy unfolding before our eyes — and we have been chosen to stand in this moment.”

A heavy silence followed. One advisor spoke hesitantly. “But at what cost, Mr. President? To lead in prophecy is to invite the judgment of nations.”

Trump's lips tightened into something between a smirk and a grim smile. "Every great chapter of history is written with sacrifice," he said. "The question is not whether there will be a cost, but whether we are willing to pay it."

Across town, the church's chants grew thunderous. "We are the chosen!" voices cried, echoing off the rafters — not just worship but defiance, a declaration that heaven itself had taken sides.

Outside, the city pulsed with unrest. Protesters pressed against barricades; police lines tightened. The air smelled of rain, sweat, and fear. A bottle shattered against a shield. Sirens wailed.

Inside the national intelligence center, the glow of screens illuminated tense faces.

"Civil volatility index just spiked," one analyst reported. "We've got simultaneous unrest in three cities. Patterns suggest coordination."

"Activate Joint Task Coordination," came the order. "Eyes on all leadership networks — political and religious."

Protocols engaged. Across the country, chaos deepened.

In the Oval Office, Trump stood once more before the Resolute Desk. He reached for the worn Bible resting beside a

stack of intelligence briefings and lifted it slowly.
"This," he said, his voice unwavering, "is our sword. We fight not against men, but for the divine purpose of this land."

For a fleeting moment, the room felt charged with something greater than power — as though heaven itself leaned near. Yet even as the words left his lips, the counsel of lesser men lingered in the corridors beyond the door — voices skilled in strategy but strangers to faith. They would soon press upon him with reason, data, and compromise, dulling what the Spirit had kindled.

Outside the White House, the storm broke — lightning flaring over the city as thunder rolled across the Potomac. And in that trembling light, America seemed to hold its breath — balanced on the thin, quivering edge between prophecy and judgment.

While chaos and prophecy stirred in the nation's capital, in a quiet Baltimore neighborhood, Dr. James Lee stood outside his small house, holding a weathered notebook in his hand. The golden hues of evening bathed the street in a soft glow, birds calling from the trees as if unaware of the turmoil gripping the world. A gentle breeze moved through the leaves, but inside Dr. Lee's chest, a storm was building.

In his study, sheet music and half-written lyrics lay scattered across his desk. The room felt heavy, the air taut with unspoken frustration. His phone buzzed — a message from Roy, sharp and insistent. Roy was asking for The Epic, the collaborative masterpiece they had once poured their hearts into.

The request struck James like a blow. *Return it?* he thought. *After all these years? After everything?* The music wasn't just notes and rhythm — it was survival, meaning, memory. His reply came quick and defensive, a mix of wounded pride and old resentment.

Three thousand miles away, Roy stood on the shoreline, the sea roaring before him and the city lights flickering behind — caught between the peace of creation and the noise of man. He stared down at his phone, the glow of the screen reflecting in his eyes. The message from James struck like a wave breaking hard against stone. The project had been their shared dream — a labor of friendship and faith.

He read the message again and felt his stomach twist. How could James see it any other way? His heart thudded with disbelief as he began typing, reminding his old friend of the years they had poured into *The Epic*, of the nights when prayer and melody had become one.

His fingers trembled as he typed back, reminding James of the years they had built *The Epic* together, of the nights when music and prayer had merged into one.

James read the reply and scoffed. To him, it felt hollow, patronizing even. He shot back another message, which was colder, sharper — declaring he was done.

Back in his room now, Roy sat down at his desk, his hands clenched around the phone. His voice trembled as he whispered aloud, "After everything..." It wasn't just a project. It was ministry, prophecy, legacy. To lose it now felt like betrayal.

He sent one more message, a plea rather than a defense: *Don't throw this away. Please.*

In Baltimore, James paced, his thoughts clashing like cymbals. He had always respected Roy's vision, but somewhere along the way he'd felt overshadowed, misunderstood. His creative spark had turned to ash under the weight of unspoken tension. He stopped, staring at Roy's last message. The anger ebbed. The night sky had deepened; stars pierced the dark. Slowly, something within him began to shift.

Meanwhile, Roy stared at a faded photograph pinned to his wall — the two of them in the studio years ago, laughing, sleeves rolled up, surrounded by microphones and sheet music. That memory softened his anger. He typed again — this time not in frustration but humility: *Without The Epic, I can't move forward. Please send it back. I won't ask again.*

James sat down, his heart heavy. He read the words twice, then a third time. The bitterness faded into sadness. He typed quietly, *I'll return it, but I'm finished. I can't do this anymore.*

Roy read the message with a sigh that seemed to drain him. It felt final. He typed one more reply — simple, regretful. *I wish it hadn't come to this.*

When James read it, his jaw tightened, then softened. His thumbs hovered before typing back: *I'm sorry for my part in this. I hope your vision comes to life.*

Roy's eyes welled. He replied gently: *Let's not end in anger. Whatever happens, I wish you peace.*

A tear slid down James's cheek. He whispered to the empty room, "And to you."

He lingered a moment longer, then placed his phone aside and sat at his piano. A blank sheet of music waited before him. His fingers touched the keys softly, forming new notes — not of conflict, but of release.

Across the country, Roy opened his laptop and began outlining a new version of *The Epic*. The melodies came slower now, deeper, tempered by loss. It would carry a different tone — one of longing, redemption, and hope. The dream wasn't dead; it was simply being reborn.

In the stillness that followed, the noise of the world narrowed to the quiet ache between two men—once united by vision, now divided by pride. Roy stood between the peace of creation and the noise of man, realizing that even sacred callings can fracture when human emotion overshadows divine purpose. Yet within that breaking, God was still at work. Like the tide reshaping the shore, loss was giving way to transformation. *The Epic* would continue—not as it began, but as it must—refined by fire, reborn through faith.

As Roy gazed upon the restless sea, his private struggle mirrored the unrest of the nations. Pride and prophecy were converging; men grasped for control while the Creator still whispered, *"Be still, and know that I am God."* In the silence between heaven and earth, the fracture between friends became a symbol of a larger truth—the tension between man's ambition and God's unyielding will.

The world, too, was being called to its shoreline. Soon it would face the same choice: to stand upon the rock of obedience or to be swept away by the tide of compromise.

"And the rain descended, the floods came, and the winds blew and beat upon that house; and it fell not, for it was founded upon a rock." *(Matthew 7:25)*

"Thou wilt keep him in perfect peace, whose mind is stayed on Thee: because he trusteth in Thee." *(Isaiah 26:3)*

The wind howled across the water, then quieted. The city lights shimmered like candles in the dark. And in that stillness—between the hum of man and the whisper of God—Roy closed his eyes. The storm had not yet come, but its shadow was lengthening.

The dream was not dead. It was simply transforming.

The city outside Angeles House slept that night, but Roy's spirit could not.

The debate with Dr. James Lee had ended hours ago, yet its echoes still reverberated through his mind like distant thunder. He had faced the machinery of human reason — sharp, proud, and certain — and glimpsed the shadow behind it. The confrontation had not been about music, nor theology, nor even the Sabbath; it had been about authority. Whose voice would define truth when the world began to tremble?

Roy's heart stirred with unease. He felt as though the veil of ordinary life had thinned, as if something vast and ancient pressed close to the fabric of his room, waiting to be revealed.

That was when the Holy Spirit came — not in a gentle whisper, but in a presence so absolute it left no space for doubt.

Chapter 25

Revelation at Angeles House

Roy sat on the edge of his chair in his room at Angeles House when the Holy Spirit came upon him with a clarity that brooked no argument. The revelation unfolded in short, terrible truths. They did not come from distant galaxies. They fell from heaven. What the world now called "aliens" were the same beings ancient texts named gods and the Bible calls fallen angels. Their names change. Their symbols evolve. But their mission has not: to deceive, to dominate, to be worshiped. They want you looking into the stars, chasing false light—gods who never made you. The Spirit showed him staged fury and convenient lies. ISIS was not merely a terrorist organization; it was a smoke screen, a convenient cover for the destruction of ancient relics, temples, and sites that held knowledge predating the Abrahamic traditions—knowledge older than empires. They filmed themselves smashing statues and burning libraries under the guise of zealous purging, but the real goal was erasure: to shatter the last remaining links to the truth of humanity's origins, to the gods we once knew and the beings who ruled over us. Is it any wonder that mankind's earliest civilizations—Sumer and Mesopotamia, Assyria and Babylon, the Levant—are now perpetual war zones? Places so volatile that legitimate archaeological digs are impossible. Every bombed-out ruin, every toppled ziggurat is another layer of truth buried in dust. The war is not just for oil or land; it is for memory. It is for history. The fallen knows this: if we remember who we are, we might remember who they are. Long ago they descended from the heavens—the Anunnaki in Sumer, the Watchers in Enoch, the "sons of God" in Genesis 6. They brought forbidden knowledge. They altered human DNA. They taught war, enchantment, and astrology. They demanded blood in return. When God flooded the earth, it was not only to punish mankind; it was to cleanse the corrupted kingdom these beings had established. But they never left—they changed tactics. Throughout history they ruled behind thrones and within temples. They gave kings their crowns and built religions in their image. And their most enduring stronghold? The Roman Catholic Church. A spiritual system that absorbed the rites and architecture of Babylon. Pinecones—symbols of spiritual control—stand in the Vatican courtyard. The papal staff and the mitre carried echoes of an older faith — the fish-crowned visage of Dagon, the god of Babylon, reborn beneath new robes.

This is not the simple church Jesus found; it is a replacement, a spiritual empire designed to mimic Christ and lead millions away from the truth. But in the twentieth century something changed. In 1947 something fell from the sky near

Roswell, New Mexico. The official story twisted within days—weather balloon, flying disc, weather balloon again. Behind the scenes, the truth was locked down and a secret group formed: Majestic Twelve. Majestic Twelve – known in classified circles as '**MAJIC-12**' – was not merely a committee; it marked a ritual handoff of earthly power from religious hierarchy to technocratic empire. The fallen, who had long ruled through temples and thrones, now embedded themselves within the very machinery of modern governance—not through altars but through briefings, not with idols but through aerospace, defense, and intelligence.

Majestic Twelve became the new priesthood; its members became the gatekeepers of forbidden knowledge. The Vatican still held spiritual sway over billions, but now the Pentagon and Langley were added to the network—two horns rising together. They reestablished communication with the same beings who had corrupted mankind. Through this network the fallen controlled both church and state. The pope spoke of unity while generals prepared for global governance—two branches, one agenda: to rule, deceive, and prepare humanity for a false kingdom. And just as they built false religions to pull people from God, they now built false ideologies to do the same. Ancient-aliens theory is not merely a quirky idea; it's a modern form of heresy repackaged. It teaches that we were created by extraterrestrials, that the gods of old were visitors, that humanity's purpose lies in evolution guided by off-world engineers. It replaces God with programmers and architects, sin with ignorance, redemption with technology. This is not science; it is Luciferianism branded for the digital age. When someone uncovers the truth—when civilization advances in ways forbidden by the new order, when archaeologists find architecture older than what authorities allow—those discoveries are destroyed, defunded, deplatformed, and discredited. To admit those structures, exist is to admit there was a kingdom before ours, to admit the Watchers were real, that the Bible was right, and that God Himself exists. Revelation tells us that the great dragon was hurled down—the ancient serpent called the devil and Satan, who leads the whole world astray. They did not come in fire. They came in light. They came offering peace, knowledge, and unity. Through government and churches, ideologies and entertainment, technology and ritual, they no longer need to be seen; they need only to be obeyed. The deception was never about green men in space. It was about taking worship from the Most High and redirecting it to the fallen. They do not want to invade; they want to be worshiped. For most of the world, they already are. Roy felt the weight of the revelation settle into him like stone. The Spirit offered no comfort—only a warning: remember, and do not be seduced by the false lights they set before you.

As the vision dimmed, a calm unlike any other filled the room. Roy's thoughts drifted to the Christian Assembly's annual men's retreat at **Forest Home;** a picturesque mountain refuge tucked deep in the **San Bernardino highlands in California**. Quiet and spiritual, its rustic cabins nestled among towering Jeffrey pines and incense cedars, the air cool and fragrant with resin and morning mist, a place where time itself seemed to pause so that men could listen for the voice of God. It was there, through the generosity of his friend **Gregg**, that eleven Servant Leadership men from the Union Rescue Mission had been given a chance to draw nearer to the Lord. For Roy, that retreat had marked a turning point; the moment when the Holy Spirit came softly, a whisper through the trees, calling him deeper into faith.

Now, in the stillness of Angeles House, that same Spirit thundered through him like living fire. **The stillness had been the quiet continuance of his anointing; this was its awakening.**

The night after the revelation at Angeles House was unlike any other. It was as though heaven itself had opened a portal above the city, and the unseen realm pressed close against the trembling earth. The winds moved strangely, carrying a stillness before the storm—a silence that was alive with expectancy. Roy could feel the pulse of something vast and unseen, a convergence between prophecy and reality.

In the vision that followed, the world appeared as a great tapestry stretched across the heavens—threads of light and shadow interwoven through time. Nations flickered like candles in the night, their flames bending as unseen forces contended for dominion. The cries of the faithful rose like incense, while the powers of darkness gathered in furious resistance. The battle was no longer confined to spirit alone—it had entered the realm of men.

Roy stood in the midst of this unfolding panorama, knowing that what he had witnessed at Angeles House was not the end of revelation but the beginning of demonstration. The truth entrusted to him was destined to confront the counterfeit kingdoms of the earth. The signs of heaven would soon collide with the skepticism of the world, and the voice of the Spirit would thunder above the noise of nations.

He understood now that the revelation must move from vision to manifestation. The time for silence had ended; the time for divine proof had come. The world was about to witness what no man could orchestrate and no power could contain.

The heavens were preparing to testify, and earth would stand as witness.

The demonstration was about to begin—and the turning point of prophecy was near.

Chapter 26

The Demonstration to the World and the Vision Turning Point

The air in the makeshift studio at the URM Angeles House hung heavy with anticipation, the faint scent of mint tea mingling with the musty pages of Roy's well-worn Bible. He sat at the cluttered table, surrounded by a chaotic array of notes, drafts, and a laptop that buzzed with life. It was a command center for a mission that felt both divinely inspired and intensely personal. The walls around him echoed with whispers of the past the laughter of family, the prayers shared with Tara, now lost in the tides of time.

Beside him, Malcolm scrolled through the latest edits for Jerusalem WON: Signed In Blood, his brow furrowed in concentration. The book was taking shape, a tapestry of prophecy interwoven with the urgent cries of a world on the brink. “Roy,” Malcolm said, breaking the silence, “have you thought about the orchestral score for the performance? The emotional depth of the music is going to be key.”

Roy nodded, his mind racing back to Dr. James Lee, and his heart sank. “I spoke with Dr. Lee yesterday. He’s tied up with his commitments at Morgan State. We need someone with a broader vision, someone who can capture the weight of what we're trying to convey in the symphony."

"John Williams," Malcolm suggested, half-jokingly. "I mean, if you can dream it, why not?"

Roy chuckled, but the thought lingered. "Why not? If we want this to resonate with the world, we need a composer who understands the power of cinematic music. Williams could bring the gravitas we need."

As they continued to work, Roy's thoughts drifted to the prophetic chapter they were drafting. The vision of the 144,000 singers rising before the Israeli Defense Forces felt like a dream that was inching closer to reality. He could almost hear their voices, a collective sound of hope, courage, and divine intervention echoing through the valleys of conflict.

"Picture it, Malcolm," Roy said, his voice a fervent whisper. "As the armies of Iran, Russia, and the Muslim confederacy encircle Israel, the 144,000 will stand with their harps and voices raised, singing the Song of Moses and the Song of the Lamb in Hebrew. God will set ambushment against the enemies of Israel, and fire and brimstone will rain down from heaven; the earth will tremble. It's a moment that will change everything."

Malcolm leaned back in his chair, eyes wide with the weight of the vision. "It could be a turning point. God will fight for His people, just as He always has," he said.

Roy's determination solidified. "Then it's our job to prepare the hearts of the people. To make them ready for what's coming. If we can get the message out if we can rally support for the symphony and the documentary the world will hear the truth."

The weeks that followed were a blur of activity. Roy and Malcolm mapped out a plan to reach out to John Williams. They crafted a proposal that outlined the vision for The Epic, emphasizing the importance of the orchestral score in conveying the emotion of the narrative. Each note would be a thread woven into the fabric of the prophecy they were heralding.

As the outreach began, Roy felt a renewed sense of purpose. He couldn't shake the feeling that they were on the cusp of something monumental. But with that excitement came the weight of reality. His relationship with Tara was a distant memory, a casualty of their shared mission. She had chosen her path, and though they still worked together, the bond they once shared was now a flickering ember, overshadowed by the urgency of The Epic.

The following week, there was a meeting with John Williams' team. The atmosphere buzzed with excitement and anxiety as Roy and Malcolm entered the luxurious Hollywood studio, adorned with gold records and memorabilia. They were ushered into a conference room, where Williams himself sat, a figure of creative genius, his presence commanding yet approachable.

"Welcome, gentlemen," John said, a warm smile spreading across his face. "I've heard intriguing things about your project. Tell me about your vision."

Roy felt the weight of his words as he spoke, sharing the story of the 144,000 singers, the orchestral score that would accompany the prophetic unfolding in Israel. He painted a vivid picture of the symphony, how it would serve as a rallying cry for hope and faith in tumultuous times.

As he spoke, he caught the glimmer of interest in Williams' eyes. "This isn't just music," Roy said passionately. "It's a divine calling. We believe it can inspire a movement, a world awakening to the truth of God's plan."

Williams leaned back, contemplating. "You're aiming for something profound, something that transcends traditional performance. It's ambitious, but I sense a deep sincerity in your mission." Silence enveloped the room, and Roy held his breath.

Williams nodded slowly. "I'm intrigued. Let's explore how we can bring this vision to life. I want to understand the emotional core of what you're aiming for."

Days turned into weeks as they worked closely with Williams and his team. The music began to take shape a blend of orchestral grandeur and haunting melodies that echoed the themes of struggle, redemption, and divine intervention. Each note was crafted with precision, aimed at stirring the hearts of those who would hear it.

But amidst the creative process, the world outside continued to unravel. News reports streamed in about rising tensions in the Middle East, the threat of war looming ever closer. Roy's heart ached with the knowledge that the prophecy they were bringing to life was not merely a story it was a reality that was unfolding before their eyes.

Back at Angeles House, Roy gathered his core team. "We need to prepare our community for what's coming," he said, urgency lacing his voice. "The 144,000 singers will be a beacon of hope, but we need to ensure they know the truth behind the prophecy and how will we support them spiritually?"

Malcolm nodded, his expression serious. "We need to organize meetings; workshops to teach them about the prophecies in Ezekiel and Revelation. Equip them with knowledge so they can stand firm in their faith."

Roy agreed, feeling the weight of their mission. "Let's also prepare for the backlash. We know the enemy will not sit idly by. We must be ready to defend our message and stand united."

As they planned, Roy felt a stirring in his spirit a sense of urgency that echoed like a drumbeat in his chest. The world was on the brink of chaos, but they were poised to shine a light in the darkness. They would rally the faithful, prepare the singers, and share the message of hope that God had entrusted to them.

With each passing day, the symphony grew closer to completion, and with it, the reality of their prophetic mission loomed larger. Roy knew they were in a race against time, but he also knew that in faith and unity, they would prevail.

Yet *The Epic* was never meant to be confined to sound alone. Behind the scenes, a small but determined technical team—handpicked by Roy and his closest advisors—worked tirelessly to bring the vision to life through film. Cameras, storyboards, and production notes filled the studio walls as they prepared to document the unfolding creation in real time. The goal was not simply to produce a symphony, but to bear witness—to capture, for all the world to see, the divine thread that wove through each note, each struggle, each prayer.

The project had become something greater than art. It was testimony—a living chronicle of redemption told through music and motion, faith and film.

And as the days grew darker beyond their walls, Roy understood that this wasn't just about composing a masterpiece. It was about arranging a message for a world on the brink of forgetting its Maker.

Roy felt the weight of responsibility settle on his shoulders. With every crescendo and every haunting melody, he realized that the music they created must carry a purpose far greater than artistic achievement. The composition was meant to awaken hearts, to remind humanity of its divine origin and calling. As chaos threatened to engulf the world outside, Roy's vision sharpened: the symphony would not simply be a work of art, but a vessel for truth, hope, and spiritual awakening. In the midst of uncertainty and upheaval, his mission became clear—to craft a message that would reach beyond the confines of their community, stirring the souls of those who had begun to lose sight of the Creator.

Meanwhile in the Middle East and Far East, the Doomsday Clock ticked… seconds away from midnight. The earth glowed with unnatural fire. From the vastness of space, it looked like many parts of the planet were in agony. Huge mushroom clouds covered these areas, almost as a premonition of what was yet to come. The Doomsday Clock, symbolic but prophetic, struck midnight.

Then chaos! The camera descended to a burning city. Screams rang out in the night. Sirens wailed. People ran through the streets as buildings crumbled and vehicles exploded. Fires fell from the sky, igniting everything they touched. It was as if the heavens had declared war on the earth.

"Sunlight disappears behind the mushroom cloud of the first nuclear explosions, leaving death and destruction everywhere."

Newsrooms around the world scrambled. Anchors appeared on screens, shaken and barely composed. Footage of devastation played behind them; ruined cities, wounded children, desperate survivors.

"This is the deadliest blast of nuclear explosions since World War II" one anchor said, her voice cracking. "Approximately three and a half billion people are estimated to be dead."

The death toll was unimaginable.

The world trembled.

And it wasn't over.

Multiple explosions followed. The earth itself seemed to groan under pressure. Mountains cracked. Oceans surged. Entire cities collapsed like sandcastles.

"The worst is still yet to come," another anchor warned. "The earth rocks like a drunkard, and no pen has ever told of the horrors we are witnessing."

More scenes of destruction flashed: blood flooding the streets, entire neighborhoods engulfed in fire, families crying in the rubble.

"Ominous signs of destruction are everywhere; there is no escape from the tragedy."

Emergency services were helpless. Sirens wailed, but they couldn't cut through the chaos. Ambulances were blocked. Hospitals were overrun. Firefighters fell to their knees, overwhelmed.

"Emergency services could never imagine the scale of this disaster," one reporter stated. "The entire planet is in danger of collapse."

In the middle of this unfolding nightmare, world leaders tried to speak to their people.

Inside **Air Force One**, enroute to the Vatican for his historic meeting with **Pope Leo**, the President sat before the cameras. The cabin lights were dimmed, the sky outside bruised with storms. His face appeared across millions of screens—tired, resolute, and lined with the weight of nations.

“My fellow Americans,” he began, his voice low but unwavering, “the world is trembling, and the earth itself seems to groan beneath the weight of what has come upon us. Yet I tell you this—we are not without hope. For every shaking in history has been followed by renewal, and every storm has given way to the dawn.”

He looked directly into the camera, eyes firm. “We are Americans—men and women born in liberty, tempered in struggle, and called to stand when others fall. We have faced darkness before, and by God’s grace, we will face this one together.”

The screen flickered as he leaned forward. “Let us not be divided by fear or hatred. Let us remember who we are—a nation under God. Let us lift our eyes from the ashes and look again toward the light. Because though the world falters, the promise of truth remains.”

His final words were steady, almost prayerful. “May this nation be again that city on a hill—shining not in pride, but in purpose. A light for the world to see, and a testament that even in chaos, faith endures.”

As the feed ended, lightning cracked beyond the aircraft window, illuminating the presidential seal—a reminder that kingdoms rise and fall, but the Word of God stands forever.

Roy turned off the television, the President's closing words echoing in his mind: *"A city on a hill..."*
He sat in silence for a long moment, the hum of the Mission generator filling the room. To most, the speech was a call for unity; to Roy, it was a signpost. He reached for his Bible and opened to Revelation 14—the passage that had shaped his calling and his message for years.

The **Three Angels' Messages** weren't merely warnings; they were Heaven's final appeal to humanity.
The first proclaimed the everlasting gospel—calling all to *"Fear God, and give glory to Him; for the hour of His judgment is come."*
The second declared, *"Babylon is fallen,"* exposing the corruption of systems that traded truth for power.
And the third warned against worshiping the beast and receiving his mark—a solemn reminder that allegiance, not appearance, defines the faithful.

To Roy, these weren't relics of prophecy—they were headlines of a spiritual reality now breaking into the world stage. The global rest mandate, the political sermons of unity, the merging of church and state—all of it echoed the very message he had spent his life trying to explain.

He whispered under his breath, *"Fear God, and give Him glory."* It was no longer a sermon. It was a summons.

In Rome, the Pope stood before a flickering crowd in St. Peter's Square, dim lights creating dancing shadows on the cobblestones, like stars clinging to earth. As he watched the crowd his thoughts turned to his anticipated announcement about Sunday worship; a decree that would be made with the leader of the free world beside him."

"We must turn back to God for the common good," he thought. "I must decree that Sunday shall be a day of rest a chance for reflection and repentance. It is the only way to bring the world back from the edge." His thoughts sent a shiver across his body as the realization of what this meant, a spark that would ignite protests across the globe.

From space, the Earth looked scorched and broken. Fires raged across the surface like angry scars. Yet amid the destruction, something began to awaken. *In the heart of the chaos, a quiet revival was taking root within the souls of many.*

"In the midst of this turmoil, a spiritual awakening began to stir within the hearts of many."

Inside dimly lit churches, people gathered. Some wept. Some sang. All prayed. One minister stood before his congregation, his voice steady and full of fire. "We must seek refuge in faith," he cried. "God is our only hope in this dark hour!"

Outside, the streets were still chaos. But inside those sacred walls, a different fire burned; one of hope, unity, and defiance against evil.

"This is it," Roy said to Malcolm. "The Epic docudrama that we anticipated to film in real-time is unfolding before our very eyes, and we are approaching the final conflict, which was prophesied at the end of days."

"The prophecies are true," he whispered to the wind. "But so is God's promise."

In a dramatic turn of events, the scene focuses on the Middle East. The battlefield was still tense, as a massive army surrounded Israel, but this time, the 144,000 singers from all the children of Israel sang boldly before the Israeli Defense Forces. Their voices rose above the tanks and missiles. Their voices echoed in praise the Epic Song of Moses and the Song of the Lamb in Hebrew, just as John Williams had envisioned, which in this unprecedented crisis invoked the wrath of God upon Israel's enemies, and the nations would not profane His name anymore.

It was a prophetic and sobering reminder that the peace of man—celebrated less than six months earlier—was not the peace of God. What had been hailed as unity was now unraveling. International alliances began to fracture, and governments, gripped by fear and desperation, turned to faith as a tool of control. Religious laws swept through legislatures under the banner of moral renewal, but beneath their pious language lay the tremor of prophecy—the warning that human peace, no matter how noble, cannot stand apart from divine truth.

In anticipation of an announcement about Sunday worship, many governments preempted the Popes expected message by issuing directives for this to happen before any Vatican decree; framed as a way to return to peace and moral order. The forced Sunday laws would only be the beginning. Those who kept the true Sabbath on Saturday would start to be treated as threats. The "Three Angels' Messages," long ignored by most churches, would now become points of conflict.

Inside a small church in downtown Long Beach, Roy stood before a group of believers. Some were elderly, some were young. All were afraid.

Roy raised his voice with conviction. "The time has come for us to proclaim the Three Angels' Messages with power and clarity. Babylon is falling. The mark of the beast is being set up in real-time. But we are called to endure."

Those that do not receive the seal of God, which is the sabbath, will be shaken out of the remnant Church because judgement starts first at the House of the Lord (Ezekiel 9) and they will receive the Mark of the Beast and there will be no divine protection when the Holy Spirit is withdrawn and God pours out his wrath of the Seven Bowls judgement as detailed in Revelation (Rev 16: 1-21) the Great Tribulation of the Apocalypse.

He looked at a young woman in the front row, eyes wide and teary. "You may lose jobs. Some of us may lose our freedom," Roy said. "But we will not lose our souls. We stand with Christ." Brothers and sisters "We will not be able to buy or sell unless we submit to worship on Sunday, which is the Mark of the Beast, 666. It tells us this in God's Word in Revelation 13 and Daniel 7, 8, and 11. Brothers and Sisters, there is a connection between modern politics and ancient prophecies; to what we are seeing happening throughout the world right now. But do not be afraid we just need to ask Him to be with us. Let us pray."

"Lord, strengthen us, Keep us faithful. And may we never deny Your truth, no matter the cost."

And His people were listening, not just in this small church community but across the world. Some did not agree, but more and more were beginning to believe that this was not just hysteria it was divine truth.

After church as Roy contemplated the state of the world, Fox News transitioned to scenes in Israel. The scene was just as he imagined it would be; the battlefield was prepared. Armies had surrounded Jerusalem. Russia, Iran, and radical Muslim jihadist forces had gathered. War was imminent.

But in front of Israel's defense forces, the 144,000 Jewish believers stood not with guns but with harps, lyres, and voices ready.

Then God's Maestro raised His hand — not man, but Spirit — and the song began: the Song of Moses and the Song of the Lamb, transcended and engulfed the battlefield, not in English but in ancient Hebrew. The same music Roy had commissioned years earlier. The same words from Scripture. The same symphonic movement from *The Celestial Resonance*. The same words God ordained before time.

"God is doing it. Just like in the days of Jehoshaphat in 2 Chronicles 20:20-23." Roy thought.

In Los Angeles, Roy fell to his knees as the sound swept through him. He heard it not with ears but with soul — the victory hymn of the 144,000, echoing across worlds. Heaven had taken the baton, and the earth trembled beneath its melody.

Around the world, the screens flickered as though Heaven itself had overridden the networks. At Fox News, Bret Baier's voice trembled as he spoke, his usual composure shaken. "Ladies and gentlemen, what we are witnessing defies all explanation. Major military coalitions are collapsing in real time... satellite feeds are failing across entire regions... there are reports of seismic events—massive, simultaneous—stretching from the Middle East to the Pacific."

For a heartbeat, the world held its breath. The footage cut from field correspondents to silent cathedrals, to trembling leaders, to weeping civilians staring skyward.

Then the scene shifted to Rome.

“We go now live to the Vatican,” Baier said, his voice low almost humbling as he waged in his mind what had just happened. The reporter on the ground struggled to speak over the swelling crowd. “There is… new hope here tonight. The Pope is about to address the world following what he has called ‘a divine intervention of peace.’ He is expected to make a historic announcement…”

The camera panned upward toward St. Peter’s Basilica, where floodlights painted the sky in gold and white. Yet somewhere behind the applause, behind the desperate grasp for meaning, the faint echo of the Song still lingered — like thunder retreating into eternity.

Roy closed his eyes. He knew what came next. When men misunderstand miracles, they build monuments to them.

Chapter 27

The Dragon's Decree and the Temple War

The sky over St. Peter's Square in Vatican City was gloomy, casting a cold shadow over the thousands who had gathered, waiting for something historic to happen. Whispers of expectation buzzed through the air, but no one knew exactly what was coming only that it would change everything.

Inside a private room of the Vatican, Pope Leo XIV stood silently by the window, waiting for President Trump, who had just arrived from Washington, D.C. He would represent the so-called "Free World" in a decree that would shake the foundations of faith itself: the proclamation of Sunday as the official day of worship. The decision would not merely mark history; it would echo through eternity. As the Pontiff gazed at the restless crowd gathering in St. Peter's Square, his heart tightened with unease. Today he would preside over a moment that carried the weight of prophecy—a choice that would send reverberations across the ages.

Suddenly, the door opened, and in walked **President Trump**, escorted by **Monsignor Gianluca Ferrari**, the Pope's personal assistant. The President's stride was confident, his smile practiced yet weary—the look of a man accustomed to command but haunted by unseen burdens.

"Your Holiness," Trump said with a grin, "the stage is set. The National Sunday Law will become the foundation of our new world."

From the outside, President Trump appeared resolute. But behind the scenes, the truth was far more complex. Both in his first and now his second term, President Trump had remained surrounded by entrenched Deep State operatives—men and women cloaked in patriotism but bound to the ambitions of the **New World Order**. They had flattered, deceived, and isolated him, feeding on his need for loyalty. A "baby Christian," Trump's faith was sincere but young—rooted in instinct more than doctrine, vulnerable to the very spiritual wolves he mistook for shepherds.

The political circles around him were no better. The Republican establishment, fractured by pride and self-preservation, often worked against his vision. Old political guards traded conviction for compromise, while career staffers angled for promotion and favor from the corporate elite. Even many spiritual leaders in his orbit—men and woman, preaching unity and progress—were steeped in 'new age' mysticism, shaping a contemporary Christianity that replaced the literal Word of God with emotional experience and globalist idealism.

Trump wanted truth and renewal, but the darkness around him disguised control as counsel, prophecy as policy. The very forces he thought he had conquered were now steering him toward the final deception: the fusion of church and state, clothed in the rhetoric of peace.

Pope Leo XIV turned slowly, his voice steady but laced with apprehension.
"Mr. President," he said, "there is much at stake. Are we ready to lead humanity down this road?"

Before Trump could respond, a strange wind howled through the ancient hall. Candles flickered violently, then extinguished as if suffocated by an unseen hand. The temperature dropped. From the darkened archway, a towering figure emerged—cloaked in shadow, eyes burning like molten fire.

It was no mere man, but the Dragon himself—the great deceiver, the very embodiment of Satan, just as Revelation 13 had forewarned.

"You've waited long enough, Pope," the Dragon hissed, its voice echoing like thunder through the marble chamber.

"Declare Sunday holy—not merely by tradition... but by law. The world stands ready."

Pope Leo staggered backward, clutching the edge of the papal throne. "And what... what do you ask in return?"

The Dragon's grin widened. "Only the allegiance of souls. Give me the people. Through you, I will rule."

A wave of dark energy rippled outward. Leo gasped, his body convulsing as an invisible force gripped his spirit. His spine arched; power like molten iron surged through his veins. "This... this isn't what I imagined," he choked. "This power... it burns."

Trump stepped forward, face pale, his instinct for control faltering.
"What the hell is going on?" he demanded, eyes darting between the Pope and the entity before him.

The Dragon turned, its gaze locking on him. "You, too, have been chosen. Lead the people. Enforce the decree. Become the voice of peace—and the hand of judgment."

Trump hesitated. He had stared down dictators, outmaneuvered billionaires, and survived political storms—but this was different. This presence didn't negotiate. **It commanded**!

"And if I refuse?" His voice was quieter now, tinged with a fear he'd never shown on camera.

The Dragon's eyes burned hotter. "Then you refuse order. You refuse unity. Peace must be enforced. Those who resist will be marked as heretics—and they will suffer."

Trump swallowed hard, jaw tightening. A part of him recoiled—but another part, one long accustomed to power, felt the seductive pull of destiny. *Was this divine purpose—or something else entirely?*

He looked to Pope Leo, seeking strength, but found only a trembling man torn between heaven and hell.
"We can't just force it," Trump said finally, his voice wavering. "This isn't how peace is made. It's... too much."

"But it will work," the Dragon said smoothly, circling him. "Isn't that all that matters? You crave order. This is how you achieve it."

Leo's eyes flared with defiance through the torment. "This is madness!" he cried. "Faith cannot be twisted into fear! The Sabbath is not ours to redefine—it belongs to the Lord!"

Trump's voice was uncertain yet searching. "But if the people demand it... if it unites the world..."

The Dragon's laughter rolled like thunder. "Is it unity, or control, Mr. President? The lines blur when your empire teeters."

Leo fell to one knee, trembling. "No," he whispered. "I will not call what is evil good. I will not yield my soul."

The Dragon's expression darkened. "Then suffer. And let the people suffer with you."

Trump stepped back, shaken. "What are you saying?"

"The Law will be enforced—with or without your blessing," the Dragon growled. "The game has begun. A game of souls—and it will not wait for your conscience."

A heavy silence followed. The storm outside raged, rattling the cathedral windows. Trump stood motionless, caught between fear and fatalism. He knew something irreversible had begun—but still didn't grasp its source.

Pope Leo slowly rose; his eyes filled with sorrow. "This is not how faith should be used," he said.

Suddenly the chamber doors burst open. Cardinals rushed in, pale and breathless.

"Your Holiness! The people are waiting—they demand your decree!"

Leo looked toward the balcony, shoulders sagging. He turned to Trump one last time. The President's face showed no triumph—only weary resignation.

Trump nodded once. This time, it wasn't confidence. It was surrender.

"Very well," said Pope Leo quietly. "I will speak—but not through fear. I will speak through love."

He stepped onto the balcony, greeted by the roar of thousands. Trump stood behind him, still and uncertain. The air around them pulsed with unseen power—the Dragon's influence heavy in the wind.

"My beloved children," Pope Leo proclaimed, his voice echoing through St. Peter's Square, "today we declare Sunday a **National Day of Worship**—a day for unity and reflection!"

The crowd erupted with applause. But scattered among them, the faithful whispered prayers of warning, sensing that something sacred had been profaned.

Trump leaned close and murmured, "We're changing the world."

The Pope's answer came low and trembling. "Yes... but at what cost?"

The sun was rising over Los Angeles, painting the city in gold, but Roy felt only the weight of a spiritual darkness creeping across the land. Outside Angeles House, he watched people come and go—many burdened, many broken. The sight reminded him why he had begun this journey in the first place. Not merely to expose deception, but to shine light into places shadowed by despair.

Later, in the community room, Roy sat with a small group of men, their stories of loss and struggle echoing in his mind. Suddenly, his phone buzzed. It was Malcolm.

"Did you see the news?" Malcolm's voice trembled. "It's everywhere. The Vatican and the White House just held a joint press conference."

Roy closed his eyes for a moment, the words confirming what his spirit already knew. "The Sunday Law," he said quietly. "They've done it."

There was silence on the line before Malcolm spoke again, his voice hushed, almost reverent. "You were right. This... it's prophetic. I didn't believe you at first, but now..."

Back in Rome, the Pope called for unity through worship, appealing to the world to observe Sunday for the sake of the planet, for families, and for God. The world press called it a beautiful act of unity. But Roy knew the truth: The implications of this blasphemous act would have dire and eternal implications for people's souls.

Roy's eyes widened. He rang Malcolm again and told him, "The message is going global."— "It's not just going global," Malcolm cut in, "it's sparking something massive. People are asking questions. They want to know what's really happening."

They then agreed to push the documentary even further translating subtitles into ten languages, broadcasting on underground networks, and DVDs smuggled into countries where digital media was restricted.

As the days darkened and laws tightened, Roy's voice spread far beyond the Mission. What began as small gatherings under freeway bridges and quiet studies in city parks had become a movement—an invisible network that stretched from Los Angeles to London, from rural prayer circles to digital sanctuaries hidden behind encrypted screens. He spoke on radio frequencies long abandoned by mainstream media, through livestreams that appeared briefly before being taken down, and in whispered assemblies where believers met by candlelight, guarded by faith and fear alike.

Across the nation—and now in many parts of the world—his message carried the same unyielding urgency: *Prepare.*

At open-air rallies and midnight vigils, his words burned like fire against the night. “They’ll call this a revival,” he said, his voice steady, “but it’s a deception. True revival doesn’t flatter the conscience—it reforms the heart. It leads to obedience to all of God’s commandments, not the selective ones that suit comfort or convenience.”

In the cities, believers gathered in basements and warehouses, reading his messages aloud when internet blackouts struck. In the countryside, families studied the Scriptures by lantern light, finding courage in his broadcasts. The underground churches became both refuge and resistance—a spiritual network that refused to trade truth for peace.

But the louder Roy’s message became, the harsher the laws grew. Surveillance expanded under the banner of “public safety.” Houses of worship were required to register with the Department of Religious Affairs. Those who refused to participate in the National Day of Worship were quietly noted in federal databases. And somewhere deep within the machinery of the state, Roy’s name moved silently—from watchlists to warrants.

Reports began to surface: small congregations raided, pastors questioned, Sabbath keepers detained “for observation.”

Emergency broadcasts warned of "dangerous sects spreading disinformation." Quietly, fear began to take root. Yet the underground church only grew stronger fueled by conviction, not fear.

"This is our message to the world," Roy said quietly into the microphone. "And if it is our last, so be it. The hour of His judgment has come. Fear God. Give Him glory. Worship the Creator, not the beast of Revelation 13:5."

The signal hissed, then steadied — a thin line of light between heaven and earth. Every syllable felt like a goodbye and a beginning all at once.

His words resonated like thunder through hidden channels. Roy continued his evangelical mission to spread the truth. "An image of the beast is forming," he said, "not just in policy but in the hearts of men. The Vatican looms large in this picture—and soon, no one will be able to buy or sell unless they submit."

He paused before a small crowd, faces lit by flickering lamps, their eyes weary but resolute. "This is your moment of decision," he said softly. "Choose this day whom you will serve."

He raised his hands and prayed, his voice trembling yet strong:

"Great and marvelous are Your works, Lord God Almighty. Just and true are Your ways, O King of saints. Prince of Peace, please control our will, bid our struggling still, bid our fears and doubting cease. Hush our spirit into peace and let us clearly hear Your words and Your will for us all. Please protect us as we follow You, seek You, and give us strength to deny the evil one's approach. We pray this in the precious name of Jesus Christ our Lord and Savior. Amen."

Roy leaned forward, eyes fierce with conviction. "This is Revelation 13 unfolding. The Dragon gave his power to the Beast—and the world follows blindly."

On the phone, Malcolm was silent for a long moment. Then his voice came low and steady: "So Roy, what do we do now?"

"We expose it," Roy replied. "With truth. With the messages of the Three Angels. This isn't just about policy—it's about worship, identity, and eternity."

Across town, screens flickered in every café and home. The Pope's announcement continued to be played on a loop: *"The National Sunday Law — a gift of unity, a family day, a spiritual rest, a climate relief measure."* The words glowed like light—but carried the weight of darkness.

Roy watched the broadcast in silence, his reflection mirrored in the glass. "They call it peace," he murmured, "but it's a spiritual war."

Meanwhile, in Jerusalem, tensions flared. The Temple Mount was now under lockdown. Israeli forces and Islamic leaders were at odds again. Reports of a Third Temple proposal had gone viral, sparking outrage among Muslims and worldwide protests.

Roy received a video call from a contact in Jerusalem a young believer named Yosef.

"They're going to do it," Yosef said, voice trembling. "The Temple Institute just announced they're ready. The red heifer ritual is scheduled for next week."

"They're rushing prophecy," Roy replied. "The dragon is pushing for global worship through force. The Beast is rising in both the West and the East."

"We need to warn the others," Yosef said. "But no one's listening."

"They will," Roy assured him. "When the image speaks, when the persecution starts they'll remember."

Later that day, Roy and his team stood on street corners; in downtown LA, in Sacramento, in San Franciso and in cities across the US, handing out flyers. He had called Malcolm, who was coordinating with teams across America; the call was more for some spiritual support rather than any specific advice. He knew he could rely on Malcolm to help keep him focused. He had been his friend and helper from the time he met him and he knew he could talk to him about his concerns.

One woman, dressed in business attire, took a flyer and asked: "Wait... are you saying the Sunday Law is the Mark?"

"Yes," Roy answered gently. "It is the mark of the beast as mentioned in Revelation 13. The Mark will come when people are forced to choose between God's commandments and man's laws."

"But Sunday's harmless," she argued. "It's good, even."

"It was never about the day," Roy said. "It's about authority. Who do you obey when the test comes?"

The woman left without answering but not before looking back with a questioning glance.

That evening, Roy went live online through his YouTube channel, *The Final Warning Project.* His camera flickered on, and within minutes, tens of thousands of viewers tuned in from across the world. Faces from every continent appeared in the live chat—families watching from candlelit rooms, pastors streaming from underground churches, and young believers logging in through encrypted links.

"Friends, brothers and sisters... we are living in prophetic times," he began. "The Sunday Law has been declared. The Temple crisis is brewing. And many are asleep. But Revelation 14 says the everlasting gospel must go to every nation, tribe, and tongue before the end."

He paused, his voice steady but urgent. "This is the final confrontation. Babylon is falling. The image is forming. And the loud cry is beginning."

The chat erupted with messages—some mocking, but most, desperate and sincere.
"What should we do?" many asked.

Roy leaned forward. "Come out of her," he said firmly. "Worship God on His terms. Keep His commandments. And be sealed by His Spirit, not deceived by false peace."

He lifted his Bible, eyes glistening in the glow of the camera. "Those who do not receive the seal of God—the Sabbath—will be shaken out of the remnant church, for judgment begins first at the house of the Lord," he said, his voice breaking with conviction. "And those who reject that seal will receive the Mark of the Beast. There will be no divine protection when the Holy

Spirit is withdrawn, and God pours out His wrath through the Seven Bowls of judgment as detailed in Revelation 16—the Great Tribulation of the Apocalypse."

A heavy silence filled the stream. Some wept in their living rooms. Others fell to their knees. The moment felt sacred—terrifying and holy at once.

"This is your call to stand," Roy continued. "Do not fear what man can do. Fear God and give Him glory. His truth will outlast every decree, every censor, and every beastly power that rises against it."

At that same moment, deep beneath the White House, a team of security officials gathered around a glowing digital map. At the center of the display pulsed a new AI-driven surveillance platform, codenamed **DRAGONWATCH.**

An aide reported briskly, "We've tracked over 4,000 content creators warning people about the Sunday Law. This one—Roy—is gaining momentum. Not just in Los Angeles, but across America and potentially sir across the world. Our intel is still being assessed in relation to his reach beyond America."

President Trump watched the screen silently, fingers steepled. Finally, he spoke. "Discredit him. Flag him. And if necessary—silence him."

Another aide hesitated. "If we push too hard, we risk turning him into a martyr."

Trump leaned back, eyes cold with calculation. "Then make him look crazy. Make the truth look like a conspiracy."

"Yes, Mr. President."

The Dragon's influence was subtle—but strong.

A few days later Roy sat alone at Angeles House, eyes closed, praying. "Lord, I'm just one man. I'm nothing. But if You can use this voice use it now."

His phone buzzed again. Another email. Another testimony. "Brother Roy, your videos changed my life. I never saw it before. I'm ready to take a stand."

Tears welled in Roy's eyes. "Thank You, Jesus," he whispered. "Let the loud cry begin."

It was Friday night in Los Angeles, but the city didn't rest. The world was in turmoil, but the 'flesh' still ruled. Music blared from clubs in Hollywood, traffic pulsed through Downtown, and somewhere beneath it all, a spiritual war was growing more intense.

Roy stood outside a small home church in South LA. 100s of people had gathered, some from shelters, others from local ministries to study prophecy. They sat on folding chairs in a dimly lit room, listening intently, dozens spilling into the car park.

Roy opened his Bible. “Revelation 13: 11-15 speaks of a beast rising from the earth an image created by the second beast, the one who looks like a lamb but speaks like a dragon. That’s what we’re seeing now: America enforcing worship through the laws of church and state.”

A man raised his hand. “But isn’t this all about protecting families and giving people rest?”

“On the surface, yes,” Roy answered. “But beneath the surface, it's about control. When government dictates worship, even if it looks good, it's a trap. God never forces worship. He invites it.”

Malcolm, sitting in the back, added: “We’re not against Sunday worshippers. We’re against forced worship. The moment it’s law it becomes rebellion against God's Word.”

A quiet hush filled the room. People were waking up. You could feel it.

After the study, a young woman approached Roy. “I left my church last week. They’re celebrating the new law like it’s a revival. But something felt wrong. When I found your video it all clicked."

Roy smiled gently. "The Holy Spirit is waking people up. Just be faithful. Keep the commandments of God and the faith of Jesus. You're not alone."

Back in Jerusalem, conflict was reaching a tipping point. Riot police guarded the Temple Mount as thousands of protestors chanted on both sides. Jewish activists called for the rebuilding of the Temple. Muslims feared their sacred site was being desecrated.

Inside a secret meeting, political and religious leaders from multiple nations gathered in a chamber beneath the Old City.

"This is our moment," one rabbi said. "The nations are ready. If we act now, we can complete the Third Temple."

"And unite the Abrahamic faiths in one location," a Catholic bishop added.

"Only if Islam agrees," Crown Prince Mohammed bin Salman interjected with an ominous word of caution, resurfacing the obvious divide between Islam and Judaism, and the problematic Palestinian two state solution.

A tense silence filled the room.

Then the doors opened. A tall, charismatic man in white robes entered. He radiated calm but commanded attention. He was known only as The Mediator, and many saw him as a rising global religious figure possibly the prophesied Man of Peace.

"Brothers," he said, "let us not fight over stones. Let us build something new. A universal temple, open to all faiths, where Sunday shall be our shared sacred day."

The room nodded in eerie agreement. Across the world, from Paris to Manila, Rio to Cairo, Sydney to San Francisco, nations began adopting Global Sunday Laws in the name of peace, climate reform, and unity. Religious leaders celebrated. The media praised it. But underground believers like Roy were sounding the alarm.

Back in LA, Roy uploaded a new video titled "The Mark, the Beast, and the Remnant." He looked tired but determined.

"What we're seeing is the rise of the Image of the Beast. They say it's about rest and unity but it's about replacing God's law with man's. The true seal of God is the Sabbath. The counterfeit is rising. We must choose."

He paused, then looked straight into the camera.

"Do not be deceived by appearances. Even if the entire world follows the beast we must follow the Lamb."

Comments flooded in:

"I'm ready to stand."

"They're shutting down my channel too."

"Jesus is coming soon."

Then came the massive arrests.

It began quietly—an isolated report buried in local news feeds, then another, and another, until the pattern could no longer be ignored. In Texas, a small Sabbath-keeping church was raided mid-service, its members dragged out under flashing lights for "violating the National Rest Ordinance." Their cries echoed through the sanctuary as authorities sealed the doors, citing "public order violations."

Within hours, footage surfaced from Canada. A youth group in Alberta, preaching the Three Angels' Messages downtown, was tackled by riot police and branded a "domestic extremist sect." Their Bibles were confiscated as evidence of "religious incitement." In Germany, entire congregations were fined for refusing to join the Ecumenical Sunday Alliance. Pastors stood in pulpits stripped of power; their sermons live-streamed and censored mid-broadcast. Across Eastern Europe, believers disappeared overnight taken for "re-education."

Across the world, people of faith, ordinary men, women, and children, were suddenly enemies of peace. And it was compounding daily.

Screens lit up with breaking headlines: *"Faith Fringe Sparks Unrest," "Government Moves to Contain Radical Sabbath Movement," "Religious Dissent Threatens Global Harmony."*

But the real story wasn't on the news. It was in the streets, in whispered prayers, in secret cellars, in the trembling hands of those clutching worn Bibles under candlelight. The persecution Roy had warned about for years was no longer prophecy. It was reality.

And still, his broadcast continued.

Roy's name appeared on an internal government memo: "Subject: Roy Ferguson – High-Risk Religious Influencer. Monitor. Disrupt. Neutralize if necessary."

But Roy remained unaware. He was focused on preparing souls, not saving himself.

Late one night, Roy sat in his small room at Angeles House. He wrote in his notebook:

"The dragon is speaking louder now. But the Lamb speaks through the faithful. We are few but the remnant has never been about numbers. Only truth."

He closed his eyes and prayed. "Lord, let the sealing begin. Let the cry go forth. And may I be found faithful, even unto death."

Outside, the city kept moving. But heaven was watching. In that moment, far above the chaos of earth, three mighty angels flew across the skies of eternity shouting messages the world had long ignored:

"Fear God and give Him glory..."

"Babylon is fallen..."

"If any man worship the beast..."

The hour of decision has come.

The angelic proclamations seemed to echo in the streets below. By dawn, the governments of earth moved as one. From Rome to Washington to Jerusalem, the Decree of Universal Rest was announced, hailed as a global covenant for peace and planetary healing. But beneath the polished rhetoric, another power stirred. The dragon's voice now spoke through parliaments and pulpits alike. What heaven had declared as warning, the world now embraced as law.

Chapter 28
The Law of Forced Decree

The sun hung low in the sky, casting an ominous glow over the landscape, as Roy gathered with a small group of believers in a secluded corner of the city. The atmosphere was thick with apprehension, as the world outside seemed to be teetering on the brink of chaos.

News had spread like wildfire; as the new decree was announced, one that declared Sunday as the official day of worship, effectively enforcing a national Sunday law. "And he causes all, both small and great, rich and poor, free and slave, to receive a mark on their right hand or on their foreheads." (Revelation 13:16). Those who accepted this decree would not only bow to a new authority but would also unwittingly accept the mark of the beast, sealing their fate for eternity.

As Roy looked into the eyes of his fellow believers, he felt a surge of urgency. A need to reinforce the meaning of what had just transpired. This was more than just a law; it was a direct affront to God's commandments, a declaration that would force individuals to choose between their faith and their livelihoods. "Remember the Sabbath day, to keep it holy," (Exodus 20:8) echoed in his mind, as he contemplated the implications of this decree.

The Pope of the Roman Catholic Church, claiming to be the Vicar of Christ, was asserting that he had the authority to change times and laws. In 321 A.D., under the reign of Roman General Constantine, Sunday had been established as a day of worship, and now, through a combination of political and religious influence, this tradition was poised to be enforced globally. “No such authority exists.” Roy declared.

“Sunday worship is not just a day; it is a mark of allegiance to the beast,” Roy said, his voice steady but filled with conviction. “The Roman Catholic Church has positioned itself as the enforcer of this decree. Those who refuse to comply will find themselves ostracized from society, unable to buy or sell.” This stark reality sent shivers through the group, but Roy pressed on, determined to instill hope amidst the fear. “But remember, God promises that our bread and water will be sure,” (Isaiah 33:16) he reassured them. “Though they may take our ability to buy and sell, they cannot take our faith!”

As the night deepened, Roy’s thoughts turned to the prophetic visions he had received. The mark of the beast was not merely a physical insignia; it was a manifestation of spiritual allegiance. “Those who do not worship the beast or its image will be persecuted," he explained, referencing (Revelation 13:15.) "They will face death, but God's faithful will endure."

The technology being developed today, from biometrics to AI tracking, was not merely a convenience; it was a mechanism for control. Roy could see how these advancements would facilitate the enforcement of the Sunday law. "The systems in place will ensure that those who refuse the mark will be completely cut off from commerce," he warned. "They will be rendered unable to provide for their families, forced into a life of hardship and persecution."

With each passing day, the tension grew. The Seventh Day Adventists stood firm, their commitment to the Sabbath acting as a powerful counter-narrative to the creeping darkness. They knew that the enforcement of the Sunday law was not simply a religious issue; it was a battle for the soul of humanity. "The enemy is preparing for a final confrontation," Roy said, recalling the words of (Revelation 16:14), which spoke of spirits of demons gathering the kings of the earth for the battle of Armageddon. "We must be vigilant and prepared!"

The Antichrist, cloaked in the guise of benevolence, would use the pretext of peace to promote Sunday worship. "For when they say, 'Peace and safety!' then sudden destruction comes upon them, as labor pains upon a pregnant woman. And they shall not escape" (1 Thessalonians 5:3 NKJV). The lure of prosperity and security would seduce many into compliance, but the faithful remnant would remain resolute, even in the face of persecution.

Roy felt the weight of the situation pressing heavily upon him. The faithful would soon be pushed to the margins of society, forced to live as outcasts. "We may become homeless, refugees in our own land," he warned. "But we must remember that God is our refuge and strength, a very present help in trouble." (Psalm 46:1).

Roy recalled, the images as the decree was announced, the streets erupted with chaos. Many hailed the new law as a return to moral order, while others recoiled in fear and anger. The Seventh Day Adventists began to mobilize, spreading the message of the impending crisis. "Come out of her, my people, lest you share in her sins, and lest you receive of her plagues," (Revelation 18:4) they urged, calling for repentance and awareness of the dangers of the new order.

Roy stood before the congregation, their faces illuminated by the flickering candlelight. "We are the remnant," he declared, conviction radiating from his voice. "We have the truth, and we must share it with the world. The mark of the beast is a spiritual mark, a sign of allegiance to a power that opposes God. We will not bow to this false god! We will worship the Creator, who made the heavens, the earth, the sea, and the springs of water!" (Revelation 14:7).

With the storm of persecution on the horizon, Roy and the faithful prepared for the trials ahead. They would not succumb to fear; instead, they would cling to the promises of God. "The Lord will fight for you, and you shall hold your peace." (Exodus 14:14). They were determined to stand against the tide of compromise, proclaiming their faith even in the darkest of times.

As the effects of the decree began to unfold, Roy felt a surge of hope amidst the encroaching darkness. The faithful would endure, and God's judgment would be revealed in all its glory. The gathering storm was upon them, but so was the promise of deliverance. "And they overcame him by the blood of the Lamb and by the word of their testimony." (Revelation 12:11).

Roy's heart swelled with determination. "Let them come," he whispered as he looked out over the assembled group. "For we will stand firm, and we will sing the songs of deliverance. Our God is greater than any power that seeks to silence us!" In that moment, the resolve of the faithful solidified, and they prepared to face whatever challenges lay ahead, united in their commitment to the truth.

Outside, the world celebrated its new covenant of peace. Fireworks burst over the great capitals, and leaders toasted the dawn of a "united humanity." But in hidden rooms across the earth, the faithful prepared to flee. The networks of truth were being erased one by one, silenced under the banner of stability.

Roy stood by the window, his eyes turned eastward toward the land where prophecy would meet fulfillment. The reports from Jerusalem were growing darker by the hour, surveillance tightened, gatherings outlawed, Scripture reclassified as subversive. The dragon's kingdom was taking shape, and time itself seemed to narrow toward an unseen edge.

He exhaled slowly, feeling the weight of providence settle upon him. "The message began in Jerusalem," he said quietly, almost to himself. "To Jerusalem it must return."

Then, turning to his team, faces illuminated by the blue glow of screens and candlelight, he spoke with the calm of conviction and the urgency of a prophet.
"We have more to say," he told them, "but this one must go out tonight."

The room hushed. Each person knew what he meant. This wasn't the final message, but it was the one that mattered most, the cry that would divide truth from delusion.

Roy stepped to the transmitter. The red light blinked like a heartbeat, waiting. He steadied his breath, his tone carrying both gravity and grace.

"This is our most vital message to the world," he said, his voice low but unyielding. "The hour of His judgment has come. Fear God. Give Him glory. Worship the Creator — not the beast of Revelation 13:5."

The transmission light steadied, and for a moment the hum of the machinery felt like the pulse of heaven itself. Then Roy turned slowly to his team, eyes fierce with quiet resolve.

"We move when the hour is ripe," he said. "Not a word beyond this room. We stay hidden, we keep our channels clean, and we obey the call — swiftly and without fanfare."

They nodded, the agreement unspoken but absolute. Outside, the world kept celebrating its fragile peace; inside, a small company of the faithful steeled themselves for the work ahead — silent, concealed, and ready.

Chapter 29

The Abomination of Desolation

They came for his editors first. Then for the servers. Within hours, *Final Warning* vanished from every platform—deleted, denounced, forgotten. Officials called it a measure of "national stability." Roy knew better. It was prophecy tightening its grip.

His private chartered jet had been on standby for this very moment. He made the call. The message would not end—it would return to its beginning: **Jerusalem.**

They were halfway across the Atlantic when the encrypted message arrived. The hum of the private jet was the only sound between Roy and Caleb, his longtime friend and advisor. Outside, the night sky stretched like a veil of dark glass, stars glinting against the curvature of the earth.

Roy's instincts had already told him to go. For weeks, subtle signs had whispered warnings—the sudden silence from friends at the Mission, the vanishing of digital channels, the tightening of border checkpoints. He had sensed something forming in the dark, a convergence that felt both inevitable and ancient.

Now the message appeared on his secured tablet, pulsing like a heartbeat across the dim cabin light:

"They've shut down the Mission. Servers confiscated. Names flagged. Get off the grid. Continue production—Jerusalem only. **DRAGONWATCH** active."

The words glowed coldly on the screen. Roy read them twice, his stomach tightening. They were no longer monitoring him—they were hunting him. The silence he had sensed was not absence; it was strategy. Yet beneath the dread, an old conviction rose from the marrow of his calling: the message must go forward.

Caleb looked up from his tablet, his voice hushed but strained. "They're wiping everything, Roy. Every broadcast, every archive. Even the off-site backups in Iceland—gone."

Roy zipped the tablet into his case and leaned back against the leather seat. "Then we start again," he said quietly, eyes fixed on the horizon beyond the glass. "On holy ground."

The rest of the flight passed in uneasy silence. Neither man spoke much, both aware of the reach DRAGONWATCH possessed. They did not know whether they would be stopped on landing—or worse. The air of anticipation thickened as the lights of the Middle East came into view below them.

When the jet finally descended into Ben Gurion airspace, their hearts pounded. The expectation of confrontation—questions, detainment, confiscation—felt inevitable.

The jet door opened to a furnace wind but the atmosphere had shifted. Heat shimmered off the runway like liquid glass, blurring the horizon, but something felt different, an unknowing shift in his own spirit. Roy paused at the top of the stairs, breathing in the heavy air—Jerusalem's air, the threshold of prophecy.

Now, stepping onto the tarmac, Roy felt a strange stillness that always came when prophecy began to unfold in real time. The atmosphere carried weight—dense, expectant, alive with spiritual voltage.

Caleb followed a few paces behind, eyes scanning the horizon. "It's too quiet," he murmured. "Even for Israel."

As they got closer to customs Roy noticed a subtle change in the airport staff and officials uniform, from when here was here in 2023. Blue insignia stitched on their sleeves: a globe encircled by olive branches, the emblem of the newly ratified *Coalition for Global Peace.* He'd seen it before—on military drones in Europe, on currency redesigns, on church banners that preached unity without repentance. An ominous sign of their inevitable show down with customs.

And so, Fourteen hours after leaving LAX in a privately chartered jet, the aircraft's wheels had finally kissed the tarmac at Ben Gurion Airport. Outside, the heat shimmered like liquid glass. The plane doors opened to a blinding sun that seemed to burn through both haze and illusion. He had left behind a world growing darker by the day—cities where faith gatherings were banned, digital speech throttled, and pastors detained under new "stability laws."

Now, stepping into Israel, he felt the strange stillness that always came when prophecy began to unfold in real time. The air itself seemed watchful, as if heaven and earth were holding their breath.

Customs and immigration—**Misrad HaPnim**, the Israeli Interior Authority—were strangely efficient that morning. The officials barely glanced at their passports, waved them through with perfunctory smiles, and stamped their clearances without a single question. Luggage passed unsearched. The silence of bureaucracy felt orchestrated, not accidental.

The air in the terminal felt different—heavier, almost electric. Announcements echoed in multiple languages, all under a single banner proclaiming *"One World. One Order. One Future."* Roy's heart tightened. What had once been the movement of nations had now become the machinery of prophecy. The world was no longer divided; it was being prepared.

As they stepped into the glaring light of the terminal, with Misrad HaPnim, praise God, behind them, Roy turned to Caleb, wonder softening the tension in his eyes. "It's almost surreal," he murmured. "As if the Lord Himself moved the hands that cleared us."

Caleb nodded, still scanning the crowd. "If DRAGONWATCH has eyes here, He just blinded them."

Screens lined the terminal. Every one of them broadcast the same feed: the Antichrist seated in the restored Temple, robed in white and gold, his eyes cold and magnetic. Behind him, the Ark's replica gleamed under a canopy of light.

His voice, calm and deliberate, rolled through the speakers:

"Peace has come at last. The age of divine unity is upon us. I am He who was promised."

Roy stopped mid-stride. The verse from Daniel flashed in his mind: *"And on the wing of abominations shall come one who makes desolate."*

Gasps rippled through the terminal. Some travelers fell to their knees; others applauded, weeping. Roy turned away, whispering to himself, "When they shall say, 'Peace and safety,' then sudden destruction..."

Caleb caught up beside him, breathing hard. "You saw it too?"

Roy nodded slowly. "It's begun. And with that they found a quiet space away from the crowd and prayed."

After they arrived, the expectation of confrontation quickly gave way to anticipation and urgency. The arrivals terminal was a rush of light, noise, and relief. As Roy and Caleb stepped into the sharp warmth of the late morning sun, the in-country team was already there—faces they hadn't seen in months, radiant with disbelief and joy.

There were quick embraces, half-laughs caught between exhaustion and relief, the kind of greetings that carried more prayer than words. Hands clasped, shoulders were gripped, and for a fleeting moment, the chaos of the world seemed to pause around them. These were not just colleagues—they were witnesses, survivors of faith and purpose reunited on foreign soil.

"Roy!" Eli called, breaking through the small crowd, his camera swinging from his shoulder. He grabbed Roy in a bear hug before pulling back with wide-eyed disbelief. "You actually made it through? We thought DragonWatch would have your passports flagged six ways to Sunday!"

Miriam, standing just behind him, clasped Roy's forearm with tears shining in her eyes. "Praise God," she said, her voice trembling. "We've been praying nonstop. The fact you cleared *Misrad HaPnim* without a single question—it's not luck. That was the Lord's hand, no doubt."

Laughter and gratitude rippled through the group, the air alive with the mingled sound of relief and faith.

Caleb smiled wearily, dropping his duffel beside the van. "If they'd run a proper scan, we'd still be in interrogation right now. But it was like... the system blinked."

Eli shook his head with a grin. "The Lord blinded their eyes. Man, He's covering you, Roy. He's covering all of us."

Roy exhaled, steady but grateful. "Then let's not waste His covering," he said. "We've got work to do."

They turned toward the waiting van, its white paint gleaming under the Mediterranean sun. That's when Roy noticed the driver. The man, lean and composed in a sand-colored cap, wore a red-banded bracelet—the *Final Warning* insignia, mark of those pledged to the regime. At first glance, it sent a jolt through Roy's chest.

But then the driver's hand moved subtly—tracing a quick sign in the air, the old signal used among the faithful.

Caleb caught it too. "He's one of ours," he murmured.

The man's eyes met Roy's in the mirror—calm, steady, and knowing. "Best keep your heads down," he said quietly. "These colors keep us invisible. The new world likes to think we're theirs."

Roy nodded, the tension easing slightly. "Then let's not prove them wrong," he replied.

Caleb hoisted his duffel into the back and climbed in beside Eli. "If they'd looked twice, we'd still be explaining our paperwork."

The driver smiled faintly and started the van moving forward. To any observer, they were just another state-approved transport under Babylon's banner—but inside that van, Heaven's mission was moving.

Miriam—ever excitable—leaned forward from the passenger seat, eyes alight. "You should've seen it, Roy—Jerusalem's electric. The city's swelling like a living prophecy. Every news crew on earth is here. They're calling it *'The Crowning of the New Age Messiah.'*"

Roy's jaw tightened. "Then we'd better move fast," he said. "Before the world crowns the wrong king."

As the van merged into traffic, the tension between prophecy and peril grew thicker. Convoys rolled toward the Holy City—luxury buses wrapped with banners reading Day of Peace, caravans of believers wearing digital wristbands synced to Vatican broadcast feeds, and drones circling overhead, their sensors blinking like eyes of judgment. Inside the van, the hum of tires blended with Roy's steady voice as he briefed the team. "We film everything—crowds, ceremonies, their language of peace. But remember: prophecy isn't political commentary; it's divine warning. We're not here to expose men—we're here to reveal the truth of God."

Miriam handed Roy a tablet showing drone footage from the Mount of Olives. "We've captured the approach. Tens of thousands have already camped outside the walls. They think the Messiah's enthronement will heal the nations." Roy studied the screen—masses waving banners, singing in unison. "They've come to witness salvation," he murmured, "and instead they'll see desecration."

“Pilgrims are pouring in by the tens of thousands,” Eli added. “Buses, drones, caravans—you name it. Every street’s jammed.”

Roy gave a faint, steady smile. “Then we’ll slip through the noise and tell the truth.”

The van turned onto the highway eastward. Convoys rolled past—luxury coaches draped with banners reading *Day of Peace*, clusters of believers wearing glowing wristbands pulsing in sync with Vatican broadcast feeds. Overhead, camera drones hovered like metallic locusts, beaming every image to a world desperate for unity.

Inside, the hum of tires mixed with murmurs of awe and determination.

It was Caleb who broke the silence first. “You realize, Roy, every kilometer we travel right now is under surveillance.”

Roy nodded. “Then let them watch. Every eye on earth will see the truth before this is done.”

A brief hush followed—half fear, half faith—before Miriam spoke again. “Still… that moment at customs. It must have felt almost supernatural.”

Roy looked out across the horizon, the Judean hills shimmering ahead. “It was. The same hand that parted the Red Sea still moves when His purpose demands it.”

Eli chuckled nervously. “Then I guess He’s our customs officer now.”

Laughter rippled through the van—brief, human, relieving. Then Roy’s tone shifted, thoughtful and low.

“Look outside, everyone. You’re not just seeing scenery—you’re passing through the corridor of prophecy.”

The road curved upward, leaving the plains of Lod behind and threading into the stony Judean rise. The heat shimmered off the asphalt like breath on glass. Roy leaned toward the window, pointing east.

“Somewhere out there,” he said, “men like **Joel**, around *835 BC*, spoke of the coming *Day of the Lord*—a day when darkness would give way to glory. Not far from here, **Amos**, around *760 BC*, cried that God would rebuild David’s fallen tent. They saw the end long before it began.”

Caleb filmed quietly from the seat beside him, panning across the ridges and terraces.

"This is **Isaiah's** country," Roy continued, his voice carrying reverence. "He walked these hills between *740 and 681 BC*, foreseeing the Prince of Peace and a new heaven and earth. And just beyond those slopes—**Bethlehem**—that's where **Micah**, about *735 BC*, said the Ruler would be born. Every stone here is a witness to what's unfolding now."

The van dipped through Kidron Valley, olive groves flashing by. Miriam whispered, "It's hard to believe how close all their words are to this moment."

Roy nodded. "The prophets never missed. We're driving through their echoes."

He gestured toward the south. "Down there, in the wilderness valleys, **Jeremiah**—around *626 to 580 BC*—wept for Israel and spoke of a new covenant written on the heart. Not far from him, **Ezekiel**, between *593 and 571 BC*, saw wheels within wheels and the vision of *Gog and Magog*. Those prophecies are breathing right now."

A highway sign flashed past: **Jericho 60 km.**
Roy's voice dropped. "Beyond that desert, **Daniel**—somewhere around *605 to 530 BC*—stood before kings and saw the rise of empires. He saw the one who would speak great things against the Most High. That's who's in the Temple today."

The crew fell silent. The van wound higher through the passes, the air thinning, the landscape glowing under the late-day sun.

"Now we're entering the territory of **Haggai** and **Zechariah**," Roy said. "*520 BC*. They urged the rebuilding of the Temple and saw the Lord returning to the Mount of Olives—right over that ridge. And **Malachi**, around *430 BC*, sealed the scrolls here, promising Elijah's return before the great and dreadful day."

Eli glanced up from his camera screen. "That's this ground, right? These same hills?"

Roy nodded. "The very same. Centuries later, **John the Baptist** stood not far from here shouting, 'Prepare the way of the Lord.' Then Jesus Himself—*around AD 30*—walked this road, warning that when the abomination stands where it ought not, His followers must flee."

Miriam turned to look at him, eyes wide. "And now we're seeing it... the fulfillment of every warning."

Roy's gaze fixed ahead as Jerusalem's outline rose in the distance—gold and fire under the waning sun. "Yes," he said softly. "**John the Apostle**, about *AD 90*, saw this city made new in Revelation. But before that New Jerusalem descends, this one will shake to its foundations."

The van fell quiet as each landmark whispered of the divine story written into the soil. It was more than a tour; it was testimony unfolding mile by mile.

As they neared the suburbs of Jerusalem, Roy's voice continued, and with it a quiet awe. "Team," he said, glancing around at the faces that had risked everything to be here, "we've just traversed nine hundred and twenty-five years of prophecy. And now it's our responsibility to show the world, in real time, the fulfillment of that prophecy and the truth of God's Word."

A deep stillness followed his words, the kind that felt like both a vow and a beginning.

The van crested a final ridge and there before them lay the city—radiant, trembling, crowned by the gleam of the rebuilt Temple.

Eli lowered his camera. "It's beautiful," he whispered.

Roy's voice tightened, almost breaking. "Beautiful—and also deceived."

For a long moment, no one spoke. The engine hummed, the city shimmered, and prophecy seemed to breathe through the very air.

Caleb broke the silence. “Then it’s begun.”

Roy nodded slowly. “Yes. And the Lord who brought us through the gate will keep us through the storm.”

The van pressed on toward Jerusalem, every mile an approach to destiny.

The van crested the ridge above the Mount of Olives. From there, Jerusalem spread beneath them—ancient and modern, holy and haunted. The Dome and the Temple glowed in the same field of light, as if eternity and delusion shared one frame.

By dusk, they reached the inner ‘sanctuary’ of the city. The ancient skyline rose against a bruised violet sky, from a nearby ridge, the air throbbed with chanting—languages from every continent, united under one false hope.

Roy’s gaze lingered on the Temple’s reflection burning in the skyline. “Beautiful,” he said, “and deceived.”

The van rolled on, winding down narrow streets toward the eastern quarter, sirens wailing faintly in the distance.

They turned onto a quiet lane flanked by limestone walls. The driver killed the headlights and coasted to a stop in front of a shuttered townhouse in the narrow streets of the eastern quarter. Roy stood as the van slowed to a stop. He could not help but here the Drones overhead, searchlights sweeping across rooftops, sirens becoming even more evident in the distance.

Miriam exited the van and walked to a side door hidden from street view. She knocked twice, paused, then once again.

The door opened a crack, revealing a sliver of lamplight and a familiar voice. “Welcome to the upper room,” said Ben, their Jerusalem contact. “You made it.”

Inside, the air was thick with the smell of coffee and dust. Maps covered one wall; a stack of portable servers hummed quietly on a table beside open cases of equipment.

Roy stepped across the threshold and paused, letting the silence soak through him. “The Lord carried us through fire and firewall,” he said softly.

Ben grinned. “We’ve kept the systems dark—off-grid. You’re clear to transmit when ready.”

Eli dropped his camera case on a bench with a sigh. “Then we’re back in business.”

Miriam gave a half-smile. "No, Eli—we're not in business anymore. We're in prophecy."

Roy looked around at the weary, faithful faces—his crew, his brothers and sisters in the work. "She's right. This isn't about production or editing anymore. Every frame we capture is a testimony. Don't wait for perfection—just truth. What we record here isn't for networks. It's for the nations."

The words settled in the quiet room like a charge in the air.

Caleb unzipped a pack and began unloading transmitters. "Then we document everything," he said. "Let history see what heaven saw first."

Roy nodded. "Exactly. The prophets wrote with ink. We write with light."

A long silence followed—holy and heavy—before Miriam's motherly instincts cut through the tension. She moved toward the small kitchenette. "You all need food before you fall over. Bread, lentil stew, and figs—that's what's left."

They ate in near silence, the quiet hum of electronics and the distant pulse of the city filling the gaps between thoughts. From the window, faint singing could be heard drifting up from the valley—the sound of pilgrims gathering below the Temple Mount.

Roy set his cup down. “We have two hours before the declaration begins,” he said. “Long enough to check the feeds and sync the relays.”

Eli nodded. “I’ll calibrate the drones for aerial capture.”

Caleb glanced toward the window. “Feels strange, doesn’t it? Like everything’s holding its breath.”

Roy looked out over Jerusalem, the lights shimmering beneath a dusky violet sky. “It’s always quiet before the Scripture breaks open.”

He turned to face them again. “Listen, everyone. What we record here tonight isn’t for us. It’s for those who will come after—the ones who will wonder how the world fell for the lie. So, film it all. Don’t worry about angles or edits. Truth doesn’t need polish—it only needs light.”

Miriam leaned against the wall, arms crossed. “Do you really think people will watch this, Roy? That they’ll see it for what it is?”

He met her gaze. “Maybe not tonight. But someday, when the final trumpet sounds and the false peace burns away, these images will testify that God warned us.”

Ben motioned toward the far side of the room. "Your station's ready—signal isolated, local relay only. We're clear to transmit once you give the word."

Roy nodded, his expression solemn but resolute. "Then we prepare. No one speaks of faith tonight—we show it."

The next two hours passed with purposeful silence. The crew worked methodically: testing mics, cleaning lenses, adjusting tripods, and syncing encrypted uplinks. Caleb drafted signal backups on a portable drive while Miriam checked the city feeds for any sign of interference.

Roy stood at the narrow window overlooking Jerusalem. The wind off the hillside carried the scent of dust and cedar, brushing through his hair like a whisper from the ages. Below, the streets pulsed with movement—streams of light converging toward the Temple Mount.

He breathed deeply and spoke almost to himself. "Every road led here."

Caleb stepped up beside him. "And the Lord led us through every gate to see it."

Roy's eyes stayed on the city. "Twenty-seven years," he murmured. "Every warning, every broadcast—it all comes down to this night."

Far below, holographic projectors shimmered above the plaza, casting the Antichrist's image across every façade. Incense smoke rose into the twilight, curling through the electric haze as choirs rehearsed the hymns of unity that would soon fill the world.

Caleb's voice was quiet, reverent. "They call this the fulfillment of prophecy—the dawn of the Eternal Sabbath."

Roy shook his head slowly. "It's the counterfeit. The real Sabbath marks God's authority, not man's."

He turned toward Eli, who was mounting his primary camera. "Keep those lenses open. No edits, no filters. Let it roll. What happens tonight must stand as witness."

Eli adjusted his focus, the faint hum of power running through the rig. "Rolling on your word."

Roy gave a single nod. "Then roll."

The soft click of the record button cut through the still air. A small red light blinked in the dim room—steady, unwavering, defiant against the coming darkness.

Outside, Jerusalem roared like a living storm. From the Temple courts rose the voice of the man the world now worshiped—his image blazing across every screen, his claim echoing through stone and soul alike.

Roy's broadcast cut quietly through the noise, a thread of truth against the fabric of deception. What they captured that night would outlive them all.

And as the lens burned its witness into light, the nations beyond were stirring—laws tightening, loyalties shifting, the stage of prophecy setting for its final act. Yet in every city and outpost, Sabbath-keepers stood like fixed stars against a darkening sky. The Seventh-day Adventists did not waver; neither did those who had newly come to the Sabbath. They prayed, they warned, they would not bow.

Roy stood among them—watchman, brother, witness—until the storm broke.

The remnant stood firm as the world bowed, their Sabbath faith unbroken, their testimony sealed in light.

And above them, unseen but certain, the gathering storm rolled toward its appointed hour.

Chapter 30

The Veil of Divinity and Opening Stanza

In the weeks that followed the Gaza Peace Plan and from the time of their arrival in Israel, the movement of Roy's team and of Roy himself vanished from public record. No satellite captured his travel; no journalist traced his steps. Even those who thought they knew his routines could only speak in whispers. The preparation for what was coming could not have survived human oversight—it had to be God's covert operation.

Hidden sanctuaries became command posts of faith: an abandoned chapel in Galilee, a shuttered studio near Jerusalem, and caves once used by shepherds. Within these secret places, small teams assembled under the cover of night—musicians, linguists, engineers, and intercessors. They were not soldiers but vessels chosen for prophecy, bound together by one purpose: to ready the 144,000.

The rehearsals were conducted in silence and prayer. Instruments were tuned only when the wind rose to drown the sound. Communications passed through coded psalms embedded in harmless digital files—each phrase of worship concealing precise instructions that only the faithful could discern. No algorithm could decode what Heaven had written.

Even the instruments themselves bore the mark of miracle. When local suppliers refused to assist, violins appeared at doorways and trumpets at border posts, left by unseen hands. Amplifiers arrived unrecorded on any shipping manifest. It was as if angels themselves had arranged the inventory, ensuring that nothing would fail when the hour struck. Every piece—every string, every wire—seemed to hum with divine intention.

An "in-country technical director," a quiet believer who never revealed his full name, oversaw the synchronization of their work. He was the unseen hand ensuring that when the appointed hour came, every note, every frequency, every channel would carry the Song of Moses and the Song of the Lamb across the valley of decision.

Authorities tried to uncover the network, but each attempt dissolved in confusion. Surveillance drones lost power mid-flight; military files erased themselves from encrypted servers; security teams reported inexplicable blindness and redirected coordinates. It was as though the entire operation existed inside a divine shield. "He shall cover thee with His feathers, and under His wings shalt thou trust." (Psalm 91:4)

By the eve of the gathering, the preparations were complete. No human credit could claim it; every thread bore the signature of Providence. Beneath the quiet stars of Israel, the stage awaited—unseen by men yet ordained by Heaven.

The sun dipped low in the sky, casting long shadows across the ancient hills of Megiddo, a place steeped in prophetic significance. Roy stood atop a ridge, his heart pounding in time with the distant drums of war. Below him, the Israeli Defense Forces were lined up, resolute yet outnumbered, facing a coalition military force of two hundred million Eastern nations led by China. They had converged like vultures on a carcass after the apocalyptic war between Israel and Iran, Russia, and the Muslim Confederacy, all believing this would be the final destruction of Israel.

And it was not lost on Roy that on June 24, 2025, the nations of Iran and Israel had agreed to a cease-fire after a brief but fierce exchange—a truce that only weeks earlier had seemed impossible. For the first time in years, sirens in Tel Aviv fell silent, and across the deserts of the Negev and the plains of Persia, soldiers stood down. The world exhaled.

That fragile calm became the seedbed for something greater—or more dangerous. On October 13, 2025, under the relentless sun of Sharm el-Sheikh, Egypt, the leaders of the world assembled. There, beneath banners proclaiming *"Peace for All Generations,"* President Trump and President el-Sisi presided over the signing of what history would call the Gaza Peace Plan. Cameras flashed, choirs sang, and from Washington to Riyadh to Brussels, the media declared *"the dawn of a new Middle East."*

But Roy saw it differently. To him, the treaty was not the end of war but the calm before prophecy's storm—a covenant built on sand, not stone. The words of Paul whispered through his mind: *"For when they shall say, 'Peace and safety,' then sudden destruction cometh upon them."* (1 Thessalonians 5:3) He knew the script of history was turning, not closing.

While diplomats toasted the accord, the faithful held their breath. Across continents, Seventh-day Adventists and Sabbath-keepers met quietly in homes and prayer circles, their conviction unshaken. They knew that the world's peace was not God's peace. Where nations bowed to the new order of unity and Sunday worship, the remnant stood firm, their allegiance to the Creator unchanged since Sinai. To them, the Gaza Peace Plan was more than politics—it was a prophetic tremor.

Roy lifted his eyes toward Jerusalem, now glowing beneath satellite lights and slogans of peace. "The ink's still wet," he murmured, "and already the thunder gathers." And indeed, far above the city, unseen but inevitable, the gathering storm began to move.

"This is it," Roy muttered, a fire igniting in his chest. He recalled the vision he had had weeks before—the Song of Moses intertwined with the Song of the Lamb, both echoing through the ages. He had translated the lyrics into Hebrew, and now they were ready to be sung by the 144,000 chosen ones, the singers of Israel, their voices rising like incense before the Almighty. The music, composed by John Williams, was not merely notes on a page; it was a battle cry, a declaration of faith, a stirring anthem of hope amidst despair.

As evening fell, the atmosphere thickened with tension. Roy could sense the presence of the unclean spirits described in Revelation—the demonic forces that had seduced the kings of the earth into believing they could conquer the land of promise. He could almost hear their whispering, like frogs croaking in a swamp, instilling doubt and destruction in the hearts of men.

He turned his gaze to the horizon, where the vast army awaited, a dark tide of uniforms and weapons surging toward Israel like a storm cloud. It was a sight that would terrify even the most stalwart of souls. But Roy was not afraid; he felt a surge of divine assurance that God was about to show His power in a way that would leave nations trembling.

With a quickened pulse, he made his way to the makeshift stage where the 144,000 singers were gathered, their faces set with determination and faith. They looked to him for direction, and he raised his hands, the words of the songs ready to spill forth like a waterfall.

Roy's voice rose above the roar of the encroaching armies. "This is our moment! Brothers and Sisters- We stand upon the very edge of history, called to declare God's glory before the nations! Lift your voices—let heaven hear us as one!"

At the first notes, a holy silence swept over the battlefield. Soldiers stilled, their weapons lowered as the haunting melody broke forth, filling the air with a sound that seemed to pierce eternity itself. The singers joined in harmony, their voices weaving a living tapestry of worship—songs of deliverance, of hope, of promises spoken by God and now echoing into the heart of the struggle.

Roy could feel the ground tremble beneath him—not from the march of the enemy, but from the power of God's presence. The armies of the world were approaching, but the King of kings was already there, ready to fight on behalf of His people.

"And I will set My glory among the nations," Roy sang, the lyrics rising with authority. "And all the nations shall see My judgment, which I have executed, and My hand that I have laid upon them." (Ezekiel 39:21)

As the singers continued, a sudden wind swept through the valley, an unseen force igniting the hearts of the Israeli soldiers. They raised their weapons not in fear but in fierce anticipation. The eyes of the world were upon them, but they were no longer outnumbered—they were backed by the very host of Heaven.

From the depths of despair, a fierce hope was born. This was not just a battle for survival; it was a divine confrontation revealing the sovereignty of God—the same God who had led Israel out of Egypt, who had delivered them from countless foes, and who would once again demonstrate His power in the face of overwhelming odds.

In that charged moment, Roy understood the magnitude of what was unfolding. The song was more than just music; it was a declaration of faith, a rallying cry for a nation poised on the brink of destruction yet clinging to the promise of deliverance.

The armies gathered in Megiddo believed they would snuff out the light of Israel once and for all, but they were about to witness the greatest display of divine power the world had ever seen.

As the last notes of the Song of Moses and the Song of the Lamb echoed across the valley, Roy felt a profound peace wash over him. God was in control, and the ultimate victory was assured. The storm was gathering, but so was the glory of God, ready to be revealed in a way that would change the course of history forever.

"Let them come," Roy whispered, a smile breaking across his face. "For we will sing, and the heavens will respond."

Chapter 31
Israel's Divine Intervention

The sun hung low in the sky, casting an eerie glow over the land of Israel. Roy stood on a hill overlooking the valley where the Israeli Defense Forces braced for a monumental clash against a vast coalition—an army forged by China and its Eastern allies. It was the culmination of centuries of prophecy, a moment that trembled on the edge of eternity. *"For I will gather all nations against Jerusalem to battle..."* (Zechariah 14:2).

As he gazed across the horizon, dread pressed against his chest like an iron weight. The words of Revelation 9:16 echoed in his mind—two hundred million soldiers massed for the final conflict. Yet another scene rose within him: Jehoshaphat's choir, marching into battle with nothing but faith and song. *"Believe in the Lord your God, so shall ye be established; believe his prophets, so shall ye prosper."* (2 Chronicles 20:20).

"Can it be?" Roy whispered. "Will God again set ambushments as He did then?"

Turning from the turmoil, he again descended toward the gathering of the 144,000—Israel's chosen singers, the faithful remnant. Their faces glowed still with unearthly calm. They knew the purpose of their song: to invite Heaven's presence into the storm.

"Brothers and sisters," Roy called, his voice steady amid the wind, "today we stand as Jehoshaphat's choir stood! As they sang, God fought. And He will fight for us again. Let your song be the weapon!"

The first notes soared heavenward, trembling in the air like lightning made of sound. Instantly the atmosphere thickened; courage filled the soldiers below. Invisible power surged across the valley. *"For the Lord your God is He who goes with you to fight for you against your enemies, to give you victory."* (Deuteronomy 20:4).

In the distance, the colossal army advanced—a tide of metal, banners, and thunder. Yet the melody cut through the roar of engines. It swirled on the wind, wrapping around the invaders like a living shroud.

Then the heavens shifted. The sky bruised black. The ground shuddered. Roy felt it before he saw it—the Spirit moving like a tempest unleashed. *"I will call for a sword against him throughout all My mountains,"* cried Ezekiel's words in his heart. *"Every man's sword shall be against his brother."* (Ezekiel 38:21).

Confusion struck the enemy lines. Command signals scrambled, machinery faltered, and the advancing ranks stumbled. The dragon's whispers turned to panic.

The singers pressed on: *"You are worthy, O Lord, to receive glory and honor and power..."* (Revelation 4:11). Their harmonies surged like tidal waves of light. Enemy commanders shouted contradictory orders; tanks fired into their own lines. Fire streaked across the plain. What had begun as an invasion became chaos incarnate.

Explosions tore the horizon. Lightning clawed at the clouds. The earth convulsed as prophecy unfolded in real time. *"The earth is utterly broken; it is violently shaken."* (Isaiah 24:19).

"Look!" cried a soldier beside Roy, pointing toward the melee. "They're turning on each other!"

Roy raised his arms toward Heaven. "Sing louder!" he shouted over the thunder. "Let all the earth hear His glory!"

The 144,000 obeyed, voices fused in perfect unity. The vibration of praise became a roar greater than artillery. The mountains trembled; the sea of soldiers froze in terror. The sun vanished behind rolling clouds as if creation itself hid its face. *"For the day of the Lord is great and very terrible; who can endure it?"* (Joel 2:11).

Blood flowed through the valley, rising like the vision of Revelation 14:20—*"up to the horse's bridle."* It was not vengeance but judgment, the reckoning of ages.

And then—amid the quake, the fire, and the storm—came the impossible.

A blinding brilliance tore through the clouds—neither lightning nor weapon fire, but a light, alive with purpose. It descended like a river of flame, folding upon itself, sweeping across the valley with a sound like a thousand trumpets. The shockwave silenced every engine, every voice, every heartbeat.

Roy fell to his knees, shielding his eyes as the brilliance enveloped him. Around him, the 144,000 also dropped to their knees, yet their voices did not falter. They continued to sing—faces lifted, hands raised, the melody trembling with tears and power. The sight was beyond mortal comprehension: a vast multitude kneeling in worship while the glory of God descended upon the earth.

The air itself vibrated with holiness. The wind stilled, the fire hung motionless in the sky, and time seemed to hesitate. In that instant, the world stood at the edge of eternity.

Out of the brilliance came the echo of a voice—not heard with ears but felt in every soul: *"Be still and know that I am God."* (Psalm 46:10).

The armies faltered, weapons slipping from trembling hands. The mountain ridges glowed like molten gold, and what began as terror became worship.

50 Miles away, in an underground control center outside Tel Aviv, the in-country technical director and his small crew fought to keep their transmission alive. "The World must begiven witness to God's power and His love for Israel" declared the 'in country' technical director.

Power grids collapsed, satellites flickered, yet their feed held steady. Their cameras—hidden, encrypted, and long since written off by the authorities—continued to stream.

Every lens captured what no network could fabricate: the visible glory of God sweeping across Megiddo. The broadcast leapt from secure servers to open frequencies without human command. Screens across the world lit up—first one, then thousands, then millions.

In New York, news anchors froze mid-sentence as live footage appeared: the valley aflame with supernatural light. In Beijing, technicians wept as their own state-controlled systems were overridden. In cathedrals, mosques, temples, and living rooms alike, humanity stopped breathing as the song filled the airwaves.

"This can't be real," whispered a BBC correspondent, tears streaming down her face.

But it was. The miracle was live.

Viewers saw the armies convulsing, then collapsing—not from weapons, but from the sheer brilliance washing over the land. They heard the 144,000 singing with such unity that even atheists felt the echo in their bones.

Around the world, miracles multiplied like ripples on water. Power returned to cities long in blackout. Storms stilled mid-tempest. A blind child in Cairo cried out that she could see. A man in Tokyo—paralyzed for decades—stood and lifted his hands toward the light on the screen.

In cities wracked by war, cease-fires erupted spontaneously. In prisons, men fell to their knees. In hospitals, dying patients opened their eyes. The broadcast had become a conduit of divine reality. And across continents, the same message spread from trembling lips: *"It is the God of Israel. He lives."*

As world leaders struggled to regain control of the narrative, "the nations raged and the people imagined vain things" (Psalm 2:1–2):, yet Heaven's decree moved forward unhindered.

Emergency networks broke into silence as translators wept openly. Some tried to cut the feed, but the transmission refused to die. Servers rebooted themselves, cameras continued to broadcast, and signals reappeared from satellites long disabled. It was as though Heaven had seized the very machinery of the modern world to bear witness.

Social media feeds filled with awe and repentance. Soldiers on foreign fronts laid down their arms. Scientists stared at readings they could not explain. And in the midst of it all, one question began to rise from every corner of the earth—spoken in every tongue:

"Who is this God, and who is the man standing in that valley?"

From the ridge overlooking the valley, Roy felt a tremor deep within his spirit. The light had not only fallen upon the land—it was moving through him, preparing something unseen. Even as the camera continued to roll, he sensed that the next miracle had already begun. The world was watching. Heaven was not finished.

Roy's heart swelled as realization struck: the world was witnessing, in real time, that the God of Israel still reigned. Every fiber of his being trembled beneath the weight of glory, as if creation itself had paused to bear witness to the hand of the Almighty. "Sing, Israel! Sing!" he cried, voice breaking with awe. "For the Lord fights for us! He will sanctify His name before the nations!" (Ezekiel 38:23).

The chorus rose once more, and as it did, the heavens blazed with unearthly radiance. The nations that had mocked now watched in silence. The shaking had begun—the unveiling of divine power foretold since Sinai. *"For the Lord your God is a consuming fire, a jealous God."* (Deuteronomy 4:24).

And the team continued to film in real time—capturing not just a battle, but the moment when Heaven invaded history.

Chapter 32

The Great Tribulation and the Unleashing of Judgment

The dawn that followed was unlike any other. The light that had filled the valley the night before lingered in the air like a living breath—soft yet potent, shimmering across the scorched ground. Smoke drifted over the plain where armies had fallen, and in the hush that followed judgment, even the wind seemed to pray.

Among the scattered remnants of the faithful, bodies began to stir. Roy lay where he had fallen, dust glowing faintly around him, his chest still. Then, with a sudden intake of breath, he awoke. A tremor passed through the valley as others rose with him—men and women of the remnant, revived by the same power that had split the heavens. They looked about in awe, realizing they were alive where death had reigned. The 144,000 knelt in reverence, singing still through tears, their voices fragile yet triumphant.

The world was still watching. The cameras had never stopped. Viewers across continents saw resurrection in real time—not a rumor or a legend but living testimony. The God of Israel had revealed His hand.

That night, the remnant spirited Roy away to a hidden refuge on the outskirts of Jerusalem. There, beneath the cracked stones of an old monastery, they tended his wounds and prayed over him. But Roy could not rest. Peace eluded him. Though the armies had fallen and miracles abounded, his spirit stirred with warning: **God was not finished.** He had seen deliverance, but he sensed wrath yet to come—justice waiting to be poured out.

He tried to sleep, but visions came instead—faces of rulers conspiring, of people rejoicing yet still blind. The Antichrist, humiliated by defeat, was tightening his grip. Through decrees and technologies, through world leaders promising order, the machinery of coercion moved again. The peace of the world had become its prison.

Then, without a step taken, Roy was *carried.*
One breath he was in the shadows of Jerusalem; the next, he stood beneath a faded awning in Hollywood.

The Loud Cry Across the Earth A sea of people stretched before him—actors, executives, families, skeptics—all drawn by a strange compulsion. The air shimmered as though charged with unseen current. When Roy stepped onto the makeshift platform beneath the theater's marquee, silence fell like the calm before thunder.

Then it came—the latter rain he had long prayed for. Not eloquence, but power. His words did not merely travel through microphones; they moved through the marrow of those who heard. Each syllable landed like a weight of light, measuring hearts before Heaven's standard.

Cameras rolled. Networks streamed. The same systems once used for vanity now carried truth like fire. The Spirit translated his message into every language at once. The **three angels' message** sounded again—first as a whisper, then as a roar:

"Fear God and give glory to Him; for the hour of His judgment is come."

As Roy spoke, the world convulsed. Markets trembled; networks crashed and revived again; governments issued denials even as their own feeds carried the revival. In studios and agencies, people wept openly. Red carpets turned into altars. Programs devoted to distraction were interrupted by testimonies of repentance. Influence that had shaped culture now bent toward conscience.

Roy did not claim the movement. Around him stood men and women—Jews of every tribe and believers from every nation—faces alight with quiet resolve. The sealed of God, the 144,000, shone not by mark but by fruit: courage, tenderness, purity of purpose. Their unity broke through cynicism like sunrise through smoke.

The crowd in Hollywood stood entranced. The air vibrated with worship and wonder, yet Roy's countenance changed. A stillness fell over him; the current of the Spirit deepened, and his eyes lifted as though listening to something vast and distant.

Then came the voice—not through speakers or sky, but through the very ground, resonating in every chest:

"Go and pour out on the earth the seven bowls of the wrath of God."

At that instant, the world itself became God's movie screen. Every satellite, every live stream, every phone and theater, every public square already tuned to the revival suddenly went still—and then, one by one, lit with the same vision Roy was seeing.

Cities, jungles, deserts, and prisons—all watched together as Heaven projected its warning across the face of the earth. The forecast of divine judgment was no longer prophecy in print; it was living revelation in motion.

Men and women froze where they stood. Newscasters fell silent mid-sentence. The vision had seized the world. The heavens parted, and the redeemed, empowered by the Holy Ghost, stood with the Angels prepared to go forth to spread the

Gospels, while healing the sick, casting out demons and raising the dead. "And they that be wise shall shine as the brightness of the firmament; and they that turn many to righteousness as the stars for ever and ever" (Danial 12:3).

Across the distant lines, soldiers who had come to wage war now stood transfixed, their weapons forgotten. The will to fight evaporated as a power beyond comprehension swept over the field — not destruction, but dominion.

In Los Angeles, Roy fell to his knees as the sound swept through him. He heard it not with ears but with soul — the victory hymn of the 144,000, echoing across worlds. Heaven had taken the baton, and the earth trembled beneath its melody.

It was not happening again — it was *being revealed*. What the world had witnessed once in Jerusalem was now replaying in divine remembrance. The heavens parted across the great screens of the world, not as breaking news but as judgment's overture — a reminder of the Lamb's triumph before the bowls of wrath were poured.

Again, images of God's Maestro raising His hand — not man, but Spirit — to conduct the 144000 in the Song of the Lamb and the Song of Moses. It began anew in vision, echoing through every nation that had refused to listen.

A tremor passed through the city. Neon lights flickered, and the people instinctively sank to their knees. Roy fell forward, shielding his eyes, the faithful beside him — those newly awakened from the Hollywood revival — still singing softly through the quake. And the vision unfolded before him, visible on the broadcast screens as though Heaven itself had seized the cameras.

The first angel poured his bowl upon the earth, and sores broke out on those who bore the mark of the beast. Roy wept, feeling both the pain and the justice of it.

The second angel poured his bowl into the sea; the waters turned to blood, and life perished within them. The third angel poured his bowl into the rivers, and they too became blood. From the altar a voice declared:

"They have shed the blood of the saints and prophets; now they are given blood to drink."

Then came the fourth: the sun flared, scorching the unrepentant. Still, they cursed God. The fifth plunged the beast's throne into darkness; people gnashed their tongues yet did not turn.

Roy cried out, "Mercy, Lord—open their eyes before it is too late!"

The sixth angel had already poured his bowl upon the Euphrates, and its waters had dried to make way for the kings of the east. The spirits of deception had risen to rally the final war, and the world had marched—unknowingly—toward Armageddon.

Now, in the vision that seized him, Roy saw it all again, not as a man watching history, but as a witness to Heaven's record. What had played out in time was being replayed in truth. The revelation was not a forecast but a confirmation—the divine commentary upon what had been fulfilled.

Across the great screens of the world, Heaven unveiled the full tapestry: the gathering of nations, the drying of the river, the rallying of kings, and the trembling of the earth beneath their march. Each scene burned with clarity, not to repeat prophecy, but to remind mankind of what they had ignored when mercy still called.

One by one, the bowls were revealed. Some unfolded as visions of what had already come to pass—echoes of wrath fulfilled, played again before the eyes of a disbelieving world so that none could say, *"We were not warned."* These were Heaven's replays, divine evidence that prophecy had not failed but been accomplished exactly as spoken.

Others, however, came as visions yet unfulfilled—previews of mercy's final countdown. They were not memories but warnings, glimpses of what still lingered on the edge of time. The world was being shown what awaited if it continued in defiance, if it hardened its heart as Pharaoh had in Egypt.

As the seventh angel lifted his bowl, a silence settled upon the earth—a silence not of peace but of suspended judgment. This was no replay. This was imminent. The vision now turned from remembrance to revelation.

The angel poured out his bowl into the air, and a voice thundered from the temple of Heaven, "*It is done!*" Lightning fractured the sky. Thunder rolled like mountains breaking. The earth convulsed and rocked like a drunkard beneath cities and seas alike. Babylon's towers shuddered; her foundations cracked. The nations who had mocked the warnings now trembled as the wrath they dismissed became reality.

Yet even in that hour, the heavens lingered on the edge of mercy, the vision hanging like a final plea: *Repent while there is breath. Turn before it is forever sealed.*

The vision pressed on—bowl after bowl, judgment after judgment—until Roy understood that this was the reckoning, the unveiling of all that remained. What the prophets had spoken and what the world had mocked now stood before them, undeniable and complete.

Finally, the seventh angel poured the contents of the bowl into the air, and a voice thundered from the throne.

Lightning split the heavens. Earthquakes shook continents. The great city fractured; the San Andreas rent from ocean to desert. Mountains fell, islands fled, and hailstones the weight of judgment crashed upon the earth.

The world had now seen what was to come—judgment unveiled before their eyes. Yet would they repent? How much more must the earth endure before man humbled himself to ask for God's grace and mercy? Would hearts still harden, or would mercy find a place before the vision became reality?

Through the vision of the coming devastation, the faithful clung together, their faces radiant with calm—the calm of those who know their Redeemer lives. Roy raised his hands and cried out above the roar:

Though the earth trembles, our God reigns! "God is our refuge and strength, a very present help in time of trouble" (Psalm 46:1).

Their song rose like defiance against despair. And then the world watched, trembling, as prophecy leapt from page to reality.

Almost in an instant, the vision dissolved into reality. What Roy had seen was no longer a revelation confined to the mind—it had become the world's stage. Time itself seemed to blur; whether moments or months had passed, none could tell. But God's final words still thundered through creation: **"It is done."**

Then, as the final echo of thunder rolled across the city, Roy's body lifted—not in spectacle, but as though drawn upward by unseen hands. A flash of light enveloped him; and in the next heartbeat, he was gone—just as Philip was caught away after baptizing the Ethiopian. "And when they were come up out of the water, the Spirit of the Lord caught away Philip, that the eunuch saw him no more: and he went on his way rejoicing..." (Acts 8:39-40)

He stood in Jerusalem. Above him rose a gleaming edifice—the Third Temple, shimmering with false promise. Crowds surged toward its gates. Upon its high platform stood the figure the prophets had warned of: the Antichrist, his smile radiant, his tone paternal. He spoke of unity, sustainability, peace—

words soft as silk, heavy as chains. Every screen on earth now relayed his image.

Roy felt his spirit rise against the deception. The Spirit gave him utterance, and his voice rang through the courtyards: "You worship not peace but power! You seek safety yet deny the Savior! Come out of Babylon and worship Him who made heaven and earth!"

The words cut like lightning through the broadcast. Some scoffed, but others staggered as if waking from hypnosis. The air vibrated between two kingdoms—the counterfeit and the divine.

Cameras found Roy again. The man from the valley was standing now before the temple of the deceiver, and the world could not look away.

Artists, politicians, soldiers—all watched as the confrontation unfolded not by sword, but by truth. The Antichrist's countenance darkened. He spoke calm words of tolerance that dripped with threat. Yet the revival's flame spread; those sealed of God moved through the streets with compassion, healing, feeding, calling. The false peace began to fracture.

The Great Tribulation had come, yet so had the certainty of deliverance. The heavens were poised for unveiling, and Roy was once more at the center of prophecy fulfilled.

Chapter 33

The Fall of Babylon

Roy stood at the lip of a yawning chasm; the world's groaning pressed into his bones.

The Great Tribulation had dimmed the sun of human courage; even stalwart hearts flickered. Beside him, the faithful waited in prayer, but in Roy's spirit **the hour tolled through his soul like iron bells of judgment**. The sound was not heard by human ear, yet every vibration carried the weight of destiny—an unrelenting summons from Heaven that the time had come.

One of the seven angels who had carried the bowls of wrath approached, radiant yet solemn. His voice rolled like thunder restrained.

"Come," he said, "and I will show you the judgment of the great prostitute who sits upon many waters."

In a heartbeat, the world dissolved. Roy was carried away in the Spirit to a barren wilderness, where silence itself seemed to recoil. Before him rose a sight both mesmerizing and dreadful: a woman enthroned upon a scarlet beast covered with blasphemous names, its seven heads and ten horns glinting like molten crowns. She was robed in purple and scarlet, adorned with gold and precious stones, holding in her jeweled hand a cup filled with abominations—the intoxicating wine of spiritual corruption.

Across her forehead burned a name written in defiance of Heaven:
"Mystery, Babylon the Great, the Mother of Prostitutes and of the Abominations of the Earth."

Roy's heart recoiled as he saw her reveling, drunk on the blood of the saints and the martyrs of Jesus. A chill of holy grief pierced his soul. Could this be what humanity had become—pleasure feeding on persecution, religion entwined with empire?

"Why do you marvel?" the angel asked, perceiving his anguish. "I will reveal the mystery of the woman and of the beast that carries her—the beast that was, and is not, and yet is to come. It shall rise from the abyss and go to destruction. Those whose names are not written in the Book of Life shall be astonished when they behold the beast that was, and is not, and yet will be."

Roy trembled as the vision deepened. The angel's words unfolded like thunder rolling over ages.

"The seven heads are seven mountains, representing Rome, upon which the woman (read Vatican) sits. They are also seven kings—five have fallen, one is, and the other has not yet come; and when he comes, he must remain but a little while. The beast that was and is not himself an eighth and belongs to the seven—and he goes to perdition."

The meaning struck Roy like fire. The structures of worldly power—kingdoms, systems, alliances—were woven into one blasphemous body, an empire built on rebellion and deception. The angel continued:

"The ten horns you saw are ten kings who have not yet received a kingdom, but they will receive authority with the beast for one hour. These will make war with the Lamb—but the Lamb will overcome them, for He is Lord of lords and King of kings, and those with Him are called, chosen, and faithful."

Roy's heart surged at those words. Amid the terror and treachery, light still reigned. The faithful would stand; the Lamb would triumph. But the vision's gravity did not relent.

"The waters you saw," the angel said, "are peoples and multitudes and nations and tongues. The ten horns and the beast will hate the prostitute "And the ten horns which thou sawest upon the beast, these shall hate the whore..." (Revelation 17:16–17); they will make her desolate and naked, devour her flesh, and burn her with fire. For God has put it into their hearts to carry out His purpose, until His words are fulfilled."

Roy understood. The very powers that once exalted corruption would turn upon it—evil devouring itself at the command of divine justice. He saw the false splendor of a global church and its empire of compromise—the wealth of cathedrals, the politics of power, the veneer of holiness masking idolatry. The angel's voice thundered again, echoing across the ages:

"Fallen! Fallen is Babylon the Great! She has become a dwelling place for demons, a haunt for every unclean spirit" (Revelation 18:2).

A radiant angel descended, his glory flooding the earth. His cry reverberated through every city and every nation:

"For all nations have drunk the wine of her passionate immorality. The kings of the earth have committed adultery with her, and the merchants have grown rich through the abundance of her luxury."

Then another voice—a voice Roy knew was not of angels but of God Himself—resounded within his heart:

"Come out of her, My people, that you may not share in her sins nor receive of her plagues. For her sins are piled up to

Heaven, and God has remembered her iniquities" (Revelation 18:4–5).

Roy's knees weakened. The message was not condemnation alone—it was mercy, urgent and unrelenting.

"We must warn them," he cried to the faithful. "We must call them out before the fire falls! God's mercy still stands between them and destruction!"

The angel lifted his hand toward the heavens.

"Render to her as she has rendered; pay her double according to her works. For her plagues will come in one day—death, mourning, and famine. She shall be utterly burned with fire, for mighty is the Lord God who judges her" (Revelation 18:6–8).

Before Roy's eyes, the vision unfolded—the great city that had sat upon seven hills, the bastion of wealth and power, suddenly engulfed in flame. The sky glowed red as gold and marble crumbled. From every corner of the earth came lamentations:

"Alas, alas, that great city, clothed in fine linen, purple, and scarlet! For in one hour such great riches came to nothing" (Revelation 18:16–17).

Kings who had once courted her wept from afar. Merchants watched their ships idle; their treasures turned to ash. The angel's lament carried across the smoke:

"The fruit you longed for has gone from you. All your dainty and splendid things are lost—never to be found again" (Revelation 18:14)

Then a mighty angel took up a stone like a great millstone and hurled it into the sea, crying,

"Thus, with violence shall Babylon the great city be thrown down and shall be found no more at all!"

A silence followed that seemed to swallow sound itself. The music of harps, the voices of craftsmen, the light of lamps—all extinguished.

Roy felt the finality settle into his spirit. The reign of deceit was over. The empire of corruption, once arrayed in gold and sanctimony, was now dust under divine judgment.

When the vision lifted, Roy found himself back in Jerusalem. Around him, the faithful stood in awe, their faces pale with holy fear. The air trembled as though creation itself was catching its breath.

Roy's voice broke through the silence.

"The fall of Babylon is not the end—it is the warning before the dawn. We must stand firm, we must speak truth, for the Lamb will soon appear!"

The people gathered closer. Their weariness melted into purpose.

"We are His witnesses," Roy continued, "the light amid the ruins. Even now, judgment gives way to mercy—for those who turn will yet be saved."

And so, they prayed—not in despair, but in defiant faith. They prayed for courage to proclaim the Gospel one final time before the end, for the strength to endure, and for hearts still lost in the ruins of Babylon to hear the call and come out before it was too late.

Above them, the heavens began to stir once more. The last seals of time trembled on their hinges. The age of the beast was ending, and the kingdom of the Lamb was about to break forth in glory.

The angel's voice lingered in Roy's mind, echoing through eternity:

"Fallen, fallen is Babylon the Great."

But beneath that echo was another—quieter, gentler, eternal:

"Behold, I make all things new."

Epilogue
The Dawn of Eternity

The air shimmered with a transcendent light as Roy stood among the throng of the redeemed, their faces radiant with joy. The Great Tribulation was a distant memory, a shadow eclipsed by the glorious promise of Christ's return, a moment foretold through the ages, "For the Lord Himself will descend from heaven with a shout, with the voice of an archangel, and with the trumpet of God." (1 Thessalonians 4:16). This was the moment when the King of kings would descend, claiming His own and ushering in a new era of hope and restoration.

As the earth trembled beneath them, the skies split open, revealing a magnificent sight: a dark cloud, the size of a man's fist, drawing nearer, illuminated by the brilliance of divine glory. Roy felt his heart race as he watched Jesus Christ descend, flanked by the celestial hosts, each angel a beacon of light. The very ground shook with the weight of His presence, a fire issuing before Him that consumed the wicked in their rebellion, leaving only the faithful to rise and embrace their destiny.

In a breathtaking moment, the dead in Christ emerged from their graves, their bodies transformed and renewed, caught up in the glory of their Savior. Roy's tears of joy flowed freely as he recognized familiar faces, radiant and alive. "Look!" he exclaimed, his voice mingling with the joyous cries of the saints. "It is the first resurrection! Blessed and holy are those who share in it!" (Revelation 20:6).

The atmosphere was electric with anticipation as Roy and the living saints were lifted into the air, soaring toward the heavens. They were enveloped in the embrace of the divine, surrounded by the angels' triumphant song. As they ascended, the voice of the heavenly host rang out in a chorus of praise, "Holy, holy, holy is the Lord God Almighty!" (Revelation 4:8).

At last, they entered the celestial realm, transformed into perfect beings, their hearts overflowing with love and gratitude. They gathered at the marriage supper of the Lamb, where joy and celebration enveloped them like a warm embrace. The first Sabbath in Heaven was a symphony of delight, a joyful harmony that echoed through eternity.

As they feasted, Roy gazed upon the light of Christ, shining infinitely brighter than the sun. He marveled at the nail-pierced hands of Jesus, the marks of love and sacrifice that would forever tell the story of redemption. The moment was profound, as he remembered the words of Zechariah, where the long-rejected Messiah revealed Himself to His people. "They will look on me, the one they have pierced, and they will mourn for him as one mourns for an only child." (Zechariah 12:10). Their wails of sorrow turned to joy as Jesus wiped away their tears, welcoming them into the eternal embrace of His grace.

"Come," said an angel, leading Roy to witness the splendor of the New Jerusalem descending from God. The city gleamed with the glory of its Creator, adorned with precious jewels, its streets of gold were as clear as crystal. It was a place where God Himself would dwell with humanity, where suffering and sorrow had no place: "And I heard a loud voice from the throne saying, 'Behold, the dwelling place of God is with man...'" (Revelation 21:3).

But the joy of heaven was tempered by the weight of truth. After a thousand years of peace, Roy was reminded of the prophecy: Satan would be released for a short time, and the enemy would gather his forces once again, surrounding the beloved city. The wicked dead rose, bewildered and filled with dread, as they faced the ultimate judgment.

The scene was both terrifying and awe-inspiring. Yet, Roy stood firm, his faith unshakeable. He remembered the promise of victory through Christ, and as the enemy rallied, fire rained down from Heaven, consuming all who had turned away from the truth. "But fire came down from heaven and consumed them." (Revelation 20:9). The devil, the beast, and the false prophet were cast into the lake of fire, where they would face eternal torment, a reminder of God's ultimate authority over evil.

As Roy beheld the great white throne, he saw the books opened, the weight of eternity resting upon each soul. "Anyone whose name was not found written in the book of life was thrown into the lake of fire." (Revelation 20:15). He whispered this truth, a wave of sorrow washing over him. The finality of judgment was profound, yet he knew that the redeemed had triumphed.

Then, a new heaven and a new earth emerged before his eyes, the holy city, the New Jerusalem, descending like a bride adorned for her husband. "Behold, God's dwelling is with humanity!" the voice proclaimed, filling Roy's heart with indescribable joy. "He will wipe away every tear from their eyes. Death will be no more; grief, crying, and pain will be no more." (Revelation 21:4).

In that moment, Roy understood the depth of God's love and the magnitude of His promises. The One seated on the throne declared, "I am making everything new. It is done! I am the Alpha and the Omega, the beginning and the end."

(Revelation 21:5-6). The victory was theirs, a testament to the perseverance of faith.

As the heavenly court rejoiced, Roy felt a sense of completion wash over him. Except where was Malcolm and his team of faithfuls? They had experienced together the trials, the tribulations, the Great Tribulation—it had all led to this moment, a glorious reunion with their Lord. They had fought the good fight, remained faithful, and now they were home. And then the Lord brought them to him for a grand reunion at the marriage supper of the Lamb with the rest of the saints in all their splendor and garments of light.

The New Jerusalem, radiant and glorious, awaited them—a city where love reigned, where peace was eternal, and where the presence of God illuminated every corner. As he gazed upon the holy city, Roy realized that this was not merely the end of suffering; it was the beginning of a new reality, one filled with hope, light, and the everlasting love of their Savior.

In that sacred moment, as the saints gathered to worship at the foot of the throne, Roy knew that peace, at last, had come to Jerusalem. ***The EPIC Quest for Lasting Peace*** had been fulfilled, signed in the blood of the Lamb, and he was forever grateful to be a part of this divine tapestry of redemption.

With hearts united in love and gratitude, they raised their voices in a song of triumph, proclaiming, "Blessed are those who wash their robes, so that they may have the right to the tree of life and may enter the city by the gates." (Revelation 22:14).

And as the echoes of their praise filled the air, Roy knew that at long last, the promise of Jerusalem WON had been realized, a reality that would echo through eternity, where God would dwell with His people, and where peace would reign forevermore.

And the watchman's call returns. The themes of prophecy, promise, and holy vigilance that opened this work now sound again as a final chord, sending the reader forth to live what has been read. Thus, the Epilogue becomes both ending and beginning: a call to watch, to believe, to walk faithfully. The pilgrimage Roy undertook, and which we mirrored in reading, is ours to continue.

For Jerusalem still stands, still speaks, and still summons the nations. ***Jerusalem had WON***. To journey with her is to journey with God's unfolding story—and the story is not yet done. Yet we see the ending, clearly in this message that has been brought to us, a message we can hear and believe, hear and deny or hear and refuse to commit to. In each of our separate journeys, our purpose is one for the salvation of Israel;

let us, in our individual pilgrimage, continue to, "Pray for the peace of Jerusalem; may they prosper that love thee" (Psalm 122:6).

Amen and Amen!

"For I testify unto every man that heareth the words of the prophecy of this book, If any man shall add unto these things, God shall add unto him the plagues that are written in this book:

And if any man shall take away from the words of the book of this prophecy, God shall take away his part out of the book of life, and out of the holy city, and from the things which are written in this book.

He which testifieth these things saith, Surely I come quickly. Amen. Even so, come, Lord Jesus.

The grace of our Lord Jesus Christ be with you all. Amen."

(Revelation 22:18–21 KJV)

ABOUT THE AUTHORS

Roy H. Ferguson, Author born in Mount Salem, Jamaica, is a passionate storyteller whose life journey is marked by resilience, faith, and redemption. Once entangled in the occult as a teenager, he ultimately found his way back to God after facing the threat of blindness. Leaving behind dreams of Hollywood fame, Roy dedicated himself to serving the homeless on Skid Row in Los Angeles, where a profound spiritual awakening transformed his path.

His journey of faith led to the creation of the sacred "Song of the Lamb" and collaborations with musical luminaries, culminating in a powerful performance at Andrews University. A mission to Israel in 2024 further solidified his vision for peace, inspiring the book *Jerusalem WON: Signed In Blood* 💧 *The Epic Quest for Lasting Peace.*

Now pursuing cinema producing at the LA Film School, Roy is committed to adapting his story into a docudrama, combining faith, prophecy, and powerful music to inspire global revival and reconciliation.

Malcolm McGough, Co-Author is a retired Australian Army Lieutenant Colonel and naturalized American citizen with a distinguished career in military leadership, political strategy, and public policy. Since moving to the U.S. in 2009, he has served in key campaign and leadership roles, including California Political Director for the 2016 Presidential Campaign and CEO of the Election Integrity Project California. He currently serves as a Senator for New California State (a new state in the making) and Interim CEO of the *Jerusalem WON* project, guiding its global vision through strategic leadership and engagement. A sought-after speaker, Malcolm is passionate about America's founding principles and spiritual heritage.

Made in the USA
Coppell, TX
10 February 2026

70948708R00273